HEINE IN ENGLAND

HEINRICH HEINE, 1797-1856
*In 1828, when Heine was thirty-one, Ludwig Gassen painted this portrait.
The original was owned by Eduard Engel of Berlin.*

Heine

IN EN·GLAND

———•———

STANTON LAWRENCE WORMLEY
ASSISTANT PROFESSOR OF GERMAN
HOWARD UNIVERSITY

With an Introduction by
WILLIAM CLYDE DeVANE
DEAN OF YALE COLLEGE
YALE UNIVERSITY

Chapel Hill

THE UNIVERSITY OF NORTH CAROLINA PRESS

1943

COPYRIGHT, 1943, BY
THE UNIVERSITY OF NORTH CAROLINA PRESS

TO

Mary Elizabeth Wormley

AND

Lawrence Riggs Wormley

MY PARENTS

Ich bin ein deutscher Dichter,
Bekannt im deutschen Land;
Nennt man die besten Namen,
So wird auch der meine genannt.
—Heine

Introduction

"THE JOYS OF PARENTS are secret, and so are their griefs and fears; they cannot utter the one, nor they will not utter the other." In this fashion Francis Bacon begins one of his most revealing essays. The joys and griefs of the teacher, though fainter, are of the same kind as those of parents, though their reticence is not so constant. The good teacher starts from a distance and his mind is usually engaged first in the intellectual aspects of his pupil's problems. If he is generous, however, as most good teachers are, his emotions gradually come to be engaged also, and he is likely to have a large stake in the success or failure of those he has trained.

I remember vividly yet that bright morning in Ithaca when the credentials and papers of Stanton L. Wormley were laid upon my desk. He was applying for entrance to the Graduate School of Cornell University, and wished to take his doctor's degree in English and German. It could hardly be said that he came as an inexperienced young man, needing to be moulded and formed. The record before me showed with unusual clearness that this young man had already achieved much, and it intimated that he was capable of a good deal of further achievement. Educated in the public schools of the District of Columbia, he had graduated from Howard University, and had already been designated as a man of promise. On his record he was nominated by the Institute of International Education as an American-German Exchange Fellow in 1931. At the end of a year he had been granted the *Sprach- und Literatur-Diplom (Summa Cum Laude)* by the University of Hamburg. He had then been appointed to the faculty of Virginia

State College and had there become Head of the Unit of Languages. He was being sent to Cornell to complete his work for the doctor's degree by the General Education Board and was to continue his work later as a Fellow of the Julius Rosenwald Foundation. Everything in the record was calculated to rouse the interest of his prospective teachers. Here was a young man who knew how to work and was notably successful at it; here was one who was obviously well equipped in the tools of his profession, versed in the languages, self-disciplined, and judicious in the use of his opportunities. Naturally we accepted him as a student at once, and the next September he came to Ithaca to begin his work with us.

We never had occasion to regret our decision. Mr. Wormley soon showed us that he was all his record said he was, and something else besides. He was able and thorough to a remarkable degree, and was meticulous and conscientious in fulfilling his obligations. Indeed, all unconsciously, his virtues caused some pain to some of the less earnest members of his classes, for Wormley set a pace which they were not capable of holding. They bore no resentment, however, because it was impossible to feel that towards Wormley. They soon saw that Wormley was a serious scholar; and almost as soon they discovered that he was a fine and gentle spirit with ideals that they could admire, and a performance that not many of them could emulate. He gained from them and from his teachers a full measure of respect.

It was not long after his arrival that Wormley found the subject which was to be the embryo of this book. He chose to work under my direction, and before long either he or I suggested the topic "Heine and the Victorians" as a suitable one for a dissertation. In any case, the project was approved, and that year and the next were spent in completing the task. The subject was appropriate and timely enough from the point of view of Heine, though it had not at the time of its inception taken on the peculiar timeliness and appropriateness in world events which it was to do when it was greatly expanded during the next several years to the scope of the present study. Heine's reputation in England by 1932 seemed finally to have settled into its permanent place. A hundred years earlier not much had been known of Heine in England, and his name was seldom heard. By 1850 he was beginning to be fairly well known in literary circles, especially in those circles where German thought and literature were appreciated. Translators of his work had begun to appear; English critics began to notice Heine; poets began to imitate him; and his name began to appear in diaries, letters, notes, and conversations—indeed, Heine had begun to make his way in English informal opinion. But those things had only begun to happen. It was in the second half of the century that Heine came into his own in England: the translators increased in numbers and competence; Arnold wrote of him in poetry and criticism; Thomson, Henley, Sharp, Owen Meredith, Dowson, Allingham, and others drew from him; in literary circles his name became a household word. His reputation was so considerable that his poetry evoked a considerable number of parodies.

This was almost too good to last; but last it did and almost at concert pitch until the First World War came in 1914. After that the drop in Heine's reputation in England was precipitous. But the poet was not entirely forgotten, and slowly, through the twenties and early thirties, Heine's reputation struggled back to what is probably its permanent position. As the English Romantic poets lost ground after the War, so did Heine. Yet he was a figure of consequence still, and had to be reckoned with. Then in 1938 came the Second World War; Heine was disowned by the Germans because he was a Jew, and his poems when they were printed at all in Germany were by "unknown" authors. This was cause enough to make the world outside of Germany think again of Heine, and perhaps read again his poems. It is this later event which gives a peculiar timeliness now to Mr. Wormley's work. If Heine is disowned, and needs a champion outside his own country, where should one rise but in America and from a group that has known oppression likewise, and still knows it, but with hope of better things. Mr. Wormley's career illustrates what might be done; that his support should come from the Julius Rosenwald Foundation has a significance that I shall not labor.

So here is the work before us, and it is most characteristic of its maker. All the qualities of Mr. Wormley's nature are here. The book is complete and exhaustive, and I venture to think more accurate and scholarly than any comparable book upon the subject. It far surpasses in these respects such books as Louis Betz's *Heine in France*, and H. B. Sachs's *Heine in America*, and all the lesser works upon the influence of Heine in other countries. Oddly enough, no one had touched the most fruitful subject of all—Heine in England. The field was large and demanded special knowledge; Mr. Wormley was the man to do it. Moreover, scores of translations of Heine which were not listed in B. Q. Morgan's *Bibliography of German Literature in English Translation* are here recorded; and numerous critical articles upon Heine are here unearthed.

The copiousness and thoroughness of the treatment reflect faithfully the virtues of the author. Yet the best I leave to the last, for it is not quantity which I would praise. The sureness, the point, the constant judiciousness of the judgments—these, in my opinion, are the superior characteristics of the work, and they, too, reflect truly the deeper qualities of the mind of the author.

I can say these things because I do not in any sense say them of myself. Mr. Wormley did the work independently and by himself. I had gone from Cornell when he completed the work, and he received from me only an occasional suggestion. I should say one thing further: there are few countries in the world as it goes now where Mr. Wormley would have been given such opportunities as he has had. To those altruistic foundations which exemplify so much of the best spirit of America, Mr. Wormley, I am sure, and I are deeply grateful.

WILLIAM C. DeVANE

Foreword

DESPITE THE REAL and spiritual kinship of England to Germany, no nation has offered a more stubborn resistance to Teutonic influences than has the little isle off the coast of the continent. For centuries, the Englishman in a spirit of singular insularity fought obstinately to stave off the inroads of Germanic culture, and it was not until the end of the eighteenth century that an appreciable amount of German culture managed to gain a foothold on British soil.

The first significant demonstration of the German spirit in England occurred when Alexander Barclay issued a version of Sebastian Brant's famous *Narrenschiff* in 1509. The impressive moral coupled with the biting sarcasm and sharp ridicule of the work so delighted English readers that by the beginning of the seventeenth century many English adaptations had been made. Christopher Marlowe and his imitators in the treatment of the Faustus legend made England for a while conscious of the great store of legendary material in German folklore. The greatest influence during the sixteenth century came, however, as the immediate consequence of the rapidly spreading ideas of the Reformation—an influence that is seen most directly, insofar as literature is concerned, in the translations and versions of the *Kirchenlieder*. The natural prejudice of the English, however, was far from broken. Did not Portia disdain the young German, the Duke of Saxony's nephew, because of his drunkenness and bestiality?

As the result of the Thirty Years' War in Germany and of Puritan oppression in England, conditions were hardly favorable for uniting the two countries in any sort of spiritual or cultural bond. Consequently, there was practically speaking no tangible evidence of German influence upon England during the seventeenth century. Even with the year 1660 when England again became semi-conscious of outside influences, it was to France she turned rather than to Germany.

The majority of the following century was nearly as barren of German influence as had been the preceding one. The politically powerless Germany was scarcely a land to call forth the admiration and respect of British eyes. German literature was not read for the simple reason that there was very little good German literature to read. William Law, who studied German in order that he might translate the mystical works of Jacob Böhme, is one of the very few Englishmen who attempted to form acquaintanceship with Teutonic culture. Lord Chesterfield, it is true, impressed upon his son the importance of studying German, but Chesterfield's own knowledge of the tongue is highly problematical. From Macaulay we learn that the members of Johnson's club had no knowledge of Lessing and Wieland. Johnson himself knew no German, and the otherwise talkative Boswell, who had studied at Utrecht and visited in Berlin, records nothing. Gibbon wrote of the antiquities of the House of Brunswick without ever troubling to learn the language.

The last half of the century saw an increasing interest in things German. Particularly is this true in the translation of German literature. Between 1761 and 1799 twenty editions of Gessner's *Death of Abel* appeared. Other translations include Klopstock's *Messiah* (1763), Haller's philosophical romance *Usong* (1772), Lessing's *Fables* (1773), *Nathan* (1781), *Minna von Barnhelm* (1786), Goethe's *Werther* (1779), and Sotheby's translation of Wieland's *Oberon* (1796). It is especially in the final decade of the century, though, that German influence was at its highest. In 1788 Henry Mackenzie, the "Scottish Sterne," read a paper before the Royal Society of

Edinburgh in which he sketched the state of the German theater. Mackenzie's interest fired Lord Woodehouslee to translate four years later Schiller's *Räuber* and indirectly influenced Scott along German lines. It was about this time that August von Kotzebue's star was in the ascendancy, and interest in German drama was at fever pitch. Schiller, Goethe, and Lessing were recognized, but only slightly so. Through the efforts of Matthew Gregory Lewis (whose *Castle Spectre* ran sixty nights), Mrs. Inchbold (who adapted Kotzebue's *Natural Son* as *A Lover's Vows*), and Sheridan (upon whose plays German influence is strong), England, while showing hardly a discriminatory taste, plunged madly into a passion for German plays and especially for the work of August von Kotzebue. Scott translated Goethe's *Götz* and the *Erlkönig* as well as Bürger's *Lenore;* Bulwer rendered in English the poems of Schiller; and William Taylor, whose *Historic Survey of German Poetry* appeared later, in 1830, translated Lessing's *Nathan* and Goethe's *Iphigenie*. Still other authors have left various translations. Through the work of DeQuincey, Coleridge, and their followers, German philosophy made its way into England.

At the very end of the eighteenth century prejudices had begun to disappear, insularity had yielded somewhat, and the barriers were beginning to fall gradually in every respect. It is in the Victorian period, however, that the influence of Germany is felt to the greatest degree. Standing as the great apostle of German culture, Thomas Carlyle threw wide the floodgates and permitted a veritable torrent of German influences to sweep through England. George Eliot, Lewes, Matthew Arnold, and scores of others joined hands with Carlyle in spreading German culture, and names like those of Fichte, Kant, Schelling, Lessing, Goethe, Schiller, became by-words in England. The music of Richard Wagner had introduced the English mind to a wealth of Germanic legend and folklore. And so England, for the first time, became truly German-conscious.[1]

The turn of the present century witnessed a still greater interest in German culture—an interest which bode well to reach in the twentieth century a heretofore unattained peak. In addition to the older German writers who had won unquestioned widespread recognition outside their native realm, new idols arose in England. Gerhart Hauptmann and Hermann Sudermann lived to see their literary works read with interest, translated, and performed with enthusiasm before British audiences. Scores of other German writers too numerous to mention were acclaimed widely by the English. Then the advent of the first great world war threatened to shatter the very foundations of a German-English literary alliance, and in the dark years of the post-war period relationships remained strained, so with far greater difficulty than before German literary influences attempted to creep into England. Under the leadership of such men as Jakob Wassermann, Thomas Mann, Frank Wedekind, Franz Werfel, Georg Kaiser, Fritz von Unruh, Ernst Toller, Erich Maria Remarque, and Stefan George, German literature strove once more to gain its rightful place in world culture and to re-establish the bonds, formerly so close, with England. A second great war now threatens again to put at naught all efforts at uniting or associating England and Germany culturally. German literature is now largely propaganda and it is only vaguely that we hear through the strains of martial music and the incessant roars of giant bombers the voices of exiled writers such as Emil Ludwig, Lion Feuchtwanger, and Heinrich Mann. But no war can long obliterate the names of Goethe, Schiller, Kant, Lessing, and the great German immortals in the annals of English literature. Once again the literary bond between Germany and England must be established.

---

1. For a fuller account of the importation of German literature, see Leslie Stephen, *Studies of a Biographer*, or Johannes Renwanz, *Matthew Arnold und Deutschland*.

Foreword

Despite the wide recognition given Goethe, Schiller, and the other German authors who have contributed so largely to the general development of English letters, one of the most powerful and important figures in German literature to exercise influence and play an impressive rôle in the literary work of England has been practically totally ignored up to the present time. Heinrich Heine, Germany's foremost singer, has been awarded but an occasional reference in relation to English poetry and letters in general. Investigation shows that Heine's songs have proved a most fertile field for translators, who apparently have never wearied of rendering in English his exquisite gems. As far as criticism is concerned, it has heretofore been taken for granted that Carlyle's terse and contemptuous term, "That blackguard Heine," is indicative of the general English attitude toward the poet. The general consensus of opinion has been that, if treated by them at all, Heine has been regarded by English critics much in the light in which Ludwig Börne regarded him—"as a dead leaf driven before the wind until at last, grown heavy with the accretions of mud, it stays on the ground and decays." Closer study, however, reveals among the eminent critics of England a startling number of writers who have treated Heine, the man and poet, adequately and intelligently, and who have rightly interpreted his significance to world literature. No less impressive is the great array of eminent Englishmen who have alluded to Heine in letters, diaries, conversations, and in other ways. Among the poets, too, Heinrich Heine has exerted no little influence and, indeed, has left his stamp indelibly on modern English literature.

The mass of material offering evidence of Heine's widespread popularity in, and deep significance for, England is all the more astounding when it is considered that, in addition to the natural barriers of insularity, ignorance, and prejudice which so long kept out German influence of any sort, well-nigh insurmountable obstacles lay in the path of Heine as an individual—obstacles which, with extreme difficulty, the British have finally overcome in accepting the German poet as a great world-figure. Heine's outspoken distaste and contempt of England and the English people has been, indeed, a bitter dose to swallow. As a Jew, a pagan, and a blasphemer of all the British hold dear and sacred, he should have been detestable in English eyes; yet study shows that Heine has been accorded an overwhelming reception despite all his undesirable traits.

Heine's significance and popularity in France have been treated admirably by Louis Betz in a thorough and diligent research monograph called *Heine in France*. H. B. Sachs has written a thesis of like nature on *Heine in America*, and similar works have appeared on the German poet's influence in Russia, Italy, and South America. At present we feel that no German poet, with the exception of Goethe, has made more friends, enjoyed more widespread popularity, and exerted greater influence among foreign nations than Heinrich Heine; nevertheless, until the present time, no treatment of Heine's significance for England has yet appeared.

This study, then, attempts to fill a long neglected gap in the consideration of Heinrich Heine's relationship to world literature. It is an extensive outgrowth of a dissertation undertaken a few years ago at Cornell University in partial fulfillment of the doctor's degree. Through the encouragement and material aid of the Julius Rosenwald Foundation I have endeavored to enlarge the limited scope of the original dissertation into a comprehensive survey of the poet Heine's significance for England. To the Julius Rosenwald Foundation I should like to express my unbounded appreciation for the unwavering and unquestioned support which has made the present study possible. I should like, too, to express my gratitude to Professor William C. DeVane, formerly Head of the Department of English in Cornell University and now Dean of Yale College in Yale University, Professor Frederick C. Prescott of the Department of English in Cornell University,

Foreword

and Professor Paul R. Pope, Head of the Department of German in Cornell University, for their encouragement and their valuable suggestions and criticisms in the preparation of the manuscript. I welcome, too, this opportunity to thank my colleagues, Professor Wolfgang S. Seiferth of the Department of German and Mr. Harold O. Lewis of the Department of History, for their untiring assistance in the reading of the proofs.

For the courtesy extended by various publishing houses and individuals in granting permission to reprint certain copyrighted material, the following acknowledgments are gratefully made: to Victor Gollancz, Ltd., and Miss Wolfe (daughter of the author) for selections from *This Blind Rose* and *Snow* by Humbert Wolfe, and to Basil Blackwell, Publisher, for the translation of "Du bist wie eine Blume" and "Heine's Last Song" from *Shylock Reasons with Mr. Chesterton* by Humbert Wolfe; to the Macmillan Company for selections from *Poems* by William E. Henley; to Henry Holt and Company, Inc., for "Once in a Saintly Passion" from *Poems of James Thomson*; to Martin Secker & Warburg, Ltd., for selections from *Days and Nights* by Arthur Symons; to George Allen & Unwin, Ltd., for selections from *Poems* by Mary Coleridge; to Thomas Y. Crowell Company for selections from the lyrics of Robert Louis Stevenson; to Little, Brown & Company for excerpts from *The Letters of Olive Schreiner*; to The Clarendon Press, Oxford, for an excerpt from the Preface of *Heine's Book of Songs* translated by John Todhunter. The selections from *Poems and Dramas* and *Poems* by William Sharp are reprinted by permission of the publishers, Dodd, Mead and Company, Inc., and a picture of Heine from *Heinrich Heine: Paradox and Poet* by Louis Untermeyer is reprinted by permission of Harcourt, Brace and Company, Inc.

STANTON L. WORMLEY

Howard University,
Washington, D. C.

Contents

INTRODUCTION, by William C. DeVane	vii
FOREWORD	xi

1.
HEINE IN ENGLISH TRANSLATION

I *Major Translators*	3
II *Minor Translators*	39

2.
HEINE IN ENGLISH CRITICISM

III *Major Critics*	105
IV *Minor Critics*	124

3.
HEINE IN ENGLISH INFORMAL OPINION

V *Letters, Diaries, Notes, Conversation*	169

4.
HEINE IN ENGLISH POETRY

VI *Major Influence*	199
VII *Minor Influence*	253
CONCLUSION	263
APPENDIX	271
BIBLIOGRAPHY	278
INDEX	301

HEINE IN ENGLAND

I.

Heine

IN ENGLISH TRANSLATION

────•·•────

1. *Major Translators*

PERHAPS NO TASK is more difficult to one interested in literature and literary history than that of evaluating the merits of translation—and particularly in estimating the value of the countless versions of the German poet, Heinrich Heine, for of all the writers who have yet lived, Heine is one of the most difficult to be rendered in English verse. All his writings are merely variations of the same little theme, the "history of Cupid and Psyche," presented in every conceivable aspect. One mood, one meaning shades off delicately into another, and it is just this nicety of shading, the intermingling of light and shadow, in the poems in their entirety and within the individual pieces themselves that creates such a difficult problem for the translator.

His poetry, "*von phantastischen Lichtern durchblitzt,*" now "*himmelhoch jauchzend,*" now "*zum Tode betrübt,*" is crammed full of graceful nuances that defy the would-be translator. Heine is essentially the subjective poet of mood, and mood is a thing that does not readily lend itself to translation, for it is a purely personal thing. With exquisite delicacy and the precision of a refined analytical spirit, the German lyricist fastens upon the lightest possible impressions and records the slightest tremblings of a soul susceptible and extremely sensitive to every influence.

The sensitivity of this soul is expressed primarily in a profound feeling of *Weltschmerz*—that intangible and elusive mood which even the best prepared translators and the deepest poetic spirits are totally unable to grasp. Heine's *Weltschmerz* is the trait that makes people care for his work. "Sweet but with a suggestion of death, like Jasmine flowers too long imprisoned in their box,"[1] it is this quality that sets him apart from all other writers. His is not the naïve, unconscious *Weltschmerz* of the idealistic Hölderlin nor the self-conscious, self-centered *Weltschmerz* of the naturalist Lenau but a *Zerrissenheit* expressed often in the form of pathos, often as vanity, and often as mere bravado and pugnacity. Lenau, the *Pathetiker* of the elusive mood, has shown that *Weltschmerz* may proceed from unrequited and unsatisfied love, but Heine, by deliberately destroying the cause through a peculiar sort of self-irony, has demonstrated that mere love-sickness is not *Weltschmerz*. Heine covers up every trace of the immediate cause of his feeling through a merciless and pitiless self-inflicted satire and calumny; yet we feel that the root nonetheless lies in unrequited love—the love for Amalie—just as surely as we sense the source of the despair and bitterness of his great prototype, Byron, in the latter's disappointed love for Mary Chaworth. The fundamental difference in the two cases is that Byron's *Weltschmerz* proceeds from the personal to the cosmic while Heine's remains ever egoistic. It is the Jew in Heine which gives the peculiar flavor to his grief.

Heine's peculiar wit, an outgrowth of his fundamental *Weltschmerz*, is still another quality which places innumerable obstacles in the way of the translator. The wit of the poet is a difficult thing to conceive and a still more difficult one to transcribe, for it is the wit of triviality. In speaking of Sir

---

1. Ludwig von Embden, *The Family Life of Heinrich Heine*, tr. by C. De-Kay, Preface, pp. xii ff.

Walter Scott, Heine unconsciously pictured himself as a jester: "Er gleicht einem Millionär, der sein ganzes Vermögen in lauter Scheidemünzen liegen hat."[2] Heine's is a nature that by some inherent twist or quirk gleefully seizes upon the ridiculous in even the most tragic of situations. "Aber es geht mir oft so, ich kann meine eigene Schmerzen nicht erzählen, ohne dass die Sache komisch wird."[3] In a statement made to Friederike Roberts is revealed how much a part of his fundamental nature this odd mental twist actually became:

Das Ungeheuerste, das Entsetzlichste, das Schaudervollste, wenn es nicht unpoetisch werden soll, kann man nur in dem buntscheckigen Gewande des Lächerlichen darstellen, gleichsam versöhnend—darum hat auch Shakespeare das Grässlichste im 'Lear' durch den Narren sagen lassen, darum hat auch Goethe zu dem furchtbarsten Stoffe, zum 'Faust,' die Puppenspielform gewählt, darum hat auch der noch grössere Poet, nämlich Unser-Herrgott, allen Schreckensszenen dieses Lebens eine gute Dosis Spasshaftigkeit beigemischt.[4]

Innumerable other obstacles, such as melody, rhythm, diction, etc., could be elaborated upon as stumbling blocks in the path of the translator, but these are difficulties encountered in the rendering of any poet.

Certain qualities are requisite to every translator of Heine's poems. He, the translator, must be an excellent German scholar in order to understand accurately and thoroughly the shades of meaning found in the originals; he must possess an extremely fine poetic taste in order to appreciate the originals; he must boast a sensitive and cultivated ear in order to catch the exquisite melodies of the German poet; he must have a genuine poetic gift of his own and the power of facile expression in order to transcribe the feeling and meaning of his subject; and he must be free of the idiosyncrasies of genius and be willing to subjugate himself entirely to his originals in an effort to enter completely into the spirit of those originals. The

2. E. Eckertz, *Heine und sein Witz*, p. 4.
3. *Heinrich Heines gesammelte Werke*, ed. by Gustav Karpeles, VIII, 408.
4. *Ibid.*, p. 468.

English versions must not be merely English versions of a great German poet but the poet himself in a different garb. Yet even if the translator possesses all the necessary qualities, he faces a well-nigh hopeless problem in attempting to render Heine. Genius itself cannot achieve the impossible, and the translation of Heine's "anguish dipped in honey," as Heine himself once said, *"c'est du clair de lune empaillé."*

For purposes of convenience of reference and clarity of subject, the translators of Heine are here divided into two large groups comprising the major and minor translators. The group of major translators includes Sir Theodore Martin, Edgar A. Bowring, Thomas Brooksbank, Margaret Armour, and John Todhunter, and eleven others who, because of the quantity and quality of their versions, form the bridge that connects the major and minor groups. Insofar as is possible the major translators are discussed in the order of their importance and general period of work. No effort is made to enter into wearisome detail, but the purpose is rather to present a general survey of the entire field of Heine translation in English, and it is hoped that such a survey will prove of value to students of comparative literature.

Theodore Martin (1816-1909).—Undeniably, the most popular of the nineteenth-century English translators of Heine was Sir Theodore Martin (1816-1909), a prodigious translator from many languages and, as an original writer, the blood-brother of Theodore Watts-Dunton, an "extremely busy man." "Bon Gaultier's" literary labors—and translations in particular—are far too numerous and varied to mention. Suffice it to say that few major Continental authors have escaped being "done into English" by this indefatigable worker. Martin's translation of Heine, published in 1878, purports to be an English version of Heine's poems and ballads contained in the *Buch der Lieder.* In reality it is merely a selection (which Martin admits) made with the scrupulous and prudish care of a Mid-Victorian gentleman who frowns with hearty disapproval on anything that so much as smacks of the *risqué*. In the *L'Envoi* of the translation, Martin writes:

The present volume contains translations of all the songs and ballads in the "Book of Songs" which the translator ventures to think are likely to be acceptable to an English reader. Perhaps a severe criticism would even say that the principle of exclusion might have been carried further. Heine, like most poets, wrote too much; and his name would rank higher in the world of letters if many of his pieces, which are either steeped in grossness or deformed by a revolting cynicism, had never seen the light. In his selections, the translator's object has been to show the poet at his best, and at the same time to illustrate the cynicism and bitter irony which are as characteristic of Heine as are his passion, his pathos, his picturesque simplicity and force.[5]

One of the chief qualities with which every successful translator must be endowed is sympathy with his original—a sympathy which is no more manifested by pity, compassion, or love than by a desire, however eager, to feel in absolute harmony with the subject. It represents a sympathy that goes far deeper —a sympathy that has its roots in understanding and is born of a kindred spirit. The translator must feel what the original poet feels; he must go further and be the poet for the time being and in a "willing suspension of disbelief" must see with the original's eyes, feel with his heart, and write with his pen. This quality Sir Theodore Martin lacks, and consequently he is not one with Heine. There is a vast, yawning chasm between the two men that nothing can bridge. Robert Buchanan, in his typically caustic fashion, presents the idea succinctly:

In all history there could hardly be two figures more violently contrasted or diametrically different than the blameless Prince Consort of England and the inspired Gnome of German poetry; and it goes without saying that the biographer of the one was ill fitted to become the translator of the other. I can hardly conceive, therefore, what species of infatuation possessed Mr. Theodore Martin when he resolved to employ his leisure, lately so admirably utilized in the editing and preparing of dainty documents of the Court, in adapting Heinrich Heine's "Poems and Ballads." I use the word adapting advisedly, for when

5. Theodore Martin, *Poems and Ballads by Heinrich Heine*, pp. vi-vii.

a Courtier, however refined and cultivated, tries to handle a revolutionary Poet, the result is certain to be adaptation, if not downright misrepresentation and mutilation. As wild as Goethe's Flea, as tricksome as an Elf, as uncertain and misleading as a Will-o'-the-Wisp, gamesome and lachrymose by turns, by turns outraging all the conventions and respecting all the proprieties, now the most doleful German that ever spun ditties to his mistress's eyebrow, and again (what Thiers called him) the wittiest Frenchman that. ever lived, Heine is the last spirit in the world to rise to the conjuration of a respectable elderly English gentleman, armed with a German dictionary, a quill pen, and an "expurgating" apparatus.[6]

Theodore Martin's translations of Heine, which first appeared in various issues of *Blackwood's Magazine* in the late seventies, probably justify more favorable criticism than the one just quoted from Robert Buchanan, and even that severe critic modifies, to some extent at least, his scathing attack a little later:

... I should do Mr. Martin gross injustice, if I failed to recognize the abundant scholarship, the great conscientiousness, and the busy earnestness, which distinguish his work. He is as just to Heine as he would be to a Prince Presumptive, and that is saying a good deal. He is rigidly fair to him, even too fair, in so much as he will suffer him to say nothing unseemly. But somehow the result is not satisfactory, and Mr. Martin's book is no more like the "Buch der Lieder" than green cheese is like the moon, or the postures of a dancing master like the leaps of Oberon on the starlit sward.[7]

Despite the fact that Theodore Martin's translations enjoyed the greatest popularity and appealed to the greatest number of readers in nineteenth-century England, we cannot help but agree—at least in part—with Buchanan's criticism. The translations of Sir Theodore Martin are in no wise superior to those of a great many of the minor writers who tried their hands at reproducing the inimitable Heine—and indeed they are quite inferior to those of more than one who laid no particular claim to the art of translation. For one who knows his

6. Robert Buchanan, *A Look Round Literature*, p. 210.
7. *Ibid.*, p. 212.

Heine, Martin's versions are a grievous disappointment, and he who is unfamiliar with the poet will get absolutely no notion of him whatsoever. It is, of course, impossible to echo Heine's exquisite melody and to capture the nuances of Heine's thought and mood, but Theodore Martin fails even in suggesting the beauties that lie in the depths of Heine's supreme poetry. The translator cannot be accused of misrepresentation or distortion of facts, for his versions are fairly literal and his loyalty and faithfulness to his original unquestioned. The problem seems to resolve itself into one of sheer inability both as an interpreter and as an English writer.

In the matter of rhythm, which is by far not the most formidable of the translator's difficulties, Martin is flagrantly lax. Where Heine's originals (as in the case of "Es treibt mich hin, es treibt mich her" and "Sterne mit den goldnen Füsschen") glide with the graceful, easy motion of the swallow, Martin's versions walk in stiff-legged fashion as if on stilts and now and then execute an awkward hop, skip, and jump merely to indicate the presence of life. Where Heine is delicate, whimsical, humorous, and pathetic as in "Als ich auf der Reise zufällig," Martin in his English version is heavy, awkward, and severe.

One of the chief errors, and unfortunately one of the chief characteristics, of Martin's work lies in his abuse of his own native tongue. This manifests itself in several ways: in the use of inappropriate, ill-chosen, and at times meaningless terms of obsolete nature (often indeed they are coined by Martin's none too fertile brain); by colloquialisms in extremely bad taste; by cumbersome and ineffectual rhymes made purely for the sake of rhyme; by poverty of vocabulary; and by use of odious and inexcusable Germanisms. It would be far too pointless and wearisome to indicate by specific references all the types of unfortunate translation, but three or four instances of the sort should be fairly indicative of the fact that Martin was unprepared to undertake the translation of such a poet as Heine. Such expressions as "tom-noddies" ("Ich stehe auf des Berges

Spitze"), "mum-chance" *(Poor Peter)*, "Agrue" (merely to rime with "knew" in "Ein Traum gar seltsam schauerlich"), "my Sweeting" (a favorite term of endearment with Martin), and countless other awkward terms not even suggested in the German—all create just the opposite of Heine's intended effect, simplicity.

Unwieldy Germanisms, too, mar Martin's work. He seems ever prone to adapt the principles of German word-order to the English language. His versions at times carry over bodily the transposed order of the German, and the reader finds himself searching in vain for the verb which is invariably to be found tucked away in some obscure spot or merely, in the German fashion, tacked on at the end. The German rhyme is not wholly to blame for Martin's awkwardness. Even in such an unrhymed poem as the *Twilight of the Gods,* the English is cumbersome; and, certainly, there is no excuse for the atrocity of allowing five of the first seven lines of *Ratcliff* to end with the pronoun "me" when there is nothing in the original to suggest it. Nor is there any excuse for the broad Scotch dialect used, in extremely poor taste, in rendering Heine's delightful and simple "Mädchen mit dem rothen Mündchen" and "Mein Kind, wir waren Kinder." Inaccuracies of translation, where diction is concerned, are too numerous to mention.

To Theodore Martin's credit, however, it must be admitted that he has made a few acceptable translations of Heine. For the most part he is incapable of catching the spirit of Heine's simple short lyrics, but in "Es liegt der heisse Sommer," "Ein Fichtenbaum steht einsam," and "Im wunderschönen Monat Mai" Theodore Martin shows far more than average skill. One of the versions is quoted as a specimen of the translator at his best:

> 'Twas in the glorious month of May
> When all the buds were blowing,
> I felt—ah me, how sweet it was!—
> Love in my heart a-growing.

> 'Twas in the glorious month of May,
> When all the birds were quiring,
> In burning words I told her all
> My yearning, my aspiring.

For the most part, however, Martin is at his best in translating the longer pieces and more particularly so in his renderings of the songs from *Die Harzreise*, which, while they leave much to be desired, are fairly capable.

All in all, though, Sir Theodore Martin is not endowed with the proper gifts of the translator and in the main shows little ability in the art. His opening stanza of Heine's immortal *Lorelei*:

> I cannot tell what's coming o'er me
> That makes me so eerie and low,
> An old world legend before me
> Keeps rising and will not go.

which an anonymous critic has described as seeming like the "premonitory symptoms of sea-sickness," and his rendering of "Die Lotosblume ängstigt" (a line admirably rendered by James Thomson as "The lotos flower doth languish") as "The lotos-flower is scared" should alone convince the reader that here is a man without a lyric gift and, as such, totally unfit as a translator of Germany's greatest singer.

Edgar A. Bowring (1826-1911).—Despite the enormous popularity of the versions of Sir Theodore Martin, it is Edgar A. Bowring (1826-1911) who, in all due justice, must be hailed as the pre-eminent and most satisfactory translator of Heine in nineteenth-century England. Two other distinctions are likewise Bowring's: he is the first great translator of Heine's poems, and he is the only translator of the period to give us the poetical works of Heinrich Heine in their entirety.

Bowring's translation appeared as early as 1859, just three years after the death of the great German lyricist. A second edition was demanded in 1881 and included still more poems of Heine, which were not available at the time of the first publication, including the "Early Poems" and "Posthumous Poems" of the poet. Bowring's professed purpose in translating the poems of Heine was to bring to public attention and notice the works of a writer "universally known and read in his native land, and highly popular in France" but "to the generality of Englishmen almost entirely unknown."[8] Bowring, who had already published translations of the poems of Schiller and Goethe, is due no little credit for singlehandedly bringing before the English public the works of Germany's third great minstrel.

To declare Bowring's translations the best made from Heine in the past century would require no little qualification. Bowring is no poet and his versions in the main lack the spontaneity and freshness of Heine. The lyric gift is lacking, and while the versions display considerable talent in versification and a thorough knowledge of German, they want the directness and simplicity of the originals. In individual translations Bowring must bow more than once to superior renderings often made by far less competent translators. It must be kept in mind, however, that his task was far more difficult than that of the rest who allowed themselves considerable freedom in the matter of selection. Those translators who, like Sir Theodore Martin, availed themselves of the opportunity to cull at will from among the poetical works of Heine enjoyed no little advantage over the man faced with the problem of assuming the entire burden. It is noticeable in no small degree that, where the power of selection is exercised, the difficult pieces—those ironically antithetic and those depending on shading and odd quirks for effect—are invariably omitted.

Heine cannot be expurgated, for to omit any part of his work is to ignore one or many sides of his complex nature. Those people who are too squeamish to read Heine in his entirety should not read him at all. The poet is not for them. Completeness is one of the chief virtues of Bowring's trans-

8. E. A. Bowring, *The Poems of Heine*, Preface, p. x.

lation, and, in daring to be complete, the translator has made a lasting contribution in giving a life-sized portrait of Heine accurate in all details, for as he says:

> There are doubtless many poems written by Heine that one could wish had never been written, and that one would willingly refrain from translating. But the omission of these would hide from the reader some of Heine's chief peculiarities, and would tend to give him an incomplete if not incorrect notion of what the poet was. A translator no more assumes the responsibility of his author's works than a faithful Editor does, and he goes beyond his province if he omits whatever does not happen to agree with his own notions.[9]

Insofar as specific criticism of the versions is concerned, it must be admitted that Bowring adequately and satisfactorily lives up to his avowed principles in translation—those principles being (1) "As close and literal an adherence to the original as is consistent with good English and with poetry, and (2) the preservation throughout the work of the original meters."[10] To point out the inaccuracies and faults of Bowring's voluminous translation would scarcely be profitable and would certainly prove tiresome. It is enough to say that occasionally his meter stumbles although in the main it is extraordinarily faithful to the originals. Now and then occur misrepresentations and awkward phrasings which, however, are to be expected. The chief faults of the translations lie in the want of poetic spirit and the too frequent use of cumbersome and out-of-place Germanisms, but as Bowring lays no claims to either the lyric gift or the power of mastery in English diction, allowance must surely be made. He writes:

> In claiming for the present work (extending over more than 20,000 verses) the abstract merits of literalness, completeness, and rigid adherence to the metrical peculiarities of the original, it is far from my intention to claim any credit for the *manner* in which I have executed that difficult task or to pretend that I have been successful in it.... The credit of conscientiousness and close application in the matter is all that I would venture to assert for myself.[11]

9. *Ibid.*   10. *Ibid.*, p. ix.   11. *Ibid.*, p. x.

While not unusually successful in reproducing the simplicity, mood, and melody of the difficult short lyrics, Bowring's versions display an evenness and accuracy to which those of Sir Theodore Martin cannot hope to aspire. Like Martin, Bowring is more successful in his longer attempts, particularly in his versions of the macabre ballad *Countess Jutta*, the curious nightmare *Marie Antoinette*, and *The God Apollo*. Bowring has, too, no little success in his versions of that powerfully pathetic group of *Lazarus* songs forming the climax of the entire *Romanzero* of which Heine himself once said: "I am well aware that it is beautiful, horribly beautiful. It is like a lamentation from the grave; in it someone buried alive is crying out in the night, or even the dead body or the grave itself. Yes, the German lyric has never yet heard such tones, and could not, in fact, for never was a poet in such a position."[12]

Thomas Brooksbank and Margaret Armour.—When Charles Godfrey Leland's translation of Heine's *Reisebilder* appeared in Philadelphia in 1855, the work was so favorably received by critics and Heine enthusiasts that Leland determined to attempt a translation of Heine's complete works. Setting to work shortly thereafter, the first volume of Leland's complete translation of Heine's works appeared in London in 1891. Volumes two and three were also printed during the same year, and the following season saw the publication of three more volumes. In 1893, there appeared a translation of *French Affairs* making up the seventh and eighth volumes of the complete works in English. Leland died before the concluding volumes could be put before the public.

William Heinemann, the publisher of the series, was determined not to leave the works incomplete and called upon Thomas Brooksbank and Margaret Armour to supply the lacking portions of the American's translation. Volume nine, comprising Heine's entire *Buch der Lieder*, was done into English by Thomas Brooksbank, and the remaining three volumes in-

---

12. F. H. Wood, *Heine as a Critic of His Own Work*, p. 100.

cluding the *Neue Gedichte, Deutschland, Romanzero,* and *Letzte Gedichte und Nachlese* were rendered by Margaret Armour. All four volumes were published during the years 1904-1905, although work on them was begun considerably earlier. The *Book of Songs* is Brooksbank's chief literary achievement; Margaret Armour, however, has also translated *Gudrun,* the *Nibelungenlied,* and Wagner's entire *Ring des Nibelungen.*

Of the two translators, who will be discussed jointly since theirs was a joint endeavor, Margaret Armour is the superior workman. Women, it would seem, have a keener insight into, and more sympathetic understanding of, the delicate, flowerlike charm and strange, bitter gall of Heine than men. Whether this is because of greater sensitivity, traditional intuition, or any other so-called purely feminine trait is, indeed, a matter of question. At any rate, it is noticeable in more than one instance that the feminine translator has had a distinct edge over the male interpreter of Heinrich Heine. Margaret Armour is in this respect no exception.

Thomas Brooksbank is out of harmony with the German poet, and his translations strike shrill dissonances and empty chords amid the beautiful music of Heine. Lacking the lyric gift altogether, Brooksbank's translations want freshness, spontaneity, and music. He does not feel with Heine; and, although in most instances he is fairly reliable as to detail and action where present, he strives in vain to reproduce mood, spirit, and idea. He strives with the tools of the blacksmith where the delicate implements of a master goldsmith are required, and he hacks with a gigantic meat-cleaver in instances that demand a surgeon's scalpel. With little feeling for the potentialities of English poetry and less sense of the significance of his German materials, he has given us mediocre renderings and no translations of Heine.

Moreover, he is notoriously unscrupulous in following his original and produces work which is highly distasteful to the reader who knows the varying moments and delicate shadings of Heine, and which gives no conception of the meaning or grace of the German to one unfamiliar with the original. It is indicated in a publisher's note that Thomas Brooksbank did not live to revise his work, but with all due consideration of this misfortune, it is hard to excuse or make light of the discrepancies of his translations. Often astonishingly careless, he is guilty of inaccuracies which make us question Brooksbank's knowledge of, and familiarity with, the German language in general. Turning more or less at random to his translations of *Die Nordsee*, we notice that the English author has rendered the second verse of *Die Nacht am Strande*, "Es gärt das Meer," with "Wide yawns the sea," and the sixth verse, "Wie'n störriger Griesgram, der gut gelaunt wird," is translated "Like a peevish old grumbler, an old acquaintance"—modifications which spoil the sense entirely. On the surface it would appear that Brooksbank had read "gärt" or "gährt" as "gähnt" and "gelaunt" as "gekannt." However, instances of the same type of misreading are too frequent merely to be excused on the grounds of hasty workmanship. Sometimes, indeed, we come across instances in which the meaning of a German passage has not only been misunderstood but so warped and distorted that the English version becomes absolutely worthless. For example, the concluding verse of the burlesque sonnet, "Dann muss ich dürsten oder ich muss—pumpen" is rendered:

> I must perish
> Of thirst, or to the pump for drink be going

where Brooksbank has fallen into the very stupid error of associating the German "pumpen" with an English "pump"!

"The last three volumes are being done by Margaret Armour (Mrs. W. B. Macdougall), and I have every confidence in presenting her work as that of a highly-gifted poetical translator." So wrote William Heinemann, and his predictions have not struck wide of the mark. Unlike the unfortunate

Thomas Brooksbank, Margaret Armour has a spark at least of the true lyric spirit and no slight talent for the art of translation. Already experienced as a translator before undertaking the task of rendering the *Neue Gedichte, Romanzero, Letzte Gedichte und Nachlese, Atta Troll,* and *Deutschland,* she writes with ease and confidence. Her versions are invariably superior and many are excellent. It would be demanding too much to expect all the translations to be of the same quality since in this case the translator was not given the right or power of selection, but, at any rate, they all show the result of training in the skill, and a pronounced gift in the art, of translation.

However, the criticism that Margaret Armour, with advantage to herself and Heine, might have adhered more closely and faithfully to the originals, may be made in all fairness. Occasionally, she has seen fit to modify details and figures of speech—perhaps with the notion that the epithets substituted were more natural and poetic to the English reader—but nevertheless to the detriment of the originals, for Heine, ever the most careful of workmen, rarely chose a term at random, but through careful selection struck upon those turns of speech that best suited the mood or idea he attempted to convey. However, such a criticism is after all a minor one, for absolute fidelity is impossible in any translation.

Particular attention should be called to Margaret Armour's versions of the celebrated epic *Atta Troll,* the mad "Midsummer Night's Dream," and the hostile, unpopular *Deutschland.* Both poems—*Atta Troll,* the "last free woodland-cry of romanticism," and *Deutschland,* a versified *tableau de voyage*—are the works of a *Tendenz-Dichter* and as such offer innumerable obstacles to the translator. Not only are both pieces full of obscure allusions to, and digressions on, the political, social, and literary situations of Heine's native land, which in themselves offer difficulties hardly to be surmounted by the translator, but the form, particularly of *Atta Troll* with the continual use of assonance in the second and fourth verses, imposes further restrictions on the interpreter. To Margaret Armour's credit, it must be admitted that she has done unusually well in attempting these seldom translated pieces. They are far from her best in the matter of translation but noteworthy, at least, for the difficulties involved.

John Todhunter (1839-1916).—In the preface of John Todhunter's volume containing a translation of Heine's *Buch der Lieder*[13] is found a statement which, despite its length, is worth citing, for not only does it relate the circumstances under which the well-known English scholar and author was induced to translate the poems of the immortal Heine, but it also outlines the general method pursued by Todhunter in his task:

> Versions of two poems from the "Book of Songs," by the late Charles Pelham Mulvany, which appeared in *Kottabos*, were my first introduction to Heine, and tempted me to try my prentice hand in the perilous art of translation, which I found a fascinating game of skill. Some of the poems seemed to go fairly easily and simply into English, while others were evidently cruxes for the translator; and even in the easier ones there were often stanzas or passages which had to wait for a happy moment before I could find a way out of the difficulties they presented—and unfortunately some of the best poems were the hardest to tackle. I had no intention at first of translating the whole Book; but made it my holiday task to pick out a poem here and there, and attempt to put it into decent English verse. It was not until I had shown what I had done to York Powell, himself a most capable translator, that I went to work seriously to revise the versions I had made, and fill the many gaps. His criticisms were most valuable, and he kept me to my task going over most of what I had done before his death. I was never satisfied until I had received his *imprimatur* in due form: "Yes, you've got that."

Of the two specific methods of dealing with poetry in a foreign tongue—"the strict method of translation, in which the sense, meter, rhythm, and emotion of the original are reproduced as accurately and sympathetically as possible" and the

---

13. John Todhunter, *Heine's Book of Songs.*

method of "free fantasia, in which the sense is rehandled in paraphrase with more or less freedom, and the meter altered if necessary"—Todhunter has elected the former:

Heine invites and eludes translation. He must be translated literally, his metres and rhythmical changes must be reproduced with all possible perfection, the very aroma of his delicate style must yield something of its fragrance, as in the process of distillation, or there is little left of him but dry bones, and he vanishes with an ironic smile. It is like trying to catch the song of a bird in a phonograph.

Since the versions of John Todhunter are easily accessible and, for the most part, quite well known, it hardly behooves us here to enter into a detailed criticism of the individual translations. Then, too, since Todhunter's work is of unusually even quality throughout, the citing of any one, or any group, of the poems as typical of a particular trait or degree of excellence is scarcely necessary. The translations, in the main, represent one of the most successful efforts—if not *the* most successful attempt—to render Heine in English verse. Certainly it would not be amiss to declare John Todhunter's work the pre-eminent version of the complete *Buch der Lieder* even though the translator has undoubtedly been surpassed in versions of individual pieces.

As in the case of every translator, Todhunter is often guilty of faulty meter, awkward phrasings, bad use of inversions, and forced rhymes; but as these faults are, in Todhunter's case, exceptions rather than the general rule, they should hardly be isolated for comment. In rare instances he fails to understand Heine's true meaning and on still rarer occasions misses the meaning of a German word or phrase. Here again, however, we have but a few isolated instances of such faults. The blunders occurring most frequently, perhaps, are the use of forced rhymes and the employment of odd, obsolete English words to render a comparatively simple German expression. While these two faults detract considerably from the naturalness and simplicity of Heine's verse, they are in insufficient frequency, when considered in relationship with the whole, to mar to any serious degree the value of Todhunter's translations *in toto*.

Throughout, the translator reveals a complete mastery of Heine's varied rhythms and intricate rhyme schemes, which are reproduced in English with complete naturalness. Heine's brief, poignant lyrics are exceptionally well handled and are in the English nearly as delicate, whimsical, humorous, satirical, or pathetic (as the case may be) as in the German. The longer poems are done with spirit and understanding and are of superior workmanship. Only in the sonnets—too often spoiled by awkward expressions and phrasings, by countless inversions, and by the use of obsolete or unfamiliar English words—does Todhunter lose his grip on the simplicity and straightforwardness less apparent here in Heine, it is true, than in the German poet's other pieces. Considering the difficulties of the sonnet form and the fact that the ideas expressed are easier to render in the German than in the English, even the sonnet translations are of better than average quality. The most difficult of all features to preserve, the tone, is preserved admirably in all the collections of the *Book of Songs*—from the strangeness, eeriness, and muffled gloom of *Junge Leiden* to the surging freedom and salt-sea-tang of the *Nordsee* cycles.

James Thomson (1822-1892).—In youth, James Thomson showed a particular aptitude for languages, learning German, French, Italian, Spanish, Latin, and Greek thoroughly. Of the modern tongues his interest centered, in the main, in Italian and German; he believed German to be one of the most necessary tools of the educated man or woman. On January 6, 1860, we find him writing in the following strain to Agnes Gray:

You say that you may study German in a few more years! Indolent and procrastinating. Give one hour a day to it regularly. "You have no partiality for it?" Did you ever have partiality for grammar, arithmetic, etc.? The language is becoming an essential in education; and it has the best modern literature in Europe. . . .[14]

Thomson's translations include selections from Leopardi, Béranger, Novalis, Goethe, and Heine. The translations from Heine first appeared in the *Jersey Independent* (1861), the *National Reformer* (1862, 1865, 1866), the *Secularist* (1876), and the *Liberal* (1879).[15] Most of the versions appeared originally in the *Secularist* and were collected and reprinted under the title of "Attempts at Translation from Heine" in the volume which contained the *City of Dreadful Night*.

For the most part, in his translations from Heine, Thomson has fared far better than the usual run of translators although his English versions of the German poet in no wise exhibit the brilliance and power of his original poems. In some of the poems, those from the *Lyrisches Intermezzo* and *Die Heimkehr*, his felicity of expression is at times astonishing. With a true feeling for the spirit of the original and an unerring sense of the appropriate English equivalent, he renders with great cleverness the almost untranslatable terms of Heine with the exact English expression. Such a poem as "Die Lotosblume ängstigt sich" taxes the translator in the extreme; yet how well does Thomson transcribe it in "The Lotos flower doth languish," where "doth languish" perfectly renders the mood, spirit, and meaning of "ängstigt sich."

Unfortunately, Thomson is not always so apt, and the hardness and coldness of such rendering as:

> The eyes and the lips and the contours
> Are all just those of my love.

for

> Die Augen, die Lippen, die Wänglein,—
> Sie gleichen der Liebsten genau—

---

14. Josefine Weissel, *James Thomson der Jüngere: Sein Leben und seine Werke*, p. 13.

15. For complete list see bibliography of Dobell & Wheeler in *The City of Dreadful Night*.

leave us unimpressed with Thomson's ability either as translator or poet. And yet, the little gem "Ja, du bist elend," "Ein Fichtenbaum steht einsam," "Du bist wie eine Blume," and "Die blauen Veilchenaugen" are nearly perfectly rendered.

Among the longer translations, attention is called particularly to two versions of *Die Götter Griechenlands*. The first, printed in December, 1862, and the second, printed in July, 1866, are entirely independent of each other. It would seem that Thomson thought his first attempt too inaccurate, for in the second he is at great pains to adhere as closely as possible to Heine's original. It is particularly in the longer poems that Thomson's ability as a translator appears in the worst light. It is here that Thomson proves absolutely unpoetic and is guilty of bringing over into English bodily the compounded forms and intricate structure natural to the German but wholly inexcusable in English. Such translations as:

> The little angel-head on the Rhine-wine-gold-ground

for

> Das Engelköpfchen auf Rheinweingoldgrund[16]

and

> And its heavenly fragrance, it has me enraptured
> It has me inspired, it has me intoxicated.

for

> Und ihr himmlischer Duft, er hat mich beseligt,
> Er hat mich begeistert, er hat mich berauscht.[17]

are typical of the atrocities committed by the British poet in rendering Heine's longer pieces. As a longer and perhaps more comprehensive example of Thomson's characteristic faults in translating the lengthier poems is the following stanza from the *Epilog* to *Die Nordsee*:

> Wie auf dem Felde die Weizenhalmen,
> So wachsen und wogen im Menschengeist

---

16. *Im Hafen.*   17. *Ibid.*

Die Gedanken.
Aber die zarten Gedanken der Liebe
Sind wie lustig dazwischenblühende,
Rot' und blaue Blumen.

As in the field grow wheatears
So grow and wave in the human mind
Thoughts.
But the delicate thoughts of Love
Are the joyous therein-between-blooming
Red and blue flowers.

Despite the opinion of Karl Marx, expressed in a letter to James Thomson shortly after the publication of the latter's first volume, in which Marx expressed his delight at the versions from Heine, which were described as "no translation but a reproduction of the original such as Heine himself, if master of the English language, would have given," we cannot but conclude that Thomson's work, while above the average, is yet full of unevenness and blemishes which prevent him from becoming a truly great interpreter of the German poet.

Julian Fane (1827-1870).—Because of a severe fever which weakened an already delicate constitution, Julian Fane was compelled to withdraw from Harrow and subsequently joined his parents in Berlin in 1841. Here he resided at the hotel of the British Legation, a cosmopolitan center where men of science, literature, politics, and fashion were wont to gather. Among the frequent visitors were Alexander von Humboldt, whose custom it was to dine there every Sunday, Rauch the sculptor, the musician Meyerbeer, Felix Mendelssohn, and the painters Begas, Hensel, and Magnus. Daily intercourse with such society further stimulated an already intelligent and eager interest in the beauties of German art, music, and literature, and Julian Fane, a sensitive, quick-witted youth, was not slow in absorbing as much of German culture as he could possibly acquire. Three years later, in 1844, the youth was officially attached to his father's mission and remained in Berlin until September, 1851, when he was transferred to Vienna.

Although the disturbing and bewildering influence of Heine had enjoyed its fullest activity during the youth's stay at Berlin, it was here, in Vienna, that Fane first devoted himself to the serious study of the works of the great German lyricist. Many of the songs of Heine he set to music of his own, and many he sang to the accompaniment of the charming music of Vesque Puttlingen, better known by the pseudonym of "Hoven."[18] In the meanwhile, he busied himself with the translation of a number of the shorter pieces of Heine which he printed[19] for private circulation only. Julian Fane's translations from Heine were never published, but they attracted, notwithstanding, considerable interest and attention on the part of Heine's English admirers—particularly Lord Houghton, in his interesting article appearing in the *Edinburgh Review* for July, 1856, and Lytton, who gives generous recognition to the translations in his *Memoir*. "The very lightness of these admirable lyrics," says Lord Houghton, "makes it most difficult to reproduce them in another tongue." Julian Fane, however, possessed unusual ability for attempting the well-nigh impossible. An excellent German scholar with a thorough mastery of the language, he was in addition an accomplished musician and a poet in his own right.

Lord Houghton's criticism that: "Mr. Julian Fane's good scholarship renders his translations the most agreeable to those who are acquainted with the originals, but his attempt to transfer to another language many of the most peculiar idioms and most vivacious turns of thought, is frequently unsuccessful," is an apt one. The first copy of Fane's German translations does abound in awkward Germanisms, and it is no doubt of this copy that Houghton spoke. In the years following, however, Fane succeeded fairly well in eliminating the un-English, unpoetic,

---

18. Robert Lytton, *Julian Fane: A Memoir*, p. 145.
19. 1854.

and unmusical terms which marred his first unpublished versions. Indeed, at the time of his death, marginal corrections in pencil showed that he was still engaged upon the task of polishing his versions. In their final form, Fane's translations, which are readily accessible, are among the best in English for sheer music, literal accuracy, and poetic spirit. His interest in Heine never waned, and, after his death, notes and materials for a projected critical biography of the German poet were found among his papers.

Richard Monckton Milnes, Lord Houghton (1809-1885).—The translations and paraphrases of Richard Monckton Milnes appeared first in his well-known article on Heine (*Edinburgh Review* for July, 1856) and were reprinted in *Monographs, Personal and Social* published in 1873. Milnes' translations, including *Die Libelle* (strophes 9-15), *Enfant Perdu*, the first eleven songs from the second *Lazarus* sequence, and *Für die Mouche*, are undertaken in a spirit of love, and what they lack in individual merits and details is more than amply compensated for by the total impression. The most significant version is that of Heine's famous swan-song—part vision and part nightmare—*Für die Mouche*, first published by Alfred Meissner in his *Erinnerungen an Heinrich Heine*. Milnes is unable to reproduce the shimmering *Mondromantik* which plays and hovers about the shadowy ruins of Heine's original, but all that is tangible and translatable in the German is faithfully transcribed. Occasionally, too, Milnes is extremely felicitous in cleverly carrying over an almost untranslatable play on words as when "der zum Sprechen gut getroffene Esel Balaams" appears as "his ass that got the power to talk like other human asses."

On the other hand, the concluding stanza falls far short of the picture presented in Heine:

> Hee-haw! hee-haw! the foolish beast out-brayed,
> Opening his jaws so wide as to provoke me

> Till, by an angry imitation swayed,
> I brayed responsive—and the effort woke me.

Characteristic of the translator is his rendering of "die Liebste" and "geliebtes Kind" as "My darling and my wife." What more could be expected of such a moralizing poet as Milnes, who says in the preface to *Palm Leaves:* "To interest and to benefit us, Poetry must be reflective, sentimental, subjective; it must accord with the conscious, analytical, spirit of present men; it must be deeper than description, more lasting than passion, more earnest than pleasure; it must help or pretend to help, the mind of men out of the struggle and entanglements of life." Respectability must be preserved and maintained at all costs!

This idea of "toning down" Heine is far more evident in the *Lazarus* poems. The "poor sick Jew" crying in anguish upon his mattress grave, scorning, blaspheming, and belittling God and mankind was too strong a dose for staid Victorian England, and in the eyes of Milnes could never have been presented to the English reading public in undiluted form. The English author has extracted from Heine all those ingredients—sarcasm, bitterness, blasphemy, coarseness, etc.—which would have offended British taste, and has made of the German poet a respectable old man making peace with the world and his Creator as he awaits the visitation of death. Let us but compare the third stanza of *Lazarus I* in Milnes' version with Heine's original, and the purpose is manifest:

> Woran liegt die Schuld? Ist etwa
> Unser Herr nicht ganz allmächtig?
> Oder treibt er selbst den Unfug?
> Ach, das wäre niederträchtig.
>
> Where the fault? By whom was sent
> The evil no one can relieve?
> Jehovah not omnipotent!
> Ah! that I never will believe.

Milnes' translation of *Enfant Perdu*, that poignant, desperate cry of the sick Heine, is his best-known rendering and one which embodies the finest virtues of the translator.

J. E. Wallis.—The translations from Heine's *Buch der Lieder* made by J. E. Wallis[20] are of exceptional caliber. The English versions are even and musical, and Wallis is most meticulous in his observance of Heine's original form. The details are accurately and faithfully transcribed and follow in nearly perfect sequence. Literal but not slavishly so, the translations of Wallis present the true spirit and mood of the German in language that is exceptionally well-chosen and adapted to convey Heine's thought. Unlike many of the English translations of Heine, the work of Wallis is steady and unbroken by lapses into bad taste, poor rhyme, or faulty meter. In no instance is the English author guilty of paraphrasing, condensation, or any of the numerous and varied liberties of which translators often avail themselves.

When we consider the fact that the translations of Heine were published as early as 1856, the year of Heine's death, and must necessarily have been undertaken several years prior to that time, the value of the English versions is further enhanced, if only from an historical standpoint, for Wallis's *Book of Songs* represents one of the very first major translations of the German poet.

The longer poems of Heine offer for the most part far less difficulty to the English translator than do the shorter ones, for in the longer ones the ballad style is employed usually—a style which finds a ready counterpart in English. Wallis has been extremely successful in reproducing these longer pieces, and his versions of a number of them, such as "Im süssen Traum, bei stiller Nacht" and "Ein Traum, gar seltsam schauerlich," are unsurpassed in any language. It is in the shorter lyrics of

20. A copy of the *Book of Songs*, tr. by J. E. Wallis (London: Chapman and Hall, 1856), was not available. However, the translations of Wallis in miscellaneous form serve just as well in arriving at a fair estimate of the value of the author as a Heine translator.

pure mood, however, that Wallis shows complete mastery. The translator stands full in the rays of Heine's genius in being able to crystallize in two or three quatrains the fleeting moments for which the German lyricist has become so famous. The gemlike quality of the German with all of Heine's shadows and flickering lights is fully and superbly preserved, and Wallis's versions of Heine's lyrics of mood such as "Wir haben viel für einander gefühlt," "Aus meinen Tränen spriessen," "Teurer Freund, du bist verliebt," and the like are unsurpassed.

Kate Freiligrath-Kroeker (1845-1904).—Kate Freiligrath-Kroeker, the daughter of the great German poet, Ferdinand Freiligrath, whose works together with the fairy tales of Brentano she translated into English, is probably best known for her *Poems Selected from Heinrich Heine* (1887) in which are included the best available translations from both English and American authors. In this admirable collection, Kate Kroeker displays the skill of a Heine, *le plus habile arrangeur*, in shaping her material to form a connected series of varying and contrasting moods ranging from love's awakening to the despair of death.

The editor has included a number of miscellaneous translations of her own in the collection, which are, in the main, attempts to reproduce in English the moments and moods of Heine's shorter lyrics. In these twenty stray lyrics, it becomes quite apparent that Kate Kroeker is definitely more at home in the unrhymed pieces "Wo ich bin, mich rings umdunkelt," "Dämmernd liegt der Sommerabend," *Heinrich*, and *Almansor*, than in those which Heine saw fit to rhyme. Rhyming appears to have been an insurmountable obstacle to this English translator, and she appears at her worst where it is demanded of her.

Her greatest undertaking, and the one which merits her inclusion among the greater translators of Heine, lies in her versions of the two cycles of *Die Nordsee*, the work in which Heine arose from the mediocrity which threatened to engulf him and built one of the greatest monuments to the versatility of his genius. It was in *Die Nordsee,* which is here unusually well translated, that Heine struck a new chord on the lyre of German poetry, for a literary treatment of the sea in German literature had been noticeably absent. Wilhelm Müller had treated it but casually, and Goethe was nearly forty when he caught his first glimpse of the sea, which only inspired in him the most banal of reflections, "and when I turned my glance to the so-called Lido—it is a narrow band of land which encloses the lagoons—I saw the sea for the first time, and on it several sails." That was all. Immediately he spoke of other matters.

Heine's love for the sea had been a love at first sight. "I love the sea as I love my own soul. Often it is as though the sea were indeed my soul."[21] Out of this passion for the sea, for its storms, roars, and deathlike stillnesses which were to Heine the symbols of the human soul, the German poet wove the varying moods of the sea into verse the like of which Germany had never known. The form of *Die Nordsee* is as interesting as its matter. Veering radically from the conventional path of versification, Heine himself doubted seriously if the public would take favorably to this new venture, for we find him writing in 1826 to Karl Simrock:

... It is doubtful if the public will find the "North Sea Pictures" to their taste. The unusual irregular meter may possibly make ordinary sugar-and-water readers sea-sick. Nothing follows the old honest level road, the old track, the old highway.[22]

Years later, Heine confessed to Fanny Lewald his motive in disregarding conventional form: "All such shrill dissonances arose from a decided feeling of antagonism to the hyper-sentimental effeminacy of the Swabian poets and their associates."[23]

Kate Freiligrath-Kroeker is at her best in the absolutely free rhythm of Heine's *Die Nordsee.* It is here that she catches

---

21. *Heinrich Heine's Memoirs.* Ed. G. Karpeles, tr. by Gilbert Canaan, I, 160.
22. *Ibid.,* I, 176.
23. H. Walter, *Heinrich Heine: A Critical Examination of the Poet and His Works,* pp. 75-76.

the true spirit and meaning of Heine. She revels with him in the surging waves, she laughs with him in the teeth of the storm, and she weeps with him at evening on the desolate strand. Her translations are nearly as free and unencumbered as the originals. She has done her work literally and painstakingly and is almost as much at ease as Heine in the loose, unfettered form employed.

Emily Pfeiffer (1827-1890).—Emily Pfeiffer's translations of Heine—nearly thirty in number—appeared in her two slender volumes *Quaterman's Grace and Other Poems* (1879) and *Flowers of the Night* (1889). Emily Pfeiffer appears at her best in her versions of the often translated *Wallfahrt nach Kevlaar* and the long, seldom attempted "Es träumte mir von einer Sommernacht" which was addressed by Heine to his *Mouche* a fortnight before his death. In the former a fairly successful attempt is made to preserve the naïve quality of the medieval tone in Heine's version; the latter is distinguished mainly by the scarcity of other versions of the same poem. In a few short translations such as those of "Ich lieb' eine Blume" (in which faithfulness of form is the chief virtue), "Die blauen Frühlingsaugen," "Ein schöner Stern geht auf," and "Was treibt dich umher" (in which the spirit is adequately if not brilliantly reproduced), the English translator has given us, too, versions above the average.

Unfortunately, the great majority of her translations is of the ordinary, uninspired type. To Heine's "Die Rose, die Lilie, die Taube, die Sonne," which appeared in the German in six lines, she has added ten verses and has succeeded only in making her paraphrase but ten times worse than it ordinarily would have been. More than once, she is guilty of using imperfect rhyme and rhyme merely for the eye, e.g. "thus—house" *(Tragödie)*, "truly—folly" and "love—sooth" ("Emma sage mir die Wahrheit"), and "flood—good" ("Das Meer erstrahlt"). Emily Pfeiffer's version of the *Lorelei* is one of her worst efforts and one of the poorest ever attempted in English. Not only does she fail to catch the note of mockery in the final stanza and the spirit of the entire poem, but her diction is most unpoetic and meaningless. The first stanza of the well-known poem is given as an example of her poor interpretation:

> I know not what should befall me,
> That I am so sad for nought,—
> For a fairy-tale so to enthrall me,
> It will not from my thought.

That Emily Pfeiffer was fully conscious of the difficulty of the task she undertook in translating Heine, is evidenced by the half-apology which precedes her efforts:

The seemingly facile beauty of the shorter poems of Heine, and the infinite difficulty of rendering them into our language, make of them a kind of vortex into which many translators are being unwarily drawn. I make no apology for having striven, for my own part, to lay hold of a few of these compromising gems; feeling that if I am to share the too-common lot of failure, I shall suffer it in the pursuit of a genuine object, and in good company.

Rennell Rodd (b. 1858).—Most of James Rennell Rodd's thirty-odd translations of Heine are to be found in his *Unknown Madonna and Other Poems* (1888), although one or two are contained in the volumes *Rose Leaf and Apple Leaf* (1906) and *Songs in the South* (1881). As a translator of Heine, Rodd belongs to that host of willing, diligent, but uninspired workers whose translations, while literal and accurate, hardly deserve the name of poetry. As in the case of so many others, Rodd has been at great effort to preserve the form and matter of Heine. Unfortunately, he is no genius; and the spirit of the originals has shied away at his coming and is totally absent in his English versions.

In a small minority of his attempts, however, he has breathed into his versions a true poetic spirit which, if not Heine's, is nevertheless a credit to the work. One of his best translations, and one which most nearly approaches the spirit of the original, is the version of "Sterne mit den goldnen Füsschen":

> Stars with little feet all golden
> Shyly pass and tread so light,
> Lest they wake the earth that slumbers
> In the bosom of the night!
>
> Each green leaf an ear that listens
> All the forests voiceless stand,
> And the mountain like a dreamer
> Reaches forth a shadow-hand!
>
> What was that across the stillness!
> Through my heart the echo rang;
> Did I hear my darling calling,
> Or a nightingale that sang?

Now and then, too, Rodd paraphrases his original material with happy result, as in the second stanza of "Der Brief, den du geschrieben," which compared with the German reads as follows:

> Zwölf Seiten, eng und zierlich!
> Ein kleines Manuskript!
> Man schreibt nicht so ausführlich,
> Wenn man den Abschied gibt.
>
> Almost a little manuscript,
> And written close and neat;
> If that were my dismissal
> Then why the second sheet?

Ernest Radford.—Ernest Radford, who has attempted a number of translations from the German—particularly from Goethe, Neumann, and Klaus Groth—has forty-four translations from Heine contained in his volumes *Chambers Twain* (1890) and *Old and New* (1895). Radford is included in the group of semi-major translators more because of the quantity than the quality of his work, which wilts pitifully under the strong, clear light of criticism. His versions are for the most part of merely average quality, displaying a fairly literal tendency, but of a very uneven merit as a whole and as individual pieces.

Occasionally, as in his version of "Mensch, verspotte nicht den Teufel," he catches a spark of Heine's genius, but far more often he is groping in the dark toward a will-o'-the-wisp which manages with perfect ease to elude his awkward grasp. In such translations as "Ein Jüngling liebt ein Mädchen" where his attempt at humor would make Heine's Muse bury her face in shame, "In den Küssen welche Lüge" where he misinterprets Heine's meaning in the last verse, and "Am Kreuzweg wird begraben" where he misinterprets the entire poem, he is definitely at his lowest ebb. Indeed, in fairness, it must be said that in all his attempts to translate the humorous or whimsical pieces of Heine, Radford could scarcely have failed with greater distinction. In a great majority of the translations, the English author shows absolute disregard for the style of the originals. Heine was ever a painstaking artist and chiseled carefully the form of each of his many gems. Whether through ignorance of versification or through sheer defiance, Radford is ever prone to gallop on none-too-sure-footed anapaests and stumble and totter on mixed and jumbled feet through Heine's carefully selected and steadily marching trochees and iambs.

Upon the appearance of Radford's translations, the versions met with a great deal of criticism ranging from the exalted opinion[24] of the *Literary World* ("Even the uninitiated can see at a glance that here is the perfection of translation") to the lowly estimate of an unknown critic that, "of course in a free Country any man may make a fool of himself if he likes, but this liberty ought to be restrained when impious hands are laid on a poet like Heine."[25] The following statements[26] more nearly characterize and evaluate the work of Ernest Radford:

It would be good for Mr. Radford, and better for Heine, if he would cease to attempt the impossible and traduce the exquisite German lyrics.—*American Traveler*

---

24. Ernest Radford, *Old and New*, p. 140.
25. *Ibid.*   26. *Ibid.*

In some translations from Heine Mr. Radford displays a very uncommon grasp of the inner meanings of poetry which almost defies adequate interpretation into English.—*Scotsman*

A fresh crop of hopeless failures in attempts to translate Heine.—*Scottish Review*

He succeeds far better in his original verses than in his translations of Heine, which are unpolished and inaccurate. Humour is certainly not Mr. Radford's strong point.—*Manchester Examiner*.

William Stigand (1825-1915).—Best known for his *Life, Work and Opinions of Heine,* William Stigand also tried his hand at translating more than forty of Heine's poems including the longer pieces: *Das Sklavenschiff, Die Wallfahrt nach Kevlaar, Poseidon, Seegespenst, Im Hafen, Bergidylle,* and *Atta Troll*. Stigand appears to have had absolutely no conception of the peculiar genius that was Heine's or of the principles of poetic production. His translations are childish and pitifully weak. With little notion of the innate beauty of Heine's verse, and less of the potentialities of English poetry, Stigand plods along with absolute disregard of the spirit of the originals and often with little care of Heine's form. License of form and inability to capture the idea may be excused, after a fashion, provided they lie beyond the capabilities of the translator; but coarse, crude, unpolished work—all too often in bad taste—offends and wearies. Stigand is neither poet nor interpreter. He is a butcher, and as such has succeeded only in mutilating Heine beyond all possible recognition.

Thomas Selby Egan.—From the standpoint of quantity of translations from Heine, Thomas Selby Egan deserves undoubtedly to be ranked among the major translators of the German poet. It would appear from the number of Egan's versions and from a statement made by him in the latter part of the past century, that he had cultivated long and assiduously an affection for the poetical flights of Heinrich Heine and was anxious to render as many of that author's pieces in English as

Major Translators   35

he possibly could. In a dedication written to A. A. Vansittart, a former Fellow of Trinity College, Cambridge, Egan expresses his indebtedness to Vansittart in becoming acquainted with the works of Heine and his accomplishment in the matter of translating the German originals:

About Christmas in the year 1868 you kindly gave me Heine's Book of Songs, and thus introduced me for the first time to his poetry, which, strange to say, I had never before read, although from early times well-acquainted with his prose writing. Since then I have translated for my amusement nearly everything he ever wrote....[27]

If Egan's statement that he had translated "nearly everything he ever wrote" can be taken as a literal one, we can only surmise that the English author published but a part of his work, for the versions from his hand do not represent anything resembling completeness. It can be said, however, that the English versions represent a fair attempt in sampling the various collections of Heine. In his volume called *Atta Troll and Other Poems by Heine*, Egan has left translations of the following pieces from the *Buch der Lieder: Vorrede*; from the *Romanzen*, Nos. 2, 6, 8, 16; from the *Junge Leiden*, Nos. 1, 2; from the *Lieder*, No. 9; the sonnets on Schlegel and B. Heine together with five of the fresco-sonnets on Christian Sethe; from the *Lyrisches Intermezzo*, Nos. 9, 18, 19, 32, 33, 43, 59, 64; from *Heimkehr*, Nos. 2, 3, 6, 7, 29, 40, 41, 44, 47, 61, 85 and *Die Wallfahrt nach Kevlaar*; from the *Harzreise, Bergidylle* and *Der Hirtenknabe*; and the two long poems *Atta Troll* and *Deutschland*.

It is perhaps as well that there exists no complete collection of Egan's translations, for in the ones listed above, which by Egan's own admission in his dedication to Vansittart are the best of his many efforts, we have translations of a very poor quality. Egan's work throughout is marred by inversions, forced rhymes, and poor choice of words. The English author tries desperately to preserve meter and form, and, in so doing,

27. Thomas S. Egan, *Atta Troll and Other Poems by Heine.*

produces tame, unpoetic, and non-inspirational pieces unworthy of bearing any poet's name. While the translator is decidedly more at home in rendering the longer, narrative pieces than the brief, lyric gems, the results are at best of such mediocre quality that they warrant little if any consideration.

Philip G. L. Webb.—The translations of Philip George Lancelot Webb include versions of the following poems by Heine:[28] poems of the *Harzreise;* from *Die Heimkehr,* Nos. 10, 18, 23, 26, 32, 42, 43, 45, 48, 50, 52, 53, 55, 56, 57, 58, 60, 63, 65, 69, 75, 76, 78, 87, 89, *Götterdämmerung, Ratcliff, Donna Clara, Almansor;* from *Romanzen, Belsazar;* from the *Sonnette, An meine Mutter* I, II; from the *Lyrisches Intermezzo,* Nos. 7, 9, 18, 19, 20, 21, 22, 24, 25, 30, 31, 35, 38, 50, 54, 58, 59, 61, 68; from the *Historien, Der Asra;* from *Neuer Frühling,* Nos. 15, 29; from *Lazarus, Bimini.*

Philip Webb's versions of Heine rank easily with the best of the many attempts to translate the German poet; among recent efforts his are without doubt second only to the masterful versions of John Todhunter. The versions of the *Harzreise* group are extremely well done and, with the possible exception of the English translation of "Ich bin die Prinzessin Ilse," which is spoiled somewhat by stumbling meter (but not enough to prevent its being a superior rendering), are among the finest yet done into English. The translator has nearly perfectly preserved the easy "open-air romanticism" of Heine throughout—as is immediately apparent in his version of the Prologue:

> Coats of black and silken stockings
> Courtly ruffles white as snow,
> Soft discourse and friendly greetings—
> If there were but hearts below!

> Hearts to beat within those bosoms,
> Hearts to love, and hearts to melt!—
> I am sick of all your ballads
> Feigning woes you never felt!

28. P. G. L. Webb, *More Translations from Heine.*

> I will hie me to the mountains,
> Where the peaceful chalets be,
> Where the lungs can breathe unstifled,
> Where the winds are blowing free.
>
> I will hie me to the mountains,
> Where the dark pine-forests lie,
> Where birds sing and streamlets whisper,
> Where the clouds sweep proudly by.
>
> Fare ye well, ye polished salons,
> Sirs and Madams, polished too!
> I will hie me to the mountains,
> And look down and laugh at you!

In the shorter lyrics from *Die Heimkehr, Lyrisches Intermezzo,* and *Neuer Frühling,* which are numbered according to the Hoffmann and Campe 1885 edition, the English versions are of more uneven quality. A great many of the translations are superior. Some, indeed, are excellent, such as the versions of "Teurer Freund, du bist verliebt":

> Dearest friend, thou art in love,
> Smitten sore with Cupid's dart;
> Ever darker grows thy brain,
> Ever brighter grows thy heart.
>
> Dearest friend, thou art in love,
> And thou wilt confess it not,
> But I see the heart's bright fire
> Through thy waistcoat growing hot.

and "Bist du wirklich mir so feindlich":

> Hast thou truly come to hate me?
> Hast thou truly altered quite?
> All the world shall be my witness
> How I suffered thy despite.
>
> O ye lips, ye lips ungrateful,
> Say, how could you slander so
> Him, who with such deep devotion
> Used to kiss you, long ago?

All too often, however, in the shorter lyrics, Webb is guilty of poor, irregular meter which spoils the music and easy simplicity of Heine's verses. At times, too, the English translator strives too desperately for rhyme and succeeds only in giving us imperfect rhyming conceived purely for the eye—as in the fiftieth poem from *Die Heimkehr* where we find combinations such as "strove—love," "proved—loved," and the like.

The versions of the sonnets written by Heine to his mother are, perhaps, the finest in English translation. The first sonnet is given here in Webb's translation as indicative of that author's excellence in handling this form of Heine:

> It is my wont to carry my head high,
> My manners oft are stiff and void of grace,
> If the king's self should look me in the face,
> I would not cast my eyes down, no, not I.
>
> Yet, mother dear, be it again confessed,
> However proud and headstrong I may be,
> In thy sweet, blessed, gentle company
> Oft-times I am with humble fear possessed.
>
> Is it thy spirit that doth my pride subdue,
> Thy lofty spirit that pierces all things through
> And flashing soars into the heavens' wide blue?
> Bitter it is, thrice bitter, to recall
> How oft my deeds have served thy heart to gall,
> That golden heart which loved me more than all.

The crowning achievement of Philip G. L. Webb lies in his handling of the longer pieces of Heine. Occasionally, the translator permits himself a few unwarranted and perhaps undesirable liberties—as in the use of rhyme in the version of *Donna Clara*—but for the most part the poems are faithfully, accurately, and spiritedly rendered. In versions such as those of *Götterdämmerung* and *Ratcliff*, the translator reveals a superb mastery, not only of Heine, but of English diction and language as well.

11. *Minor Translators*

THE NUMBER of minor translators of Heine is amazingly large. In this group are included those English authors who attempted in round numbers from one to twenty-five versions of Heine's poems. The group includes many well-known names in the field of literary endeavor as well as others whose primary claim to immortality lies in the fact that their names have been coupled with that of Heinrich Heine. The average number of translations ranges from five to eight. As the translations vary in respect to quantity, so do they vary as to quality when considered both as a whole and in regard to the individual authors. A great many prove to be of an unusually high standard of excellence while others are the merest excuse for literature of any type. Regardless, however, of the quality, the number of versions alone attests the popularity of Heine among the poets and poetasters of England.

For purposes of convenient reference, the translators are arranged in alphabetical order. A chronological order would perhaps be preferable; however, it is impossible to determine from the dates of publication when the vast majority of versions was undertaken. Rather than list them indiscriminately or in inaccurate chronological sequence, the alphabetical arrangement is used and should prove of great benefit in the matter of hasty reference.

"*John Ackerlos.*"[1]—John Stores Smith, writing under the pseudonym of "John Ackerlos," has four translations quoted in

---

1. *Selections from the Poetry of Heinrich Heine*, tr. by John Ackerlos (London: John Chapman, 1854). This volume, listed in the bibliography contained in Sharp's *Life of Heine*, is not available.

the Kroeker collection: "Ich lache ob den abgeschmackten Laffen" (*Junge Leiden*, B. d. L.*), "Es erklingen alle Bäume" (*Neuer Frühling*, B. d. L.), and *Wartet Nur* and *Warnung* (*Romanzen*, N. G.). Smith's translations are literal and for the most part well rendered although *Wartet Nur* and *Warnung* lack spirit. The difficult sardonic sonnet, "Ich lache ob den abgeschmackten Laffen," is exceptionally well rendered. As a specimen of Smith at his best, the translation of "Es erklingen alle Bäume" is given:

> All their nests with song are ringing,
> Forest music fills the land;
> Who may be the concert-leader
> In the feathered woodland band?
>
> Is it that grey Plover yonder,
> Who keeps nodding quick and strong?
> Or the Pedant who, incessant,
> With his "cuckoo" times the song?
>
> Or is it the Stork, that gravely
> Still keeps tapping with his bill,
> Just as though he were conductor,
> While the rest their music trill?
>
> No, in mine own heart is sitting
> The song-leader of the grove,
> And I feel how he the time beats,
> And I think his name is—Love![2]

David Anderson.—In a slender volume which bears the title *Edith Cavell and Other Poems*, David Anderson, a little-known poet of the First World War era, has attempted four translations from the German: one of Goethe's immortal "Über allen Gipfeln" and three short lyrics of Heine.[3] The versions of Heine are of three of his most popular songs: "Du bist wie eine Blume" and "Du schönes Fischermädchen" from

---

* The titles of Heine's books will hereinafter sometimes be abbreviated as: B. d. L. for *Buch der Lieder*; N. G. for *Neue Gedichte*; L. G. for *Letzte Gedichte*; L. G. u. N. for *Letzte Gedichte und Nachlese*; R. for *Romanzero*.

2. Kroeker, *op. cit.*, p. 195.   3. Pp. 79-80.

Die Heimkehr and "Wenn zwei von einander scheiden" from the *Lyrisches Intermezzo*. While Anderson makes a valiant attempt to be as literal as possible in his versions, he fails altogether in transcribing the mood and delicacy of Heine's songs through his stumbling, awkward meter and his want of simplicity and true poetic feeling. The finest of the small group is his version of "Du schönes Fischermädchen" which, given below as indicative of the translator at his best, still leaves much to be desired:

THE FISHER MAIDEN

O beauteous maiden of the sea,
Pray draw thy bark to land,
And hither come and sit by me;
We'll prattle hand in hand.

And on my breast all fearless lay
Thy little head, sweet child.
Dost thou not trust thee every day
Upon the ocean wild?

My heart, dear maid, is like the deep,
Has storm and ebb and flow,
And many a priceless pearl doth sleep
Far in its depth below.

William Archer (1856-1924).—William Archer, a prolific writer of the early part of the present century, is best known probably for translating and editing the works of Ibsen. Among his other translations, perhaps the most significant is his English version of Gerhart Hauptmann's *Hanneles Himmelfahrt*. The only other significant work of Archer in connection with German literature comprises his selection of "Five Hundred and One Gems of German Thought" (1917) and a translation of Heine's "Das Glück ist eine leichte Dirne" attempted in 1881. Archer's version of Heine's foreword to the *Lamentationen* (R.) is undoubtedly a superior one, which not only is especially faithful to the original lyric in content, but which likewise preserves admirably both the form and spirit of the

German. Unquestionably it is the best dialect version of the little poem yet attempted, and because of its unusualness in this respect it is cited here:

> O Joy is but a lichtsome hizzy,
> She winna bide wi' ye ava;
> She stroks yer broo an' makes ye dizzy,
> Then kisses ye, an' flees awa.
>
> Dame Sorrow is a canty kimmer,
> A warm embrace ye's hae frae her;
> She vows she isna thrang—the limmer!
> Knits by your bed an' winna stir.[4]

Thomas Ashe (1836-1889).—The numerous and varied attempts at translation on the part of Thomas Ashe attest to that writer's interest in and knowledge of languages in general. The poet has left among his extant works scattered translations: from the Greek of Theocritus, Moschus, and Bion; from the Latin of Catullus, Vergil, Horace, Ovid, and Richard Crashaw; one translation from the Italian of Dante; and poems from French writers too numerous to mention. With the exception of Heine, Goethe, from whom Ashe has given us nine short poems, seems to be the only German writer with whom the English poet is familiar. Ashe's translations from Heine[5] are: from the *Junge Leiden*, "Morgens steh' ich auf und frage"; from *Die Heimkehr*, "In mein gar zu dunkles Leben," "Du schönes Fischermädchen," "Wenn ich auf dem Lager liege," "Ich weiss nicht was soll es bedeuten"; from *Neuer Frühling*, "Wenn du gute Augen hast," "Die blauen Frühlingsaugen," "Ich lieb' eine Blume"; from *Verschiedene, Katharina*.

Thomas Ashe makes in his translations a definite and fairly successful attempt to preserve as far as possible the form and substance of the originals. The rhythm is true and the thought is accurately transcribed. Occasionally, Ashe is a bit too literal and allows the unwieldy German word-order to creep into his

---

4. Charles Archer, *William Archer: Life Work and Friendships*, p. 95.
5. Thomas Ashe, *Poems*.

verse. The translations from the earlier poems of Heine are far superior to those from the later collections with the exception of *Katharina* which, unlike the others, is a comparatively loose translation and the equal if not the superior of the original German poem. With the exception of the first stanza, which limps along dreadfully in Ashe's translation, the *Lorelei* represents one of the better English versions of Heine's most popular song. All in all, *The Fisher-Girl (Du schönes Fischermädchen)* is Ashe's finest rendering if we can excuse the unfortunate rhyme of the second stanza:

> You lovely fisher-maiden,
> Draw in your boat to land;
> Come near me, sit beside me;
> We'll prattle hand in hand.
>
> Your little head lean on me,
> And have no fear of me:
> Each day you venture boldly
> To trust the lawless sea.
>
> A sea as well my heart is,
> With storm and ebb and flow;
> And many a pearl unheeded,
> Rests in the depths below.

William E. A. Axon (1846-1913).—William E. A. Axon, in *The Ancoats Skylark and other Verses,* has translated into English ten poems from the German—two from Schiller and one each from Fr. Bodenstedt, Rabbi Stern, Uhland, August Schwarzkopf, Paul Förster, Mendelssohn, Herder, and Heine. His translation from Heine, that of the ever popular, undying lyric, "Du bist wie eine Blume," is better than average. Axon's version, which is unknown to the majority of English readers, is given below:

> Thou art as yonder flower
> So pure, and fair and kind,
> Yet when I see thy face
> Grief in my heart I find.

> And fain upon thy head
> My hands would lay in prayer,
> That God will keep thee still
> So kind and pure and fair.[6]

William Blathwayt (b. 1882).—In *Collected Poems*[7] of William Blathwayt appear a great number of translations from the French and German including versions of Heine's "Der Brief, den du geschrieben" *(Neuer Frühling)*, "Herz, mein Herz, sei nicht beklommen" *(Die Heimkehr)*, and "Mein Kind, wir waren Kinder" *(Die Heimkehr)*. Blathwayt's translation of "Herz, mein Herz" is fairly accurate but totally unimpressive. In the ever popular "Mein Kind, wir waren Kinder," the translator has attempted, in the main, to be literal but has spoiled the version by the liberties taken in form and meaning. Heine's easy quatrains appear in Blathwayt's version as unwieldy and unpoetic couplets, and at times the meaning of the German is stupidly ignored as in the last stanza where the philosophical import of the German is absolutely lost in the English:

> Vorbei sind die Kinderspiele,
> Und alles rollt vorbei—
> Das Geld und die Welt und die Zeiten,
> Und Glauben und Lieb' und Treu!

> But these wonderful hours have vanished and all has faded away,
> The fairyland of the hen-coops, the cat and the cocks and the hay.

The best of Blathwayt's translations is his version of the delicately humorous "Der Brief, den du geschrieben"—one of the finest of the many English renderings of the little gem:

> The letter that you lately wrote
> Will never make me fear;
> You love no more, so says your note,
> But it is long, my dear.

---

6. W. E. A. Axon, *The Ancoats Skylark and Other Verses*, p. 93.
7. Pp. 119-121.

Twelve pages penned so neatly
Must other thoughts imply;
One does not write so fully
When one would say "good-bye."

F. W. Bourdillon (1852-1921).—In the slender volume, *Verses*, by Francis William Bourdillon, are to be found, scattered among the original poems, translations from Feuchtersleben, Rückert, Victor Hugo, Jordi, Lemoine, Lucan, and, of course, Heine. The volume contains, in addition, poems addressed to Albert Dürer and Bismarck. Bourdillon has left us but one translation of Heine, that of "Das Meer erglänzte weit hinaus"[8] from *Die Heimkehr*. The English poet has remained throughout faithful to the German, and in some instances, it must be admitted, has improved upon the original meter. Considered as a whole, however, Bourdillon's translations are flat and stale when compared with the original versions.

Percy Boyd (d. 1876).—As a translator of Heine, Percy Boyd is deserving of no special notice other than the mere observation of the fact that his are among the earliest attempts to render Heine in English verse. In 1848, Boyd published a *Book of Ballads from the German* in which are found some six or seven scattered translations of shorter poems drawn from the *Buch der Lieder*, such as "Ein Fichtenbaum steht einsam," "Du liegst mir so gern im Arme," "Mein süsses Lieb, wenn du im Grab," *Lorelei*, and *Bergstimme*. All of Boyd's versions are marred by awkward Germanisms and infidelity to the originals and are at best but weak and uninspired attempts.

John Le Gay Brereton (1871-1933).—John Le Gay Brereton, a former assistant librarian in the University of Sydney, has but one poem after Heinrich Heine. Brereton has had unusual success in this little poem in maintaining throughout the true Heine spirit and atmosphere:

I know thou dost not love me,
Nor carest for my fate;

---

8. F. W. Bourdillon, *Verses*.

I would that thou wert worthy
Either of love or hate.

I rave so much about thee,
Pitiless heart of stone!
Who never wept at another's plight,
And never knew thine own.

Who couldst smile, and make a heaven,
With a woman's cunning spell,
And turn, and with another smile,
Couldst make my life a hell.

I was a fool, I know it,
To deem myself forlorn;
Alas, thou art not worthy
Even of my scorn![9]

Elizabeth Barrett Browning (1806-1861).—It is quite notable that among Elizabeth Barrett Browning's paraphrases or translations but one modern poet is represented, and that one is Heine. Yet Elizabeth Barrett Browning had more than a speaking knowledge of several of the modern continental authors including many German ones. She mentions Goethe by name on several occasions,[10] read *Die Leiden des jungen Werthers* in her youth, and among her poems is one entitled *To Bettina the Child Friend of Goethe*. In *A Vision of Poets*, too, she speaks of Goethe as well as of Schiller. Martin Luther is likewise mentioned in her correspondence. Indeed, Elizabeth Barrett Browning was no stranger to the works of German authors. Among her many readings are found Freytag's *Soll und Haben*,[11] an English translation of *Jung Stilling*,[12] and the works of Alexander Humboldt and David Straus.[13]

Despite the intense popularity of Goethe in England, more extensive mention is made of Heine than of any other German

---

9. John Le Gay Brereton, *Travels of Prince Legion and Other Poems*, p. 141.
10. F. G. Kenyon, ed., *The Letters of Elizabeth Barrett Browning*, I, 474. See also *Letters of R. B. and E. B. B.*, I, 273; II, 315.
11. Kenyon, *Letters*, II, 282, 288.
12. *Letters of R. B. and E. B. B.*, I, 112.
13. Kenyon, *Letters of E. B. B.*, II, 426.

poet. As early as November 5, 1846, in a letter to Mrs. Martin written from Pisa, the poetess says:

> ... As to our domestic affairs, it is not to *my* honor and glory that the "bills" are made up every week and paid more regularly "than the bard beseems," while dear Mrs. Jameson laughs outright at our miraculous prudence and economy, and declares that it is past belief and precedent that we should not burn the candles at both ends, and the next moment will have it that we remind her of the children in a poem of Heine's who set up housekeeping in a tub, and inquired gravely as to the price of coffee.[14]

The "children who set up housekeeping in a tub" are obviously taken from Heine's delightful lyric "Mein Kind, wir waren Kinder," a poem which Elizabeth Barrett Browning translated in 1860 and of which more will be said later.

In spite of Heine's desperate effort to conceal his agonizing sufferings from the world during his life-time, Elizabeth Barrett Browning shows that she was not only well acquainted with the poet's works, but was also well informed as to the intimate details concerning Heine the man. Dated from Florence, September 4, 1854 (two years prior to Heine's death), a letter was written by the poetess in an attempt to console Miss Mitford, who had requested Elizabeth Barrett Browning to pray for her:

> ... You know how that brilliant, witty, true poet Heine, who was an atheist (as much as a man can pretend to be), has made a public profession of a change of opinion which was pathetic to my eyes and heart the other day as I read it. He has joined no church, but simply (to use his own words) has "returned home to God like the prodigal son after a long tending of the swine." It is delightful to go home to God, even after a tending of the sheep. Poor Heine has lived a sort of living death for years, quite deprived of his limbs, and suffering tortures to boot, I understand.[15]

The "poor sick Jew," Heinrich Heine, with his terrible sufferings, both physical and spiritual, was quite the type to awaken the wholehearted and genuine sympathy of such a

14. *Ibid.*, I, 301.   15. *Ibid.*, II, 301.

person as was Elizabeth Barrett Browning who, herself, was no stranger, at least, to physical discomfiture. It is little wonder that the emaciated Mephistopheles with the face of Christ should be singled out by Elizabeth Barrett Browning from among a host of nineteenth-century poets for purposes of translation. Among her many poems, six paraphrases from Heine stand as mute testimony to the sympathy and interest of the English writer. The paraphrases are dated from Rome, 1860; but it is quite likely that they were undertaken one or two years earlier, for from Rome on December 8, 1858, in a letter to her beloved sister, Henrietta, she wrote:

... The most delightful journey we had from Florence,—seven days of it. So strange it is, living on the road in that way. We had books in the carriage, and I read through poems in German, and translated two or three of them.[16]

At any rate, two years later, the translations were completed. They represent versions of the following poems: from *Lyrisches Intermezzo*, "Du liebst mich nicht, du liebst mich nicht," "Mein süsses Lieb, wenn du im Grab," "Aus meinen grossen Schmerzen"; from *Die Heimkehr*, "Die Jahre kommen und gehen," "Bist du wirklich mir so feindlich?" "Mein Kind, wir waren Kinder."

It must be truthfully admitted that Elizabeth Barrett Browning's paraphrases are far from satisfactory. In "The Years Come and Go," she has missed entirely the delightful irony of Heine's concluding stanza:

> Nur einmal noch möcht' ich dich sehen,
> Und sinken vor dir aufs Knie,
> Und sterbend zu dir sprechen:
> Madame, ich liebe Sie!

which she translates as follows:

> Could I see thee but once, one day,
> And sink down so on my knee

---

[16]. *Elizabeth Barrett Browning: Letters to Her Sister*, ed. by Leonard Huxley, p. 303.

And die in thy sight while I say,
"Lady, I love but thee!"[17]

The paraphrase for which she is best known, and the one which is included in most anthologies of Heine in English verse (on what basis it is hard to determine), is "My Child, We Were Two Children," an attempt at translation of "Mein Kind, wir waren Kinder." Elizabeth Barrett Browning's translation has been over-estimated and over-emphasized. It is at best but a mediocre translation of Heine's delightful lyric and one that is surpassed by more than one English poet of far less ability.

The best of the lot is the little poem "Thou Lovest Me Not" (from Heine's "Du liebst mich nicht") which is quoted below:

Thou lovest me not, thou lovest me not!
'Tis scarcely worth a sigh,
Let me look in thy face and no king in his peace
Is a gladder man than I.

Thou hatest me well, thou hatest me well,
Thy little red mouth has told.
Let it reach me a kiss and however it is,
My child, I am well consoled.[18]

All in all, the paraphrases of Elizabeth Barrett Browning are hardly worth the effort required to read them. She has tried too consciously, too desperately for exactness, and, as a result, the poetical quality is lacking. Her verses are mere prose utterances hobbling along on crutches. It is as if she had translated with one hand while the other thumbed diligently through a pocket dictionary.

George Browning (1813-1878).—George Browning is one of the few minor translators of Heine and other German authors whose expressed purpose in putting into English verse poems selected from the German masters was to disseminate and encourage the study of German culture—particularly as

17. *Poetical Works*, p. 596.   18. *Ibid.*

represented through literary forms. While residing in the little Saxon-Weimar capital, he tells us, the glory and beauty of German poetry made so deep an impression upon his mind that as soon as his knowledge of the German language permitted, he set himself the task of rendering into English verse some of those poems which had already gained a world-wide renown. In doing so, he "endeavored to adhere as closely to the original as is compatible with poetical principles." He tells us further that "it is for the translations that I hope to receive some small share of public attention because I think they may be the indirect cause of inducing many to court a closer acquaintance with that richest of modern languages, the German; and I can assure them that in so doing the time will never be regretted, and the knowledge gained will be a life-long gratification."[19]

Browning, true to his word, has rendered in English verse versions of poems by Goethe, Schiller, Stobbe, Beck, Rückert, Storm, Sturm, Tanner, Kerner, and—last but not least—Heine, from whom we have seven translations: from *Die Heimkehr*, "Mein Kind, wir waren Kinder," "Du hast Diamanten," "Du bist wie eine Blume," "Auf den Wällen Salamancas"; from the *Lyrisches Intermezzo*, "Ich hab' im Traum geweinet"; from *Die Nordsee*, Erster Zyklus, "Das Meer hat seine Perlen."

Browning has taken rather full advantage of his idea of adhering as closely to the original "as is compatible with poetical principles." Although he manages to remain fairly constant to the general impression that Heine would have us receive, he has taken more than a few liberties with the details that go to make up that impression. In his rendering of "Das Meer hat seine Perlen,"[20] Browning has missed entirely the underlying idea of the entire *Nordsee* volume. In his translation, which bears the title "Pearls hath the Ocean," he has cramped and forced Heine's great lyric into the typical

---

19. George Browning, *Footprints*, Introduction, pp. v-vi.
20. *Ibid.*, p. 37.

Heinesque quatrains of the poet's earlier days. Browning seems to have overlooked the fact that Heine, in the *Nordsee*, had abandoned the popular form employed to such great extent in the earlier volumes and had become here for the first time completely original in his use of *freie Rhythmen* in which he makes a radical departure from the conventional forms prevalent at the time. To attempt to rhyme any part of *Die Nordsee* cycles is to attempt to chain the wind or to control the movement of the waves twisting and surging restlessly and ceaselessly throughout the entire volume.

Nor has Browning failed to take liberties with his other translations—liberties which undoubtedly are more excusable but which, nevertheless, keep his versions from rising above the mediocre. There is one translation, however, which deserves particular commendation for its likeness to the original; it is his version of "Du hast Diamanten und Perlen," which is worthy of being cited:

> Pearls and diamonds hast thou, loved one,
> Also all that men adore,
> And thine eyes, none can be brighter—
> So I ask—what will'st thou more?
>
> For thine eyes have such a radiance,
> Such a brilliancy before
> Ne'er inspired a poet's verses—
> Maiden say—what will'st thou more?
>
> With those stars of heavenly beauty
> Hast thou touched the tender core
> Of my heart—and now I'm ruined
> At thy feet—what will'st thou more?[21]

Mary Anne Burt.—In what appears to have been the only work written by Mary Anne Burt, *Specimens of the Choicest Lyrical Productions of the Most Celebrated German Poets*, first published in Zürich and then re-issued under the title of *The German Parnassus in Twelve Different Languages*, the

21. *Ibid.*, p. 24.

author has left splendid translations of six poems[22] all found originally in Heine's *Neue Gedichte*—*Bertrand de Born, Katharina,* "Es war ein alter König," *Ritter Olaf, Die Nixen* and "Morgens send' ich dir die Veilchen." All of the translations are done with genuine feeling for the thought, mood, and form of the originals. In each of the poems attempted, the author has worked carefully and painstakingly to reproduce the originals in a form as nearly perfect as possible; without exception each effort represents superior craftsmanship. As a specimen of Mary Anne Burt's ability as a translator, her version of "Es war ein alter König" is cited here:

> Once on a time there lived a King,
> Splenetic with the cares of life,
> And this infirm and aged King
> Espoused a youthful wife.
>
> A gentle Page, of graceful mien,
> With spirit light, and golden hair,
> Attended on that beauteous Queen,
> Her silken train to bear.—
>
> An ancient legend shall I tell?
> Tender, yet sad, the history!—
> The Page and Lady loved too well,
> And both were doomed to die.

Prefacing her translations of Heine, Mary Anne Burt has included a short biographical sketch of the German poet.

Wathen Mark Wilks Call (1817-1890).—Wathen Mark Wilks Call has included in his *Golden Histories* several scattered translations from Anacreon, Moschus, Catullus, and Heine. Although the book was not published until the turn of the seventies, it is fairly evident that the majority of the translations were undertaken a few years earlier, for pasted to the flyleaf of the copy examined, there is the following original note addressed to A. J. Ellis:

---

22. *Specimens of the Choicest Lyrical Productions of the Most Celebrated German Poets,* pp. 218-222.

Will you kindly accept the little volume of poems—some of them written in early life and none of them, save a bit of translation, written since 1859—which will accompany or perhaps follow this note?

The translations from Heine number three: from *Die Heimkehr*, "Das Herz ist mir bedrückt," "Mein Kind, wir waren Kinder"; from *Die Harzreise, Bergidylle*.

Call's translations are undoubtedly among the best of the century. He has given us as accurate and faithful a translation as could be desired. The thought, mood, tone, and rhythm are as true to the original lines as it is possible to be in reproductions of this sort. His "My Child, We Were Children" preserves admirably the delicate, whimsical humor of Heine's original poem and sacrifices to no appreciable extent the light touches of Heinesque satire so difficult to reproduce in English verse. All in all, however, Call's undertaking of the three rather lengthy sections of the *Bergidylle* is his finest effort. Here again, the spirit, matter, and form of the original are faithfully adhered to. But little is lost of Heine's tender pathos, vivid power of description, and feather-touch. The translations are a bit too lengthy to quote, but as they are readily accessible, perhaps quotation is scarcely necessary.

Charles Stuart Calverley (1831-1884).—Charles Stuart Calverley is known, as a translator, primarily for his adaptations from the ancients, Theocritus and Virgil. In his *Literary Remains*, however, we do find one translation from Heine—a reproduction of the German poet's *Anno 1829*.[23] Calverley's choice of the *Anno 1829* from the *Romanzen* (N. G.) is not a particularly happy one, for, in reality, the poem belongs to that type of *Zeitgedichte* which does not reveal to us the true lyric quality of Heine. Nevertheless, to Calverley's credit it must be admitted that he has done a better than average job in translation. With the exception of the first stanza, which is rather freely rendered, and the fifth stanza, which is omitted entirely (probably because of the fact that it presents tremendous

23. W. J. Sendall, *The Literary Remains of Charles Stuart Calverley*, p. 238.

difficulties to the translator), the version is accurately if not brilliantly undertaken.

William Henry Charlton (b. 1814).—William H. Charlton, who has made translations from Bürger, Anastasius Grün, and Friedrich Halm, has attempted but two translations from the works of Heine[24]—the world-famous *Lorelei*, and the poem *Begegnung (Romanzen)*. Charlton's versions of Heine are as varied in quality as any two attempts from the pen of the same author can be. In the *Lorelei*, an extremely mediocre rendering, not only has the translator failed altogether in capturing the charm and full significance of the old legend, but he is guilty as well of failing to recognize the beauties and possibilities of his own native tongue. The version abounds in awkward, unpoetic expressions couched in a stilted and unimpressive style. The translation of *Begegnung*, on the other hand, is a fine piece of work. Here Charlton exhibits true poetic feeling and an understanding of his original.

Edward Chawner.—In a collection of translations from numerous sources, published in 1879,[25] Edward Chawner has included eleven poems from Heine: "Und wüssten's die Blumen," "Warum sind denn die Rosen," "Vergiftet sind meine Lieder," and "Ein Jüngling liebt ein Mädchen" *(Lyrisches Intermezzo)*; "Du schönes Fischermädchen," "Wie kannst du ruhig schlafen," and "Am fernen Horizonte" *(Die Heimkehr)*; *Die Grenadiere (Romanzen)*; "Ein Traum gar seltsam schauerlich" *(Junge Leiden)*; *Bergidylle (Die Harzreise)*; and a version, *The Chapel*. With the exception of the versions of "Und wüssten's die Blumen" and "Du schönes Fischermädchen," which are of inferior workmanship and quality, Chawner's translations have no better than average merit in all respects.

Henry Bernard Cotterill (b. 1846).—H. B. Cotterill, a classical and medieval scholar of the later nineteenth century,

---

24. William H. Charlton, *Poems and Plays Original and Translated*, pp. 113-114, 117-118.
25. Edward Chawner, *Gleanings from the German and French Poets*.

is best known (as a Heine translator) for his rendering of *Der Schiffbrüchige (Die Nordsee)*. Cotterill's version is by far the best in English. The translator has been unusually successful in reproducing the felicity, the spirit, and the deep significance of Heine's original. The form, too, is studiously and zealously adhered to. In more than apt language, Cotterill has given us all of the many details of the original—each in its proper sequence. Cotterill's splendid diction cannot be overestimated nor his faithfulness overpraised.

Of Heine's "Welch ein zierlich Ebenmass" *(Nachlese)*, the English author has attempted a condensed paraphrase which lacks much of the spirit of the original and fails altogether in giving a true concept of Heine's poem. The English quatrain, "In God's great cattle stable," is deserving of no particular merit or mention. Because of the length of Cotterill's finest translation, *Der Schiffbrüchige*, the shorter translation of *Wo? (Lazarus)*, is given here as an exceptional translation—perhaps the best English version of the German lyric:

> Where shall be from weary wandering
> That last resting-place of mine?
> In the south beneath the palm-tree?
> Under linden on the Rhine?
>
> Shall I be in some far desert
> Buried by a stranger's hand?
> Or upon a beach of ocean
> Lie in peace below the sand?
>
> Nay, it matters not: God's heaven,
> There as here shall cover me,
> And at night as coffin-tapers
> Stars shall hover over me.

All the translations of Cotterill are found in the volume *Proems* (1873).

Elizabeth Craigmyle.—In *German Ballads*, Elizabeth Craigmyle undertook the translation of selected pieces of Goethe, Schiller, Bürger, Uhland, Rückert, Platen, Freiligrath,

Herder, Heine,[26] and a few miscellaneous poets of lesser significance. With the exception of *The Asra,* which is taken from the *Romanzero* of Heine, Elizabeth Craigmyle's translations from Heine are chosen from the earlier poems of the *Buch der Lieder* and include: "Im süssen Traum, bei stiller Nacht," "Was treibt und tobt mein tolles Blut," "Ein Traum gar seltsam schauerlich," *Die Wallfahrt nach Kevlaar, Don Ramiro, Love's Burial.*

In one of the few attempts made to translate the whole of *Don Ramiro,* Elizabeth Craigmyle has succeeded fairly well, although she omits several stanzas appearing in the original version. The translation of "Im süssen Traum, bei stiller Nacht" is perhaps her best, and *The Asra* and *The Story of a Night* are of superior quality. The remaining translations are little better than average. The popular *Pilgrimage to Kevlaar* is especially weak.

Alexander William Crawford (1812-1880).—The twenty-fifth earl of Crawford, Alexander William Crawford Lindsay, a rather busy writer on a variety of subjects ranging from religion to genealogy, has translated Heine's *Seegespenst* from the first cycle of *Die Nordsee.*[27] There is little to be said either for or against the English version; for, while it preserves the unusual form of its original and is for the most part accurate in its details, it wants the inspiration and feeling of the German.

"*G. E. D.*"—*A Song of Caedmon* (1871) by "G. E. D." contains the following translations from Heine: from the *Lyrisches Intermezzo,* "Im Rhein, im schönen Strome" (p. 70), "Ich will meine Seele tauchen" (p. 88), "Im wunderschönen Monat Mai" (p. 56), "Allnächtlich im Traume seh' ich dich" (p. 66); from *Die Heimkehr,* "Du schönes Fischermädchen" (p. 67), "Mir träumte: traurig schaute der Mond" (p. 69).

"G. E. D." has yet to be identified, but to take a shot in the

26. Pp. 161-184.
27. Alexander W. Crawford, *Ballads, Songs, and Poems Translated from the German*, p. 106.

dark (which is in all probability close to the mark) the initials in all likelihood stand for two of England's foremost engravers of the nineteenth century who also dabbled a bit in verse: George Dalziel (1815-1902) and Edward Dalziel (1817-1905). If the conjecture as to the identity of the mysterious "G. E. D." is correct, there is no doubt but that George and Edward Dalziel should have confined themselves to the tools of their trade, for their efforts at translation are among the most pitiable imaginable. "Thou lovely fishermaiden" is their supreme effort, and it is and will always remain merely an effort. The two brothers are entirely without the slightest conception of poetry, and what they have given us in the matter of translation is merely doggerel dignified by the name of Heine.

Francis D'Anvers.—In *English Echoes,* a collection of translations of German authors by various hands, Francis D'Anvers [pseud.] contributed an undistinguished version of Heine called *The Lotos and the Water-Lily*.[28] There is a definite attempt at correctness in the translation, but the English lyric can boast otherwise of little else. It remains but a mediocre effort when considered as a whole.

John Dennis.—In *Verses* (1898)[29] John Dennis has done what comparatively few translators have attempted; he has rendered into English verse one of the sonnets of Heine, *An meine Mutter, B. Heine,* No. II:

>I left thee once in mad desire to find
>The Love for which my spirit yearned with pain,
>At many a door I knocked and knocked in vain,
>Craving Love's alms which none to grant inclined,
>But laughing, treated me with cold disdain;—
>Yet still I wandered, eager in the quest,
>For ever seeking, and for aye unblest,
>Since no one gave the boon for which I pined.
>Then, Mother! turning to my home I went

28. *English Echoes of German Song,* ed. by N. D'Anvers, p. 50.
29. P. 52.

> With weary steps and sorrow-numbing care,
> And lo! my pain was lost in sweet content,
> For what I sought came to me unaware;
> In the dear eyes that on thy son were bent
> All I had asked I found, for home was there!

The spirit of Heine's tribute to his mother is undeniably present in the sonnet of John Dennis, but the form and words of the English version are entirely divorced from the German. Heine's sonnet form, the Italian with internal rhyme scheme, becomes an irregular one under the pen of Dennis. The word-rendering is extremely loose, and the succession of ideas changed at will. Despite the literal unfaithfulness to the original, the total significance of the English version is fully in accord with the German sonnet.

Charles Dexter.—In *Versions and Verses* (1865) Charles Dexter did into English the following poems by Heine:[30] from *Romanzen, Bergstimme, Die Botschaft;* from *Die Heimkehr,* "Du bist wie eine Blume"; from *Lyrisches Intermezzo,* "Und wüssten's die Blumen, die kleinen," "Ich hab' im Traum geweinet"; from *Neuer Frühling,* "Es war ein alter König."

Dexter's translations, with the exception of his version of "Es war ein alter König" which is spoiled unfortunately by the too frequent use of un-English inversions, are all of the better sort. In the two lovely lyrics chosen from the *Lyrisches Intermezzo,* the translator has permitted himself a few liberties with the text and form, but has managed nevertheless to preserve admirably the mood of the German poems. In the remaining versions, Dexter has worked with consistent poetic urge, accuracy, and understanding of Heine's originals. "The Errand," which cannot be called the best of Dexter's efforts, is given here as a fair specimen of the translator's ability.

> Up, laggard! arise, and saddle in haste
> The fleetest steed in the stall,
> And ride for dear life over forest and field,
> To King Duncan's lordly Hall!

---

30. Pp. 15-23.

Await at the gate till there comes to thee
Some one at his serving train,
Then ask him at once, "Quick! tell me which weds,
Which of the daughters twain?"

And if he replies, "'Tis the dark-eyed one,"
Then haste with all speed to me;
But if he replies, "'Tis the fair-eyed maid,"
Ride back to me leisurely.

Stop as thou comest so leisurely back,
And buy me a rope right stout,
And slowly ride home, but say not a word
Of what thou hast been about!

Sir Francis Hastings Doyle (1810-1888).—In spite of Sir Francis Hastings Doyle's statement, "one of the greatest mischiefs resulting from my weakness of will and want of definite aims, is that I have never made any real progress in the German language," and his further assertion that although he calls himself an educated man, he is unable to "grapple with the works of Goethe" and is barely able to determine that the great universal genius is a splendid lyric poet only "by the help of cribs and dictionaries,"[31] he has left a better than average translation of Heine's "Ein Fichtenbaum steht einsam":

A Pine-Tree standeth lonely
On a bleak and northern hill,
And sleeps with ice surrounded
With snow that falleth still.

There is one palm he dreams of,
Far in the morning land,
Who mourns alone, and silent,
Mid rocks and burning sand.[32]

Henry W. Dulcken (1832-1894).—Nine of Heine's most popular songs from the *Buch der Lieder* have been translated into English by Henry W. Dulcken: *Die Grenadiere (Roman-*

---

31. Francis H. Doyle, *Reminiscences and Opinions of Sir Francis H. Doyle*, p. 230.
32. F. H. Doyle, *Lectures on Poetry*, Second Series, p. 282.

zen), Nos. 22, 39, 51 *(Lyrisches Intermezzo)*; Nos. 2, 8, 21, 28 and *Die Wallfahrt nach Kevlaar (Die Heimkehr)*. All of Dulcken's translations are quite correct from the standpoint of the faithful carrying over of words and ideas and are done apparently with great care, but they lack true poetic fire and redound little to the English author's credit. Dulcken is either no poet or has striven too desperately to render his originals word for word. His translations are mediocre and undistinguished.

Sophia May Eckley.—Sophia May Eckley, in *Minor Chords* (1869), has a paraphrase on Heine's "Lieb Liebchen, leg's Händchen aufs Herze mein" *(Junge Leiden)*. The paraphrase represents a fairly faithful attempt to reproduce one of the lesser known lyrics of Heine. Because of its inaccessibility, the translation is given below:

> O, lay thy hand, Dear, on my heart,
> Dost hear it in its chamber beat?
> For there a secret carpenter
> Is making me my coffin neat.
>
> There hammers he all night and day,
> From happy sleep my eyes to keep,
> Make haste then, master carpenter,
> For I am ready now to sleep.[33]

Havelock Ellis (1859-1939).—In 1877, while still in his eighteenth year, Havelock Ellis[34] went to teach in a small, private school located just three hundred and fifty miles north of Sydney in the little town of Grafton. It was here that the youth first began to take serious interest in languages, translating Alfred de Musset's *Rolla* and several lyrics of Heine, who was second only to the immortal Shelley in his affections. Wandering over the primitive hills of Australia, he shouted German poetry to the skies above and was hardly ever known to be without a copy of Goethe, Montaigne, or Heine in his

---

33. P. 271.   34. See also section on Criticism.

pocket.³⁵ "The translations from Heine and Renan," says Goldberg, "must have satisfied the youth in a double capacity. They were, in the first place, an outlet for his deep, if unconventional and unacademic instincts of scholarship. In the German lyrist, moreover, young Ellis found a kindred love and yearning, a kindred passion for the sea."³⁶ The stray pieces from Heine, begun in 1877, were finished on February 27, 1880, shortly after the youth had passed his twenty-first birthday.³⁷ Six years later, Ellis edited an excellent selection of *Heine's Prose Writings* and a new translation of the *Florentine Nights*. In 1925, Ellis published a collection of sonnets together with folk songs from the Spanish, which included Heine's sonnet *An meine Mutter*.³⁸ Ellis' eight other translations from Heine are of the following poems: from *Lyrisches Intermezzo*, "Ein Fichtenbaum steht einsam"; from *Die Heimkehr*, "Du schönes Fischermädchen," "Mein Herz, mein Herz"; from *Neuer Frühling*, "Ich lieb' eine Blume," "In meiner Errinnerung erblühen"; from *Die Harzreise*, "Ich bin die Prinzessin Ilse"; from *Verschiedene*, "Mit schwarzen Segeln"; from *Letzte Gedichte*, "Das gelbe Laub erzittert."

"Only Heine has grasped the glory and loveliness of the sea in any degree approximate to Swinburne," said Havelock Ellis and continued: " 'Ich liebe das Meer wie eine Geliebte,' Heine says somewhere. There is something almost filial in Swinburne's love. My own love for the sea and all its manifestations makes these two poets dear to me."³⁹ It is little wonder, then, that Ellis' finest translation should be that which most nearly embodies the spirit of the sea. The version of "Mit schwarzen Segeln," an example of Ellis at his best in the rôle of translator, reads:

---

35. Houston Peterson, *Havelock Ellis: Philosopher of Love*, p. 97.
36. Isaac Goldberg, *Havelock Ellis: A Biographical and Critical Study*, pp. 66-67.
37. *Ibid.*, p. 61.
38. *Sonnets with Folk Songs from the Spanish*, p. 23.
39. Goldberg, *op. cit.*, p. 298.

>With sail of black my ship sails on
>Far over the stormy sea;
>Thou knowest that my soul with grief
>Is laden heavily.
>
>Thy heart as faithless as the wind,
>Turns as inconstantly,
>With sails of black my ship sails on
>Far over the stormy sea.[40]

The other translations of Ellis are very average in quality. The two men, Heine and Ellis, possessed a great deal in common—particularly in their passion for the sea and their love of life. A passage from Ellis' translation of Heine's "Ich bin die Prinzessin Ilse" might serve almost as the creed by which Ellis lived:

>The living only are living
>And the dead are forever dead.

"C. K. F."—The unidentified "C. K. F.," who translated Schiller's *Song of the Bell*, translated in 1873 three of Heine's popular longer poems: *Die Grenadiere, Lorelei,* and *Belsatzar*.[41] Few translators have permitted themselves the liberties assumed by "C. K. F." In the *Lorelei*, for example, not only is one entire stanza omitted, but the translator has seen fit to change Heine's ballad form to one of rhyming couplets. A similar liberty is taken in *Belsatzar* where Heine's couplet form is brought over into English in the form of blank verse. Such liberties are, perhaps, to be excused if justified by the net results, but (in the instances cited) the entire effect of the originals is lost in the translations. Not only have the poems suffered by the modified form employed, but through indiscriminate omissions and improper and inaccurate sequences of ideas, the originals are merely shadowed forth in the English versions. The first two stanzas of *Lorelei* are cited as indicative of the license assumed:

---

40. Ellis' translations are found in Goldberg, *op. cit.*, pp. 293-296.
41. C. K. F., *Selection of Ballads Translated Chiefly from German Authors*, pp. 143-144, 130-131, 161.

My heart is sad, I know not why—
The passing Zephyr seems a sigh!
The shadow of a tale of woe
Rests on my mind from long ago.—

'Tis twilight—on the banks of Rhine
The stars like glittering diamonds shine—
The sun-set on the mountains glows,
While at their feet the current flows.—

Thomas Campbell Finlayson (1836-1893).—Thomas Campbell Finlayson, minister of Rusholme Congregational Church, Manchester, was advised by his brother, James Finlayson, to take up literary work to relieve the strain of preaching, which had no doubt contributed to his state of chronic ill health. The advice was given in either 1876 or 1877, but it was not until 1879 that the minister began to compile various prose selections and poetical works which were published posthumously (1893) under the title of *Essays, Addresses, and Lyrical Translations*. In this miscellaneous collection of prose and poetry were published translations from a number of German poets, including Goethe, Schiller, Uhland, Freiligrath, Geibel, Hermann Neumann, J. M. Götz, Halm, Gleim, Emil Rittershaus, Grün, R. Gottsched, Ferrand, Chamisso, Rückert, Körner, K. E. Ebert, and Heine.

Finlayson's translations from Heine are: from *Junge Leiden*, "An meine Mutter" I and II, "Schöne Wiege"; from *Lyrisches Intermezzo*, "Hör' ich das Liedchen klingen," "Wenn zwei von einander scheiden," "Ich hab' im Traum geweinet," "Allnächtlich im Traume," "Sie haben mich gequälet," "Der Herbstwind rüttelt die Bäume," "Ein Jüngling liebt ein Mädchen," "Und wüssten's die Blumen, die kleinen," "Ein Fichtenbaum steht einsam," "Aus meinen Thränen spriessen," "Im wunderschönen Monat Mai," "Es stehen unbeweglich," "Die Lotosblume ängstigt," "Auf Flügeln des Gesanges"; from *Die Heimkehr*, "Herz, mein Herz," "Du bist wie eine Blume," "Am fernen Horizonte," "Mein Kind, wir waren

Kinder," "In mein gar zu dunkles Leben," "Die Lorelei," "Du schönes Fischermädchen," "Wenn ich an deinem Hause," "Das Meer erglänzte weit hinaus"; from *Neuer Frühling*, "Wie des Mondes Abbild zittert," "Leise zieht," "Der Brief"; from *Letzte Gedichte und Nachlese*, "Das gelbe Laub erzittert."

In the two sonnets "To My Mother," Finlayson has preserved better than any other translator Heine's use of the Italian sonnet, although the English author has seen fit to shorten the second sonnet by one verse. The translations are literal, spirited, and in unusually good taste throughout. Indeed, T. C. Finlayson is, speaking by and large, one of the most skilful of Heine's translators. He seems to be one with the poet and reproduces the exquisite melodies with remarkable accuracy, ingenuity, and studious zeal. He has even managed to preserve Heine's frequent use of repetition and alliteration with the effectiveness and naturalness of the original, for example:

>   And 'tis she herself that hath torn—
>   Hath torn my bleeding heart:

for

>   Sie hat ja selbst zerrissen,
>   Zerrissen mir das Herz"[42]

or

>   The violets twitter and titter

for

>   Die Veilchen kichern und kosen[43]

What a pity James Finlayson did not urge his brother earlier to take up the avocation of writing! There is scarcely a translation of Heine among the works of T. C. Finlayson that does not rank with the best ever attempted. Finlayson is a true poet and responds as such to the slightest touch of the

42. "Und wüssten's die Blumen, die kleinen."
43. "Auf Flügeln des Gesanges."

original. Occasionally, it must be admitted, he varies somewhat from the original, as in his version of "Die Lotosblume ängstigt" where the line "And shyly stands up again" misses entirely the meaning of *Und starret stumm in die Höh'*, or in his version of "Im wunderschönen Monat Mai" which is quite freely transcribed:

> When all the buds were blowing
> In the wondrous month of May,
> Then also in my bosom
> Love blossomed in a day.
>
> When all the birds were singing
> In the wondrous month of May,
> Then I confessed my passion
> As at her feet I lay.

Unlike many other translators of Heine, Finlayson has not fallen into the error of over-ornamentation but has striven always to maintain the simplicity of style and language for which Heine is so famous. Finlayson's translations of "Du bist wie eine Blume" and "Ein Fichtenbaum steht einsam" are given below as examples of his easy, accurate workmanship:

> DU BIST WIE EINE BLUME
> As sweet and pure and lovely
> As any flower thou art;
> I look on thee, and sadness
> Doth creep into my heart.
>
> On thy dear head it seemeth,
> As if my hands must meet
> Beseeching God to keep thee
> Thus lovely, pure, and sweet.
>
> . . . . .
>
> EIN FICHTENBAUM STEHT EINSAM
> Far north a lonely pine-tree
> Stands on a barren height,
> And the snow and ice enwrap it
> With a coverlet of white.

> It sleeps, and dreams of a palm-tree
> Far off in the Eastern land,
> That, all alone in silence,
> Mourns on the burning sand.

Finlayson, too, manages quite cleverly to catch the subtle humor of Heine, which has so often proved the undoing of many translators, as in this passage:

> ### Der Brief
>
> The letter you have written
> Has done my heart no wrong;
> You say you'll no more love me,
> But then—your letter's long!
>
> 'Tis quite a little manuscript,
> Close-written to the marge!
> One does not pen twelve pages,
> In giving a discharge.

The translations cited above are by no means the best that T. C. Finlayson has done; yet it cannot be gainsaid that they are among the best, for, in reality, all of his translations are of superior merit and of lasting significance.

Richard Garnett (1835-1906).—In *Poems from the German* (1859),[44] Richard Garnett included specimen translations of the masters of German song: Goethe, Hölderlin, Uhland, Rückert, Platen, Brentano, Lenau, Freiligrath, Lingg, Schefer, Hebbel, Deutsch, and Heine. His translations from Heine include Nos. 3, 14, 23, 41, 59, 63, and 77 from the *Lyrisches Intermezzo*, the larger poems *Agnes, Valkyrs, Ottillia, Asra, The Tempest, Three and Two,* and the lyric "Sag' mir wer einst die Uhren erfund" from *Neuer Frühling.*

Garnett's translations are those of the better sort. With the diligence of a scholar and the inspiration of a more than average poet, he has captured the better part of Heine in his English versions although more than a few of the subtleties and graces of the German lyricist have eluded him. Among

---

44. Pp. 76-94.

his best versions are a spirited translation of *Walküren, Ottillia (Böses Geträume)*, Nos. 63 and 77 from the *Lyrisches Intermezzo*, and "Sag' mir wer einst."

Joseph Gostwick (1814-1887).—Joseph Gostwick, a literary historian and author of several books on German literature, has left the following critical and annotated translations of Heine: *The Lorelei*,[45] *The Grenadiers*,[46] *The Preacher's Family*,[47] *The Pilgrimage to Kevlaar*,[48] *On the Rhine*,[49] and an excerpt from the *Mountain Idylls*.[50]

Of the *Lorelei*, Gostwick says: "The originality, simplicity, and apparent carelessness of Heine's lyrical poems are well exemplified in his tale of *The Lorelei*. . . . The original poem is so perfectly easy and careless in its style that it reads like an impromptu."[51] Heine's ease and carelessness lie far beyond the ability of Gostwick. As in the case of so many translators, Gostwick misses entirely the note of mockery which creeps in, in the last stanza. Gostwick's translation of *Die Grenadiere*, concerning the original of which he says that it contains verses "as spirited as anything to be found in all the poetry that has been devoted to Napoleon,"[52] begins in spirited fashion but wilts as it proceeds. The pathos of the heart-rending stanzas containing the verse "Was schert mich Weib, was schert mich Kind!" is entirely lost, and the whole translation peters out to a close which is pathetically weak.

Concerning "Der bleiche, herbstliche Halbmond" *(The Preacher's Family)*, Gostwick says: "There is the true dramatic and laconic power of poetry in these few verses. They suggest a whole domestic history. . . . The gloom and misery of the picture is perfect and the ghost at the window seems in perfect keeping with the rest of the scene, for the misery of such a

---

45. Joseph Gostwick, *Outline of German Literature*, p. 456.
46. J. Gostwick, *Spirit of German Poetry*, p. 92.
47. Ibid., p. 94.   48. Ibid., p. 93.
49. J. Gostwick, *German Poets*, p. 262.   50. Ibid., p. 257.
51. Gostwick, *German Literature*, p. 454.
52. Ibid., p. 453.

family was enough to call the dead up from his grave."[53] Gostwick's understanding of the poem is far superior to his translation[54] of this "little gloomy picture of domestic misery." Gostwick's translation of *Die Wallfahrt nach Kevlaar* is his best. The version is literal and simple and more nearly approaches Heine's poetry than any of his other attempts. The English writer regards the original as "a good instance of Heine's versatility" and says further that "it might be accepted as an authentic miraculous legend written in old times by some devout Catholic."[55]

Joseph Gostwick's general estimate of Heine both as a prose writer and a poet reveals a biased, prudish nature—one that is much more aware of Heine's faults than of his virtues. The following criticism is a bitter but in some respects true picture of the peculiar genius of Heine:

... He [Heine] belongs to the class of negative writers and satirists, who declaim against all existing institutions, while the objects for which they contend are only vague generalities. Heine's writings are often humorous and piquant, but disfigured by the affectation of a coarse cynicism and an irreverent temper which confounds together things sacred and profane.

He is like a harlequin, who, rather than fail of attracting notice, will daub his face with the coarsest pigments. He makes himself vile to be notable. He is aware of this as he has assumed cap and bells and styled himself arch-foe and jester for Germany. His jests and ironies are sometimes bitter, often foolish; but we shall not meddle with them: they do no good.

Heine's verse, as well as his prose, is often disfigured by the coarsest sentiments and most irreverent expressions, apparently thrown in with no other motive than to excite attention, by offending good taste.[56]

Alexander Gray (b. 1882).—Alexander Gray, author of a number of books on German political, economic, and military theory and translator from the German, has left a version of

53. Gostwick, *Spirit of German Poetry*, p. 94.
54. *Ibid.*, p. 94.
55. Gostwick, *German Literature*, p. 454.
56. Gostwick, *Spirit of German Poetry*, p. 92.

"Es fiel ein Reif in der Frühlingsnacht," which Heine claimed was a genuine folk-song he heard on the Rhine, and which Gray claims to be traceable to Zuccalmaglio (1803-1869).[57] Gray's translation of the little lyric which is *Tragödie II* of the *Verschiedene* represents a fair attempt to render the poem in Scottish dialect:

> There cam a frost in a nicht in May;
> It fell on the tender and bonnie blumes.
> They withered awa and wallowed.
>
> A young lad dearly lo'ed a lass;
> They raise at nicht and quat their hames.
> The auld fowk didna hear them.
>
> They wandered here and they wandered there;
> They had neither starn nor a guidin' hand.
> God githered them hame the gither.

Thomas Hardy (1840-1928).—Among the *Collected Poems* of the well-known novelist and poet, Thomas Hardy, is found a translation of "Ich stand in dunkeln Träumen" *(Die Heimkehr)*. With all due respect to Hardy, whose fame is spread to the corners of the earth, it must be said that, as in the case of many a famous writer, as a translator he is more or less completely at a loss. To quote Hardy's translation would be useless. It has few faults, but then again it has likewise few merits. It simply is not Heine.

Frances Ridley Havergal (1836-1879).—Frances Ridley Havergal, who attended school in Düsseldorf (Heine's native city) while her father spent the winter under the care of a skilful oculist there, composed hymns in French and German, and in December, 1853, made an English version of Heine's famous *Lorelei*. Evidently, with the idea in mind of improving on Heine's nearly perfect poem, Frances Havergal has gone to extraordinary pains to enlarge upon Heine's opening lines and makes of the one stanza in the German two in English:

---

57. Alexander Gray, *Arrows*, p. 57.

> Ich weiss nicht was soll es bedeuten,
> Dass ich so traurig bin;
> Ein Märchen aus alten Zeiten,
> Das kommt mir nicht aus dem Sinn.

> Ah, where are the echoes of gladness
> Which dwell in my listening mind?
> What meaneth the whisper of sadness,
> Like the moan of the autumn wind?

> I am chained by an often told story,
> Come down from the olden time
> When fairydom saw its glory,
> A haunting, saddening chime.[58]

The enlarged introduction not only is irrelevant to the story to be unfolded and in bad taste but spoils her remaining stanzas, which, at best, but fairly well convey Heine's thought, drawing the whole translation down to the level of ridiculous and exceedingly poor workmanship.

Heinrich Herz.—The following quatrain, representing a translation of "Ich hab' dich geliebet und liebe dich noch" (*Lyrisches Intermezzo*), is the only translation from Heine by Herz found:

> I loved thee once, I love thee still,
> And, fell this world asunder,
> My love's eternal flame would rise
> 'Midst chaos, crash, and thunder![59]

Mary Howitt (1799-1888).—Mary Howitt, who has numerous translations from the Danish and Swedish and from the German of Freiligrath, is best known (as a German translator) for her version of Heine's *Die Wallfahrt nach Kevlaar*. Mary Howitt had the advantage of having lived in Germany and of being thoroughly familiar with the language and literature of the people of the country. In 1840 the question of the education of her older children became more or less urgent, and the Howitts, who had learned of the advantages of a resi-

---

58. F. R. Havergal, *Poetical Works*, I, 223.
59. Kroeker, *op. cit.*, p. 72.

dence in Germany from their friends, Mrs. Hemans, Mrs. Jameson, and Henry Chorley, gave up their cottage at Esher and decided to spend two or three years at Heidelberg. Armed with letters of introduction from Jameson they effected an entrée into German society, which they found more to their taste than that of England. "For the sake of our children," writes Mary, "we sought German acquaintances, we read German, we followed German customs. The life seemed to me easier, the customs simpler and less expensive than in England."[60]

In the course of the three years spent at Heidelberg, William Howitt wrote his *Student Life in Germany, German Experiences,* and *Rural and Domestic Life in Germany* while Mary busied herself with translations from the Swedish—chiefly from the work of Frederica Bremer. With their elder daughter, Anna, the Howitts made a tour of Germany and Austria. At Stuttgart they visited the German poet Gustav Schwab; at Tübingen they made the acquaintance of Uhland and at Munich that of Kaulbach—then at the height of his fame. In Berlin they made friends with Tieck, who had been made the recipient of a pension and a house at Potsdam, and during their visit to Weimar they were the guests of Frau von Goethe. All in all, then, Mary Howitt enjoyed an intimate acquaintanceship with German mores and people, an acquaintanceship that continued to grow with the years. From the Pension Felsberg, Lucerne, as late as July 4, 1870, we find her writing to her sister Elizabeth that, "Frau Henriette Heine, the widow of Heinrich Heine's first cousin and fellow student, was staying at the pension."[61]

But to return to the years spent in Heidelberg, we find the following statement in Mary Howitt's *Autobiography:*

... in that period of mental activity I could often write a poem in a day. Some of my pieces were English renderings of German poetry

60. George Paston, *Little Memories of the Nineteenth Century,* pp. 354-356.
61. Mary Howitt, *An Autobiography,* II, 201.

by Freiligrath and Clemens Brentano. Heine's exquisite lines of a mother taking her sick son to be cured by the Virgin Mary at the holy shrine of Kevlaar I translated in 1841.[62]

Her translation of the popular medieval picture is probably the best-known one in the English tongue. Because of the widespread popularity of the translation, it is surely unnecessary to make more than a passing comment on the version of Mary Howitt. She has tried to adhere fairly closely to the original poem and through the use of the simplest English words and phrases has managed quite well to preserve the true medieval simplicity and naturalness of Heine's poem. Despite a few occasional loose constructions, the medieval atmosphere in all its naïvety (which is after all the chief thing) lives in the English version.[63] Mary Howitt has also a lesser known translation of "Wir sassen am Fischerhause."

Francis Franz Hueffer (1845-1889).—Franz Hueffer, editor of the *New Quarterly Magazine* (1879-1880) and an authority on music during the nineteenth century, has left five translations from Heine. His translation of *Tragödie*, appearing first in the periodical *Dark Blue*,[64] is of extremely average quality and makes but poor attempt to preserve the meter and spirit of the original. His remaining translations[65] are versions of "Morgens steh' ich auf und frage" *(Junge Leiden)*, "Im Rhein, im schönen Strome" *(Lyrisches Intermezzo)*, and "Die blauen Frühlingsaugen" and "Durch den Wald *(Neuer Frühling)*. The remaining translations are of better quality and more nearly approach the originals in form and substance, but they, too, are far from superior. Hueffer's best translation is his version of the little gem, "Morgens steh' ich auf und frage":

> Rising when the dawn still faint is,
> Asking, "Will she come?"

62. *Ibid.*, II, 22.
63. Mary Howitt, *Ballads and Others Poems*, p. 267.
64. *Dark Blue Magazine*, I (1871), 163.
65. Kroeker, *op. cit.*, pp. 15, 59, 196, 200.

Minor Translators 73

Late at eventide my plaint is,
"Ah! She did not come!"

In the night time with my sorrow
Waking still I lie,
And the day dream of the morrow
Passes sadly by.

Henry Crossley Irwin.—H. C. Irwin, who also translated selections from Uhland, Schiller, Goethe, Gottschall, Hammer, Hamlin, F. von Sallet, and Platen, has in his volume *Rhymes and Renderings* (1886)[66] the following translations from Heine: from the *Junge Leiden,* "Ein Traum gar seltsam schauerlich"; from the *Lyrisches Intermezzo,* Nos. 13, 14, 18, 19, 31, 33, 44; from *Die Nordsee, Die Götter Griechenlands;* from *Neuer Frühling,* "Wie des Mondes Abbild zittert," "Die Rose duftet"; from *Verschiedene,* "Es kommt zu spät"; miscellanies, "Freundschaft, Liebe, Stein der Weisen," "Bleich Blümchen."

Irwin ranks among the finest of Heine's many English translators. In his faithful and spirited versions of the longer poems, "Ein Traum gar seltsam schauerlich" (in many respects his finest translation) and *Die Götter Griechenlands,* he is unsurpassed. In the short lyrics, Irwin's renderings have the gemlike quality of Heine, and each facet, regardless of how minute, reflects truly the image of the German originals. With the exception of two lyrics—"Die Rose duftet," in which the alternate rhyme of Heine is changed to internal rhyme in the English version, and "Die Welt ist so schön," in which the consecutive rhyme of the German appears as alternate rhyme in English—the form is as perfectly adhered to as is possible in translation. Irwin has the feel of the language and exercises his poetic powers, which are by no means slight, to the full. The results are highly gratifying, and Heine loses but little in translation. As specimens of Irwin's exceptional ability, two short lyrics are cited:

66. Pp. 110-125.

O SCHWÖRE NICHT UND KÜSSE NUR
Ah, kiss me still and vow no more,
What woman ever truly swore?
Thy words are sweet, but sweeter 'tis
To me thy rosy lips to kiss,
For there a sure delight I find,
And what are words but idle wind?

Nay, sweet, vow evermore; to me
Thy simple word shall sacred be.
So let me lean upon thy breast
And feel that I indeed am blest;
I love thee, sweet, eternally,
And longer yet shalt thou love me.

EIN FICHTENBAUM STEHT EINSAM
In Norland wastes mid barren crags
A pine-tree stands alone,
Asleep beneath the mantel white
By winter o'er him thrown.

He dreams of a palm-tree tall and slim
In some far Eastern land,
That desolate and silent grieves
Mid plains of burning sand.

Alexander H. Japp (1839-1905).—A. H. Japp, who is discussed elsewhere,[67] has but three specimen translations in all: one from Goethe, two sonnets from Petrarch, and a version[68] of Heine's *Die Zwei Grenadiere*—the poem conceived when Heine, going from Göttingen to Düsseldorf, met, in 1820, those prisoners of war who, in their dejection, re-awakened in the poet his fierce love of Napoleon. One of the most difficult poems of Heine to translate is the *Two Grenadiers,* for the meter of each verse is wedded completely to the meaning of the line and the significance of the mood. The slow, dragging, mournful iambics, "Der andre sprach: das Lied ist aus," changing suddenly to the fiery anapaests, "Dann reitet mein Kaiser

---

67. See section on Criticism.
68. A. H. Japp, *Occasional Verses*, p. 124.

wohl über mein Grab," are difficult to produce. Japp has tried and failed. The wild grief of "Was schert mich Weib, was schert mich Kind" is but weakly indicated by Japp's "Oh, what care I for wife or child."

Henry George Keene (1825-1915).—As in the case of A. Rogers, who will be discussed later, Henry George Keene busied himself primarily with oriental matters, contributing a number of histories concerning the countries and peoples of the Eastern lands. In spare moments, it seems, he found opportunity to translate a stray lyric or two from Schiller, Freiligrath, von Salis, and Heine. His translation of "Aus meinen Tränen spriessen" *(Lyrisches Intermezzo)* is in reality in the nature of a paraphrase in which Keene attempts to convey the spirit of Heine's mood but does not attempt to make a literal translation:

>Fed by my scalding tears
>A wreath of blossoms springs,
>And in my sigh one hears
>A nightingale that sings.
>If thou wilt love me, I
>Will give thee those sweet things,
>And the nightingale to thee shall fly
>To tell my sorrowings.[69]

Keene's other attempt is a translation of the concluding stanza of "Du schönes Fischermädchen":

>My heart is like the ocean,
>Has storm, has ebb and flow;
>And many lovely pearls lie
>Hid in the depths below.[70]

Charles R. Lambert.—Five very mediocre translations from Heine are those attempted by Charles R. Lambert, in his *Poems and Translations from the German,* of "Die blauen Frühlingsaugen" and "Der Schmetterling ist in die Rose verliebt" *(Neuer Frühling), Die Wallfahrt nach Kevlaar* and

69. H. G. Keene, *Verses Original and Translated,* p. 30.
70. *Ibid.*

"Herz, mein Herz, sei nicht beklommen" *(Die Heimkehr)*, and "Ein Fichtenbaum steht einsam." Without exception, Lambert's translations are marred by countless inversions, clumsy Germanisms, ungrammatical constructions, and poor rhythm. Spiritless and without merit, they represent but another effort to translate words only.

John Alfred Langford (1823-1903).—John Alfred Langford, translator of two poems by Uhland and one each by J. Körner and Oehlenschläger, has undertaken three translations from Heine.[71] Two are from *Die Heimkehr: Die Lorelei* and "Wie kannst du ruhig schlafen"; the other is from the *Lyrisches Intermezzo:* "Es fällt ein Stern herunter." Langford's translation of *Die Lorelei* is of a better than average quality, but not nearly so well done as the two shorter lyrics of which the better is "A star is hitherward falling." All three are fairly well rendered as to form and matter, and the spirit of Heine is definitely present even if muffled and veiled to some degree.

Sir Alexander W. Lawrence (1874-1939).—A contemporary translator of stray pieces from the Latin, Greek, French, Spanish, Italian, Swedish, and German, Sir Alexander W. Lawrence has made a fine effort in translating Heine's "Mein Kind, wir waren Kinder."[72] The late Sir Lawrence has proved in his one effort from Heine that his understanding and sympathy were one with his original. The version is excellent and deserving of quotation were it not for its length; it is, however, easily accessible.

J. D. Lester.—Perhaps the poorest translation of *Die Wallfahrt nach Kevlaar* ever attempted is that of J. D. Lester, also to be discussed as a critic of Heine.[73] Heine's poem, written in quatrains of iambic trimeter (the first and third lines containing an added syllable) has been changed under Lester's hand to a poem in prose—and not very good prose at

---

71. J. A. Langford, *The Lily of the West and Other Poems*, pp. 124-127.
72. Sir Alexander W. Lawrence, *Aliunde*, pp. 69-71.
73. See section on Criticism.

that. The charm and spell of the Middle Ages is utterly destroyed by Lester's radical form as illustrated in the following verses representing a quatrain each in Heine:

The mother stood at her lattice, the son lay upon his couch. "Wilt thou not arise, Wilhelm, to see the holy procession?"

"I am so ill, my mother, that I cannot see or hear; I think of my dead Margaret, and my heart is heavy."[74]

Amy Levy (1861-1889).—Amy Levy translated but two of Heine's poems, "Sie haben dir viel erzählet"[75] and "Lebewohl,"[76] so far as has been determined. Of far less than average quality, Amy Levy's translations represent, at best, a poor effort to catch the elusive spirit of Heine. The English versions limp in meter and are flat in spirit.

Frank Laurence Lucas (b. 1894).—The literary historian and very active writer, editor, and translator, Frank L. Lucas, has made, in all, four translations from Heine, which he calls *Tea, Fin de Siècle, Billeting,* and *Prose and Verse.*[77] The two last named are fragmentary bits and of no unusual quality. In *Tea*, which is a version of "Sie sassen und tranken am Teetisch" *(Lyrisches Intermezzo)*, and *Fin de Siècle*, a translation of "Das Herz ist mir bedrückt" *(Die Heimkehr)*, the English author has contributed translations of the better sort. He appears to have complete grasp of his material and to be fully in accord with Heine. *Tea* is given here as an example of complete understanding of Heine's whimsicality:

> With love their talk was dealing
> As they sat and sipped their tea;
> The ladies spoke with feeling,
> The men aesthetically.
>
> "All love should be platonic"
> The wizened Councillor cried,
> His lady smiled ironic;
> And yet "Ay me!" she sighed.

74. "Heinrich Heine," *Fortnightly Review*, XII, 302-303.
75. Katie Magnus, *Jewish Portraits*, p. 73.
76. Amy Levy, *A Minor Poet and Other Verse*, p. 86.
77. *Marionettes*, pp. 29, 54, 56, 76.

Said the wide-mouthed Dean replying:
"Love should not run too high,
One's health finds that so trying!"
The young Miss whispered "Why?"

"Ah love's a wild, wild passion,"
Said the Countess mournfully,
And passed in gracious fashion
The Herr Baron his tea.

One place was void at table,
How I missed thee, love of mine!
Thou hadst so well been able
To tell that love of thine.

George MacDonald (1824-1905).—George MacDonald, one of the century's most prolific writers of novels, romances, and tales, translated the following poems[78] from Heine: from *Junge Leiden*, "Lieb Liebchen, leg's Händchen"; from *Lyrisches Intermezzo*, Nos. 38, 41, 45, 64; from *Die Heimkehr*, "Du hast Diamanten und Perlen," "Sie haben heut' Abend Gesellschaft"; from *Die Nordsee, Frieden.*

MacDonald's translations show Heine, and, indeed, the translator himself, to very poor advantage. MacDonald's mere doggerel gives one absolutely no impression of the supreme genius and talent of Heine. The English author has "plugged away" doggedly at his subject and has succeeded only in giving us, in the form of jingles, verse with poor rhymes and childish expressions ("send"—"stand," "foot"—"mute," "uncheerly," "love"—"stilly," etc.). Everything is sacrificed for the sake of the rhyme. Even in Heine's unrhymed poem *Frieden* from the first cycle of *Die Nordsee*, MacDonald employs rhyme although it would appear that he later regretted the freedom he took, for he wrote years afterward of his translation: "I have here used rhymes although the original has none. With severer notions of translating than when I did this, many years ago, I should not now take

---

78. *Exotics*, pp. 153-165.

such a liberty. In a few other points also the translation is not quite close enough to please me; but it must stand."[79]

Archibald MacMechan (b. 1862).—Archibald McKellar MacMechan, best known for his Canadian pieces and as an editor of Carlyle and Tennyson, has done little in the field of German literature save a study of Hans Sachs and a translation of Heine's "Der Herbstwind rüttelt die Bäume" *(Lyrisches Intermezzo).*[80] There is little to be said of MacMechan's version, for it is a commonplace, insignificant piece of work.

Alexander MacMillan (1818-1896).—The oddest, and incidentally one of the best, translations of Heine's world-famous *Lorelei* is that of Alexander MacMillan, who has given us a dialect version of the poem.[81] Because of the remarkable adherence of the poem in every fashion to the German song, it is quoted here:

> I canna tell what has come over me
> That I am sae eerie and wae;
> An auld-warld tale comes before me,
> It haunts me by nicht and by day.
>
> From the cool life the gloamin' draps dimmer,
> And the Rhine slips saftly by;
> The taps of the mountains shimmer
> I' the lowe o' the sunset sky.
>
> Up there, in a glamour entrancin',
> Sits a maiden wondrous fair;
> Her gowden adoraments are glancing,
> She is kaimin' her gowden hair.
>
> As she kaims it the gowd kaim glistens,
> The while she is singin' a song
> That hauds the rapt soul that listens,
> With its melody sweet and strong.
>
> The boy, floating by in vague wonder,
> Is seized with a wild weird love;
> He sees na the black rocks under,—
> He sees but the vision above.

---

79. *Ibid.*, p. 163.
80. *Late Harvest*, p. 33. 81. Kroeker, *op. cit.*, p. 86.

The waters their waves are flingin',
Ower boatie and boatman anon;
And this with her airtful singin',
The Waterwitch Lurley hath done.

Laurie Magnus (1872-1933).—Laurie Magnus, a well-known scholar in European literature, published in the *Fortnightly Review* for September, 1903, nine translations from Heine:[82] from *Lyrisches Intermezzo*, Nos. 4, 8, 12, 36; from *Die Heimkehr, Die Lorelei,* "Mein Kind wir waren Kinder," "Du bist wie eine Blume," "Du hast Diamanten und Perlen," "Wer zum ersten Male liebt."

The translations of Magnus are less than ordinary. Only in three instances—Nos. 4 and 12 of the *Lyrisches Intermezzo* and in "Wer zum ersten Male liebt" does he in any way call forth the shade of Heine. The diction throughout is poor and unpoetic; the versions are those of a layman.

James Clarence Mangan (1803-1849).—James Clarence Mangan's only work published during his lifetime was the *Anthologia Germanica* in two volumes, which, having first run its course in a magazine, appeared in 1845. Perhaps no other translator—major or minor—had the passion for the German enjoyed by Mangan. His readings in German metaphysics and poetry were endless, and there is no doubt that his vast familiarity with things German colored his entire intellectual life and established the trend of his own writings. At the time, the star of German poetry was definitely in the ascendancy, and Mangan basked in its light. Often his views on German literature are highly interesting and most amusing. He insists humorously upon calling Klopstock "Clockstop" and "Stopclock" and just as humorously describes the German poet's Miltonic style as "Mill-stone-ic." He makes merry at the expense of Tieck and even Justinus Kerner, a particular favorite of his. Of German epigrams he says with a great deal of truth, despite the humorous nature of the statement, that "The

---
82. LXXX, 525-528.

humour of three fourths of their number consists altogether in their want of point, but giants cannot be expected to excell at pushpin."[83]

When his article on Hindoo poetry was rejected by the editor of the *Dublin University Magazine*, Mangan bewailed in the following fashion the fact that he was left alone to struggle with the German muse:

> Where art thou, soul of Per-Version?
> Where be thy fantasies jinglish?
> Why lies intact so much Prussian and Persian?
> And whither has fled the phrase, "Done into English?"
>
> . . . .
>
> Oh, when translation's no feasible,
> Where is the scamp would be scheming off?
> Bowring, you sponge, you have ceased to be squeezable,
> Anster the Bland, what the deuce are you dreaming of?[84]

One of the reasons for Mangan's love of German poetry lies in his passion for the ballad form, a form in which the German poets excel so well. Mangan, who had probably been incited to his interest in German poetry through the activities of Carlyle, believed that there was no greater poet than Schiller; and he has left numerous translations from this author. Mangan's translations from Schiller, Goethe, and Heine are not far above the average. All in all, he is most in sympathy with Schiller and probably least in sympathy with Heine whom he misunderstands. There is no better criticism of Mangan as a translator than that given by Lionel Johnson in his introduction to the *Prose Writings of James C. Mangan:*

> . . . Beside his own Ireland there were two chief worlds in which he loved to wander; the moonlit forests of German poetry, often painfully full of "moonshine," and the glowing gardens of glittering deserts of the Eastern, the "Saracenic" world. He wished, half-whimsically and half-seriously, to make his readers believe that he knew some dozen languages; certain it is that he has a strong philolog-

---

83. D. J. O'Donoghue, *Life and Writings of J. C. Mangan*, p. 75.
84. J. C. Mangan, *Poems*, ed. by D. J. O'Donoghue, Preface, p. xxi.

ical instinct, and much of that aptitude for acquiring a vast half-knowledge of many things not commonly known, which he shares with the very similar, and dissimilar, Poe. But his "translations" from many tongues, even when, as in the case of German, he knew his originals well, were wont to be either frank paraphrases or imitations, often to his original's advantage.[85]

W. Wilsey Martin (b. 1833).—In the collection *By Solent and Danube* (1885), W. Wilsey Martin offers a translation of "Du bist wie eine Blume,"[86] which, while not extraordinary, is quoted below because of the comparative rarity of the volume containing it. There is great similarity between the last stanza of Martin's version and that of Charles Russell, which is also given:

> I look on thee, sweet floweret,
> So fresh, and pure, and fair;
> While on my heart creeps slowly
> The shadow of a care.
>
> I'd lay my hands devoutly
> Upon thy golden hair;
> And pray God keep them ever,
> As fresh, and pure, and fair.
> (Martin's translation)
>
> . . . .
>
> I could stretch my hands toward thee
> And lightly touch thy hair,
> Praying God ever to keep thee
> So sweet and pure and fair.
> (Russell's translation)

Annie Matheson (b. 1853).—Annie Matheson, who has made translations from miscellaneous poems of Rückert, Julius Rodenberg, Halm, Goethe, Uhland, and Jacobi, has done into English two lyrics by Heine: "Ich stand in dunkeln Träumen"[87] (*Die Heimkehr*) and "Auf ihrem Grab, da steht eine Linde"[88] (*Verschiedene*). Annie Matheson's two translations, while

---

85. Ed. by D. J. O'Donoghue, p. xiv. 86. P. 138.
87. Annie Matheson, *The Religion of Humanity and Other Poems*, p. 174.
88. *Ibid.*, p. 182.

Minor Translators

they are far above the average in accuracy and spirit, fall far short of the original lyrics. The form and substance are adhered to strictly, and the choice of diction used by the author is quite above reproach, yet the total effect of each of the two attempts is wanting.

A. Bernard Miall.—A. Bernard Miall, one of the past century's most prolific translators,[89] has left but one translation of Heine, that of "Sterne mit den goldnen Füsschen."[90] Miall's translation is exceptionally literal, and the spirit of the original breathes through his version to great extent. The version, quoted below, is one of the best of Heine's delightful lyrics:

> Stars with golden feet are creeping,
> Wandering sad with footsteps light,
> Lest they wake the tired earth sleeping,
> Sleeping in the lap of Night.
>
> Every leaf a green ear seeming
> List the woodlands, still and calm,
> And the mountain as if dreaming,
> Stretches up its shadowy arm.
>
> But who calls there? Echoes ringing
> Pierce within my breast and fail:
> Was it the Beloved singing?
> Was it but the Nightingale?

J. Saxon Mills.—J. Saxon Mills has left but two translations, one from Uhland and the other from Heine's "Die Erde war so lange geizig"[91] *(Lyrisches Intermezzo).* Mills has made an unfortunate choice from among the many lyrics of Heine, for in the one chosen it is absolutely impossible to convey the impression Heine wishes to give by his use of words derived from the French at the end of practically each verse, i.e., *spendabel, kapabel, miserabel, passabel, aimabel,* and *ennuyieret, titulieret.* The general effect is the same as in the

---

89. Miall has translations from the Russian, the French, the German, the Spanish, and the Dutch.
90. *Nocturnes & Pastorals,* p. 10.   91. *Fasiculus Versiculorum,* p. 52.

German poem, but that added odd quirk produced by the use of French derivatives is impossible to reproduce.

Thomas Herbert Noyes (b. 1827).—Thomas Herbert Noyes, who shows unusual familiarity with German poets of the first rank,[92] has undertaken but one translation of Heine, rendering into English verse the seldom attempted *Ritter Olaf*[93] *(Romanzen).* Sir Olave represents a bold effort on the part of Noyes to re-tell one of Heine's most spirited ballads, and no small modicum of success is due the translator. With consummate art, Noyes manages to match Heine's atmosphere of the Middle Ages and follows the German completely in his succession of events and ideas. The form of the first and third parts is strictly adhered to while that of the second, which varies slightly from that of Heine, is a superb attempt to "get the feel" of the peculiar five-line stanza employed by Heine. With the exception of a few awkward English expressions, Noyes has given an exceedingly meritorious version.

Francis Turner Palgrave (1824-1897).—Francis Turner Palgrave has attempted but one translation of Heine, that of "Wenn ich in deine Augen seh'"[94] *(Lyrisches Intermezzo).* Palgrave's version is among the best translations of Heine's charming lyric. The comparative freedom with which the first stanza is rendered in no wise detracts from the truly Heinesque effect of the whole. We are inclined to excuse Palgrave for the liberties taken since the spirit of the moment presented is so thoroughly captured:

> As within thine eyes I look,
> All my pain the heart forsook:
> When my lips with thine are seal'd,
> All the wounds of life are heal'd.
>
> On thy heart when I recline
> Heaven's happiness is mine:

---

92. Noyes, in *An Idyll of the Weald*, has translations from Heinrich Hoffmann, E. Geibel, Schiller, Rückert, Graf von Auersperg, Uhland, Herder, Tieck, Matthison, Platen, Chamisso, and Heine.

93. *Ibid.*, p. 86.   94. *Idylls and Songs*, p. 136.

When thou say'st, I love but thee:—
Bitter tears fall fast and free.

Charles Kegan Paul (1828-1902).—The former editor of the *New Quarterly Magazine* (1873-1878), Charles Kegan Paul, has attempted quite a few translations from both the French and German including *En Route* from the French of J. K. Huysmans, *The Thoughts of Blaise Pascal* from the text of Auguste Molimer, Goethe's *Faust*, and one or two miscellaneous pieces. He has but one translation from Heine, *The Pilgrimage to Kevlaar*.[95] This translation of *Die Wallfahrt nach Kevlaar*, while better than average for this ever-popular song, scarcely merits discussion at any length. The English version is fairly literal; the form is preserved; but the delicacy and pathos of the original are sadly lacking.

John Payne (1842-1916).—Proclaimed by no less an authority than Richard Garnett as "literally without a rival in the field of translation,"[96] John Payne, largely through the Villon Society, has rendered, in English, works representing a remarkable range of interest and activity. In his *Autobiography*, Payne tells us that as a mere schoolboy, "Between the years of 14 and 21 I translated into English verse the *Divina Commedia* of Dante, the Second Part of Goethe's *Faust*, the *Hermann and Dorothea*, Lessing's *Nathan der Weise*, Calderon's *Magico Prodigioso* and countless short poems by Goethe, Schiller, Heine and other German poets."[97]

According to Payne's own statement, the translations of Heine together with "other worthless exercises" were subsequently destroyed and forgotten. There is no doubt that a number of the English versions did perish, but there is equally no doubt that a great many of them survived, for in an account by Thomas Wright of a visit to John Payne on August 29, 1910, is related a rather detailed conversation of the two men regarding the efforts of Payne to translate Heine. Indeed,

---

95. *On the Wayside*, p. 60.
96. John Payne, *Autobiography*, p. 19.   97. *Ibid.*, pp. 10-11.

at the request of Wright, Payne read a number of the poems, "all of which were written on folio sheets of flimsy paper," and stated that the work owed its completion "to the urgent instance of Sir Edward Burne-Jones" to whom a work proper on Heine and the English translations are dedicated.[98]

Payne's translations, which are for the most part inaccessible but from which many passages are cited in the *Life* of Thomas Wright, show a spontaneity and freshness completely in accord with the original pieces. Payne, who, indeed, considered himself "Heine *redivivus*," reveals an understanding of the German poet's many-sided nature rarely found among his English readers, as evidenced not only by his translations but his expressed opinions as well.[99]

A. Rogers.—A. Rogers, a scholar of oriental tongues and translator from the Persian and Indian, as well as from the German of Goethe, has four translations from Heine cited in the Kroeker collection.[100] Two are taken from Heine's *Junge Leiden: Der Traurige* and *Zwei Brüder;* and two are from the *Lyrisches Intermezzo:* "O schwöre nicht und küsse nur" and "Vergiftet sind meine Lieder." Rogers has proved himself here an exceptional translator, and his versions cannot be praised too highly. Of nearly equal merit, his four translations reveal a hand that is fully in accord and sympathy with that of Heine. His version of "Vergiftet sind meine Lieder" is chosen arbitrarily as a fair specimen of Rogers' ability as a translator:

> All of my songs are poisoned—
> How could it otherwise be?
> The bloom of my very existence
> Hast thou e'en poisoned for me.
>
> All of my songs are poisoned—
> How could it otherwise be?
> In my bosom I've many a serpent;
> There, too, my love, I have thee.

98. Thomas Wright, *Life of John Payne*, pp. 230 ff.
99. See section on Informal Opinion.
100. Kroeker, *op. cit.*, pp. 22, 29, 60, 75.

Franciska Ruge.—Franciska Ruge's version of *Der Asra* (*Historien*, R.) quoted in the excellent selection of Heine's poems by Kate Freiligrath Kroeker[101] is the finest of the many translations of the poem read. Franciska Ruge has preserved admirably Heine's use of *freier Rhythmus*, and in spirited fashion has remained in all ways faithful to the original:

> Every day the wondrous lovely
> Sultan's daughter paced the courtyard,
> At the hour of sunset glory,
> Where the foaming fountains whiten.
>
> Every day the youthful slave stood
> By the fountain's foam at sunset,
> Where the snowy waters murmur,—
> Daily grew he pale and paler.
>
> Till one even stept the Princess
> To his side with rapid question:
> "Tell thy name, and tell thy country!
> Tell thy clan, for I would know them!"
>
> And the slave replied, "My name is
> Mahomet, my home is Yemen,
> And my clan is that of Asra,
> Whom Love slayeth by its ardour."

Charles Russell (1872-1917).—Charles Russell appears to have been particularly fond of the German poets, for he offers in *Sonnets, Poems, and Translations,* paraphrases of Goethe, Schiller, Stolberg, and Heine. His translations from Heine[102] number three in all: "Wie des Mondes Abbild zittert" (*Neuer Frühling*), "Du bist wie eine Blume," and "Du schönes Fischermädchen." Of the three, "My Child, Thou Art a Flower" is the best and most nearly approaches the true Heinesque form. The remaining two stumble and halt a bit in their rhythm and are but of average merit in general. The best of the lot is a superior but far from perfect transcription of Heine's well-known short lyric:

101. *Ibid.*, p. 232.
102. *Sonnets, Poems and Translations*, pp. 39-40.

My child, thou art a flower
So fair and pure and sweet,
That unawares a sadness
Creeps o'er me when we meet.

I could stretch my hands toward thee,
And lightly touch thy hair,
Praying God ever to keep thee
So sweet and pure and fair.

Rollo Russell (1849-1914).—Francis Albert Rollo Russell, in a slender volume, *Break of Day*, translated two of the shorter lyrics of Heine, "Anfangs wollt' ich fast verzagen"[103] *(Junge Leiden)* and "Du bist wie eine Blume."[104] The translator has made little attempt to capture Heine's form or substance and has put forth quite a shabby effort, which falls miserably short of the quality of the originals. As is true in the case of a number of Heine's translators, Russell has "overdressed" the German lyricist's naïve and genuine expression, and the result is mere ostentation and nonsense. Particularly is this true of the English version of "Du bist wie eine Blume":

Thou art a flower's image
So holy, pure and kind,
Thy tenderness beholding
Love hallows all my mind.

It seems as though a blessing
Arose and filled my heart,
A prayer that God possessing,
Would keep thee as thou art.

Ernest Rhys.—In *A London Rose and Other Poems*, Ernest Rhys attempted but one translation of Heine, a version of *Geheimnis*[105] *(Zeitgedichte*, N. G.). It is at best but a mediocre paraphrase, loosely and carelessly done, and misses entirely the grace and significance of Heine's poem. The first stanza quoted below, together with the original, is a fair sample of

---

103. *Break of Day and Other Verses*, p. 116.
104. *Ibid.*, p. 118. 105. P. 96.

Minor Translators

poor interpretation on the part of Rhys. Note the entirely false conception given by the second verse:

> We do not sigh, our eyes are tearless;
> And if we smile, we laugh no more;
> Never shall the hidden secret
> From our eyes gleam as of yore.

> Wir seufzen nicht, das Aug' ist trocken,
> Wir lächeln oft, wir lachen gar!
> In keinem Blick, in keiner Miene,
> Wird das Geheimnis offenbar.

J. M. W. Schwartz (1858-1915).—"Maarten Maartens," whose real name was J. M. W. Schwartz, began his literary career as a maker of English lyrics and ended it as a maker of Dutch songs. In the interim, he translated a great deal from German, Dutch, French, Norse, and Italian. Schwartz, born of Jewish parents in Prussian Poland, worked for five years in Berlin and lived thereafter many years in the famous town of Bonn. His letters reveal a decided interest in German literature, and Heine in particular. On October 23, 1898, in a letter to Mrs. Gosse, Schwartz wrote: "It is a pity you cannot read Heine, for in my opinion, he is the wittiest writer that ever—yes, ever—wrote. And no one that has not read him can form any conception of the exquisite possibilities of German prose."[106] Maarten, or Schwartz, has translated five of Heine's superb songs in his *Morning of a Love and Other Poems:* from *Junge Leiden*, "Anfangs wollt' ich fast verzagen" (p. 27), "Lieb Liebchen" (p. 25); from *Lyrisches Intermezzo*, "Es liegt der heisse Sommer" (p. 271), "Wenn zwei von einander scheiden" (p. 272); from *Die Heimkehr*, "Du bist wie eine Blume" (p. 270), *Lorelei* (p. 267).

The translations of Schwartz are of no great consequence. They are literally done and are of merely average quality. His one translation, however, which does evoke a bit of criticism at any rate, is that of the *Lorelei*, of which he gives two versions.

106. J. M. W. Schwartz, *The Letters of Maarten Maartens*, p. 162.

The first is a quite conventional poem representing a half-hearted attempt to do Heine's splendid piece into English. It is an unusually loose paraphrase reflecting credit neither on Heine nor on Schwartz. The second version is an attempt to parody Heine's poem in Heine's manner. It is given below—not for any literary merit but for its singularity, which may be of interest to the many who have read the original:

> I can't think whatever's the matter;
> I'm duller and heavier than lead;
> Some stupid old nursery chatter
> Has got itself wedged in my head.
> The evening gets hotter and hotter
> It's dark, though the sun's shining still;
> He's poking his rays at the water,
> And winking his eyes at the hill.
>
> A fine-looking girl sits up yonder,—
> She's made that old mountain her home;
> She's combing her hair out—O wonder!—
> Up there with a glittering comb.
> It's a fact that I scarce like to mention,
> But she's got nothing on but her hair,
> And she's really attracting attention,
> A-sitting and combing it there.
>
> The fisherman cannot help viewing
> The scene, and it gives him a shock;
> He don't look to what he is doing,
> He'll get into trouble on a rock.
> It's really extremely improper,
> Unless she's "Permission to kill";
> They ought to do something to stop her
> From making that noise on the hill.

William Charles Scully (b. 1855).—William C. Scully has translations from Earl Beck Arndt, Julius Moser, and eighteen translations from Heine in his volume *Poems*,[107] among which are English versions from *Junge Leiden*,

107. See pp. 194-206.

Lyrisches Intermezzo, Die Heimkehr, and *Neuer Frühling.* Scully's translations from Heine deserve no special mention. The English writer has taken great pains to preserve as much of Heine as he could. The form is especially well adhered to; and the idea of the English versions is that of the German; but Scully is unable to weep and laugh with Heine, and, as a result, his versions leave us unaffected. The total effect of each poem is lost despite the fact that nearly all the details are faithfully given.

E. B. Shuldham.—E. B. Shuldham, who is also a Heine critic,[108] has but one translation of Heine (cited in the Kroeker collection), which appeared first in *Temple Bar.* It is a translation of "Mir lodert und wogt im Gehirn eine Fluth" (*Nachlese,* L. G.). The rhythm of the original presents a few difficulties with its constantly shifting iambs and anapaests, but Shuldham manages fairly well to give us at least a decent version[109] of the seldom attempted German poem.

John Snodgrass (1850-1888).—John Snodgrass is best known for his admirable translation, *Religion and Philosophy in Germany: A Fragment,* the original of which was first published in the *Revue des Deux Mondes* in 1834. In the French version (1835) of Heine's works it appears as the first part of the two volumes *De L'Allemagne.* Snodgrass followed his first translation of Heine by a second, calling it *Wit, Wisdom and Pathos from the Prose of Heinrich Heine,* which appeared several years later (1879) and met with wide acclaim in England and elsewhere. Typical of the criticisms of the work of Snodgrass are the following:

No Englishman of culture who is unacquainted with Heine can fail to derive a new intellectual pleasure from Mr. Snodgrass's pages.—*Contemporary Review,* September, 1880.

... One of the most successful books of the season.—*Aberdeen Journal,* March, 1879.

---

108. See section on Criticism.   109. Kroeker, *op. cit.,* p. 268.

He has performed his task with skill, tact and judgment; and it is easy to perceive that he has a thorough acquaintance with his author and sympathy for his matter.—*Notes and Queries*, April, 1879.

Probably the best of the criticisms of Snodgrass's translations of Heine in general is the following:

Mr. Snodgrass would appear to have saturated himself with Heine literature, to have so caught Heine's mode of thought and his turns of expression—quaint, droll, swift, and scathing by turns—that the translator would appear to have had no more difficulty in presenting Heine as he was to the reader than he would have in presenting his own thoughts.—*Glasgow Herald*, March 31, 1879.

In addition to his prose translations, Snodgrass has put into English versions of "Wenn Du mir vorüberwandelst" *(Neuer Frühling)*, "Der Tod, das ist die kühle Nacht" *(Die Heimkehr)*, and "Wenn zwei von einander scheiden" *(Lyrisches Intermezzo)*. The verse translations[110] of Snodgrass, while not nearly so fine as his prose ones, are yet of more than a little interest. Snodgrass is no poet; but he has managed far better than some who lay claim to the title, to convey Heine's mood and thought in Heine's form. As a specimen of the verse translation of Heine, the short, popular lyric, "Wenn zwei von einander scheiden," may be quoted:

> When two that are dear must part,
> In sorrow the hands are pressed;
> Their tears begin to flow,
> Their sighing knows no rest.
>
> With us there was no weeping,
> Nor had we aught to say—
> Our sighing and our weeping
> Came on an after-day.

"*Stratheir.*"—Colonel H. S. Jarrett, writing under the pseudonym of "Stratheir,"[111] has contributed six of the trans-

---

110. Kroeker, *op. cit.*, pp. 75, 122, 197.

111. *The Book of Songs*, tr. by "Stratheir" (London: Constable & Co., 1882), is listed in the bibliography in William Sharp's *Life of Heinrich Heine*. Copies are not available.

lations in the Kroeker collection: from *Junge Leiden, Die Minnesänger*, "Im Hirne spukt mir," "Ich möchte weinen"; from *Die Heimkehr*, "Wie dunkle Träume stehen," "Ich wollt' meine Schmerzen ergössen"; from *Verschiedene*, "Das Meer erglänzte weit hinaus." Jarrett's translations are of fairly even quality throughout. Effort is made to be as literal as possible, and the form of the originals is in the main observed; but the spirit of Heine is definitely absent.

Alma Strettell.—In the admirable collection of Kate Freiligrath-Kroeker are included sixteen translations of Heine by Alma Strettell.[112] They are of the following poems: from *Junge Leiden*, "Hüt' Dich, mein Freund" (p. 50), "Im nächtigen Traum" (p. 9), *Der arme Peter* (p. 23); from *Lyrisches Intermezzo*, Nos. 4, 5, 22, 25 (pp. 56, 66); from *Die Heimkehr*, "Saphire sind die Augen dein" (p. 111), "Kaum sahen wir uns" (p. 121); from *Neuer Frühling*, "Sterne mit den goldnen Füsschen" (p. 201); from *Verschiedene*, "Entflieh mit mir" (p. 210); from *Romanzen*, *Ritter Olaf* (p. 235), *Altes Kaminstück* (p. 215); from *Lamentationen* (R.), *Auto-da-fé* (p. 237), *Altes Lied* (p. 236); from *Letzte Gedichte und Nachlese*, "Ich war, o Lamm, als Hirt bestellt" (p. 249).

Alma Strettell's work is of slightly uneven quality. Her translations of Nos. 4, 5, and 25 of the *Lyrisches Intermezzo* are of exceptional merit. She is in accord with Heine in both mood and form. The version of the faint last glimmer of Heine's passionate love, *Auto-da-fé*, is also excellent. Occasionally, as in "Kaum sahen wir uns," *Altes Kaminstück*, and *Altes Lied*, her rhythm is faulty and poorly applied. All too often, too, Alma Strettell falls into the habit of rhyming purely for the eye, which spoils utterly Heine's melodious music—as in the concluding stanzas of "Entflieh mit mir" ("gone"—

---

112. In the course of reading, I came across a reference to *Selections from the Poetical Works of Heinrich Heine* (London: Macmillan & Co., 1898), by Alma Strettell, a copy of which I have been unable to find.

"alone"), "Saphire sind die Augen dein" ("lover"—"over"), and "Sterne mit den goldnen Füsschen" ("fell"—"nightingale"). Her finest translations are those already mentioned from the *Lyrisches Intermezzo* and an extremely clever, accurate, and superior version of *Der arme Peter*, which is undoubtedly one of the finest in English. Because of the length of *Poor Peter*, the shorter lyric (No. 25 in the *Lyrisches Intermezzo*) is quoted as a sample specimen of Alma Strettell at her best:

> When the lime-trees bloomed, and the sun shone bright;
> And the nightingale sang in the morning light,
> You kissed me then, and your soft arm pressed
> And clasped me close to your throbbing breast.
>
> When the sun shone pale, and the leaves were dead,
> And the raven croaked in the trees o'er head,
> We wished one another a cold "Good-day,"
> You made me a courtesy, and went your way.

John Addington Symonds (1840-1893).—Best known for his studies of renaissance Italy, and particularly for his translation of the *Memoirs* of Cellini, whom he regarded as a sort of human touchstone for the Renaissance, John Addington Symonds cultivated also a definite interest in German literature—particularly that of the modern era. While still at Oxford, he became intensely interested in Goethe, whose works were given to him by his father on his twenty-first birthday, and whose Proemium to *Gott und Welt* he later translated in 1870. Indeed, Goethe appears to have been the guiding star of Symond's life; and Goethe's maxim, "To live resolvedly in the Whole, the Good, the Beautiful," became the creed by which the English author lived.[113] No little credit is due to Madame Goldschmidt, the celebrated singer, for having further stimulated the interest of Symonds in German music and

---

113. Van Wyck Brooks, *John Addington Symonds: A Biographical Study*, p. 216.

literature. As a direct result of the many discussions with the musician, we find Symonds making comparisons and contrasts between the nature of German and English literature, the most interesting of which to us is the following statement of the comparative merits of Heine and Tennyson: "Tennyson takes all the solid sharp words and puts them together. Music cannot come between. He does not flow. He cannot like music. Heine's songs run into music at once; they are music."[114]

Immediately after taking his degree, Symonds accompanied by his father and sister made an extensive trip through Europe—including, of course, a visit to Germany. It was the first of many trips abroad. Upon his return to London, he wrote to H. G. Dalkyrs on March 23, 1865: "We have read many books, the best being Lewes' 'Goethe.' . . . Gaps are filled up by Dante, Heine's Songs, and the learning of some poems of Goethe."[115]

At the suggestion of Jowett, for whom he had an unbounded admiration, Symonds undertook the translation of Zeller's history of Aristotelianism, upon which much time was wasted and which proved in the end "intolerably irksome" and was done "abominably ill."[116] While engaged upon this irksome task, Symonds continued his studies, read Heine's letters, and even projected a sort of original version of Hegel's *Aesthetics*. In a letter to W. J. Courthope, dated from Cannes, December 28, 1867, he wrote:

. . . I have also been reading the correspondence of Heine. Do you know him? I mean, of course, the poet, or patriot, as he preferred to be called. It is good to find anything so purely fresh in this century—such a source of tears and laughter, bitter, sweet, ironical and tender, ribald and religious, all in one gush. Why do not the gods give humor to more of us, and make a better world? We do for the most part carry about our sorrows and our purposes in such sadness— like Dante's hypocrites beneath their leaden cowls.[117]

---
114. H. F. Brown, *John Addington Symonds: A Biography*, I, 207.
115. *Ibid.*, I, 316.
116. Brooks, *op. cit.*, p. 69.   117. Brown, *op. cit.*, II, 29.

96 *Heine in England*

Seven months later, in a letter to "H. S." (July 25, 1868), he revealed further interest in Heine:

> ... I have read very little except German for the good of my mind; and the German has been Heine's "Reisebilder." It is a very amusing book, certainly, and of a good style. But his particular humor in which so much absolute filth is mingled with faded rose-leaves on the one side and satiric stinging nettles on the other, with exquisite lyrical interbreathings of the true poet and many wise remarks, wearies me. I like the "Harzreise" best of all. It is so fresh, the joy of the wood is so strong and unaffected in it, and the humorous picture of the Brocken supper and of the two young men who mistook a clothes cupboard for a window opening on moon and mountain, is natural. Next, I think, I like the satire on Platen: because it is as genuine and unmixed in its antique abusiveness.[118]

Despite Symonds's avowed interest in Heine, he attempted but one translation from him—"Ein Fichtenbaum steht einsam" —and has given us but a poor version of the often-quoted and translated poem. The English version is unpoetic and unmusical and a distinct disappointment coming from one whose interest in and knowledge of German was far beyond the average.

Arthur Symons (b. 1865).—Arthur Symons,[119] whose translations are for the most part confined to the French of Baudelaire, Gauthier, and Du Bellay, has made a very creditable version[120] of *Die Wallfahrt nach Kevlaar*. This translation preserves unusually well the spirit of the Middle Ages that permeates Heine's poem. The soul with its naïve beliefs and its innocent simplicity is everywhere in the English version as in the German. The translation is literal and well rendered. Occasionally, Symons, through carelessness, falters in the matter of meter, and the easy-flowing form of the German poem is interrupted and broken. Particularly is this true of the second stanza of the middle section, which is compared below with

---

118. *Ibid.*, II, 28-29.
119. See also section on Influence.
120. *Days and Nights*, pp. 144-147.

the original in which Heine, through the careful use of elision and slurring, maintains his flawless rhythm:

> Die kranken Leute bringen
> Ihr dar, als Opferspend',
> Aus Wachs gebildete Glieder,
> Viel wächserne Füss' und Händ'.

> The sick folk all of them bring her,
> As thanksgiving most meet,
> Wax limbs cunningly moulded,
> Waxen hands and feet.

Edward Locke Tomlin.—Edward Locke Tomlin has but one translation of Heine—a version of the popular quatrain beginning "Anfangs wollt' ich fast verzagen" *(Junge Leiden)*. Tomlin has failed to preserve the meter of the original, as is evident by the following comparison:

> Anfangs wollt' ich fast verzagen,
> Und ich glaubt' ich trüg' es nie;
> Und ich hab' es doch getragen—
> Aber fragt mich nur nicht, wie?

> Once I thought my heart must sever,
> Never should I bear it, never;
> I have borne it all—but now
> Ask not how.[121]

Richard Chenevix Trench (1807-1886).—Richard Trench, former Archbishop of Dublin and sometime authority on linguistics, spent his leisure time composing poems original and otherwise. Among his non-original poems are found translations from Rückert, Goethe, Platen, and a version of Heine's *Lorelei*.[122] As in the case of the vast majority of other translators of Heine's well-known song, Trench loses entirely the faint gleam of mocking gaiety which the German poet injects in the concluding stanza. Otherwise the poem is rather creditably done into English; the translation is literal, and the spirit of the original is fairly well maintained throughout.

121. *Gleanings*, p. 107. 122. *Poems*, II, 37.

Bernard Freeman Trotter (1890-1917).—In an only work, Bernard Freeman Trotter, a former army officer killed in action in France during the last World War, has left a better than average translation of Heine's "Dass du mich liebst, das wusst' ich" *(Verschiedene).*[123] The translation is given here largely because of the fact that it is, in all probability, unknown to most readers:

> I knew, sweetheart, you loved me,
> I guessed it long ago;
> Yet your confession moved me
> As this had not been so.
>
> I strode upon the mountains,
> I shouted to the skies—
> The sunset on the ocean
> Brought tears into my eyes.
>
> My heart aglow with passion,
> A blazing sun I bear,
> And in love's boundless waters
> 'Tis sinking, great and fair.

R. E. Wallis (1820-1900).—Rev. R. E. Wallis, translator of a few religious works from the German of F. J. Delitzsch, J. Peter Lange, and H. A. W. Meyer, contributed to the collection of F. D'Anvers translations of Heine's "Wir sassen am Fischerhause" and "Du schönes Fischermädchen," both from *Die Heimkehr.*[124] The versions of Wallis are for the most part correct in form and meaning and manage fairly well to preserve the spirit and tone of the originals; but as they are undistinguished in any other way, it is hardly necessary to quote a specimen.

Frederick E. Weatherly (b. 1848).—"Wenn zwei von einander scheiden" was done into English verse by Frederick E. Weatherly, and represents the only translation by that author found. The version, as can be readily seen, is but average:

123. *A Canadian Twilight,* p. 86.
124. F. D'Anvers, *op. cit.,* pp. 46, 83.

Minor Translators 99

When two fond hearts are parting
They clasp sad hands in pain,
And they fall a-weeping
And sigh and weep again.

But we wept not at parting,
No sighs from our lips fell,
The weeping and the sighing
Came after our farewell.

Edward Wilberforce (b. 1834).—Edward Wilberforce, a translator of no little note,[125] undertook to put into English verse three of the longer poems of Heine: *Rhampsenit*[126] and *Der Ex-Nachtwächter*[127] from the *Historien* (R.) and *Lamentationen* respectively and *Das Sklavenschiff*[128] from the *Letzte Gedichte*. Wilberforce's three translations cannot be praised too highly. He has entered thoroughly into the spirit of his author and has managed to catch more than the proverbial spark of Heine's genius. With the precision and thoroughgoing accuracy of a scholar of no mean repute, he has studied each situation unfolded by Heine in an exhaustive manner; for not only are his translations as perfect as could be humanly possible, but he calls attention to an anachronism in *Rhampsenit* which even the most intelligent reader might pass without notice.

With consummate skill he has caught all the nuances of Heine's peculiar brand of irony in his literary satire on the poet Dingelstedt, *Der Ex-Nachtwächter*. Each poisoned dart is there and strikes in Wilberforce's version with the same potency of effect as in Heine's original. *Das Sklavenschiff* with its cutting yet humorous satire is as brilliant and effective in the English version as Heine intended it to be in the German. No one of the three translations is in any way far inferior to

---

125. Wilberforce has translated H. von Hellborn's biography of Franz Schubert, Dante's *Inferno*, and songs from Goethe, Schiller, Hermann Lingg, Bodenstedt, Giusti, Alfieri, and Alfred de Musset.
126. *Dante's Inferno and Other Translations*, p. 271.
127. *Ibid.*, p. 257.   128. *Ibid.*, p. 267.

the originals. The length of each forbids quotation as a whole, and the even quality of the whole does not justify the excerpting of a single stanza as better or worse than any other. It probably should be noted that from *Der Ex-Nachtwächter* five stanzas are omitted in the English version, but the absence of the stanzas does not lessen to any degree the value of the English translation. Translation of the quality of Wilberforce's is indeed an art that bespeaks genius.

Mrs. James Glenny Wilson.—So radically has Mrs. James Glenny Wilson departed from Heine's "Mit Rosen, Zypressen und Flittergold" *(Junge Leiden)* and "Am leuchtenden Sommermorgen" *(Lyrisches Intermezzo),* that her versions can in no wise be called translations. In the first mentioned poem, she has succeeded in completely butchering Heine's six-strophe song, and from the scraps left upon her chopping-block she has assembled the nine-line monstrosity:

> With myrtle and roses
> Perfumed and cold,
> With weeping laburnum
> And marigold
> I will garland this book
> Like some holy shrine,
> And wrap in its shroud
> These sad songs of mind.
> Oh, if Love, too, could sleep in its funeral fold![129]

In the other poem (we dare not call it paraphrase) she has made an obvious attempt to translate the first stanza—without success—but in the last verses we are unable to find or infer the slightest resemblance to the original:

> Am leuchtenden Sommermorgen
> Geh' ich im Garten herum.
> Es flüstern und sprechen die Blumen,
> Ich aber wandle stumm.
>
> Es flüstern und sprechen die Blumen,
> Und schaun mitleidig mich an:

---

129. *A Book of Verses,* p. 681.

Sei unserer Schwester nicht böse,
Du trauriger, blasser Mann!

This sunshiny summer morning
The trees by the south wind are stirred.
The roses are whispering together;
I only have never a word.

The roses are nodding and whispering,
"O Love! Let us love while we may,
Reproach not our sister, our darling,
Though lonely she leaves us today."[130]

James H. Wilson.—In *Zalmoxis and Other Poems* (1892),[131] James H. Wilson has included ten translations from the German—one each from Kerner, Lenau, Eichendorff, and Uhland, and the following four from Heine: from *Lyrisches Intermezzo,* "Aus meinen Tränen spriessen" (p. 182), "Nacht lag auf meinen Augen" (p. 179); from *Die Heimkehr,* "Sie haben heut' Abend Gesellschaft" (p. 184), "Du bist wie eine Blume" (p. 183). Wilson's translations are all carefully undertaken, and the author has been at pains to adhere as closely as possible to the originals in practically all respects. The meter is preserved, and a definite effort is made to capture the spirit of the German; yet the language is but ordinary, and the verses lack tone.

Humbert Wolfe (b. 1886).—The contemporary poet Humbert Wolfe, who is discussed more fully elsewhere,[132] has written four English poems from Heine which in no wise merit the title "translations." Three of the so-called versions —those based upon the first three songs in the *Lyrisches Intermezzo* proper—appeared in the *Spectator* in 1927;[133] and the fourth, based upon "Du bist wie eine Blume" is to be found in Wolfe's *Shylock Reasons with Mr. Chesterton.*[134] The pieces are called advisedly "English poems from Heine," for the

---

130. *Ibid.,* p. 68.   131. *Passim.*
132. See section on Informal Opinion.
133. "Three Poems from Heine," *Spectator,* CXXXIX, 661.
134. P. 54.

English poet makes no effort whatsoever to translate Heine's lyrics but has written extremely loose versions bordering on parodies and twisted at will to suit his own desires. The pieces neither detract credit from Heine since they bear such slight resemblance to the German originals, nor add credit to the English poet since they are at best pointless and mediocre. The version of "Du bist wie eine Blume" is given here as a sample of "Wolfesque Heine":

> You have the way of a blossom,
> Gold petal with April green,
> And you melt the heart in the bosom
> As your beauty enters in.
>
> I will fold my hands together,
> Asking of God for you
> Always in April weather
> Cold petals and colder dew.

John Dennistoun Wood (b. 1829).—"Du bist wie eine Blume" will ever prove a fruitful source for translators. Another English version of the celebrated gem has been attempted by John Wood, who also has one or two translations from Goethe and Uhland. Wood's version represents but another effort to translate the popular song:

> As is a flower new-opened,
> Pure, sweet, and fair thou art,
> But as I view thee sadness
> Comes stealing o'er my heart.
>
> With hand on thy head resting
> Should I not breathe a prayer
> That God will keep thee ever
> As pure, and sweet, and fair.[135]

Other Translators.—Two minor translators of Heine who are discussed elsewhere in this study, Lady Lucie Duff Gordon and George Meredith, are merely listed here in order to avoid needless repetition. Meredith has four translations in the

---

135. *Poems in Rhyme and Blank Verse*, p. 114.

Monthly Observer for 1849, and Lady Duff Gordon eight scattered paraphrases of miscellaneous lyrics. In the *Notebooks* of Stopford A. Brooke (1832-1916), too, are found,[136] mingled with his sketches in crayon of scenery in Switzerland and Italy, experiments in verse including a few translations from Heine made during the 1850's.[137]

136. L. P. Jacks, *Life and Letters of Stopford Brooke*, I, 142.
137. Listed in the bibliographies of B. Q. Morgan and/or H. G. Atkins are collections by Robert Levy, J. Geike, H. B. Briggs, J. W. Oddie, G. Tyrell, and M. P. Turnbull containing miscellaneous translations from Heine, together with volumes by "Stratheir," J. E. Wallis, P. G. L. Webb, and "J. Ackerlos." I have been unable to locate any of these volumes.

2.

Heine

IN ENGLISH CRITICISM

III. *Major Critics*

"*Tu deviendras sûrement illustre, mais tu ne réussiras point à te faire aimer*," predicted Professor Sartorius in speaking of the brilliant young scholar and artist Heinrich Heine.[1] How accurate the prediction was is attested by the great bulk of English criticism dealing with the German poet. The great number of English critics of Heine—nearly as great as that of Heine's English translators—have paid ample tribute to the genius of the German lyricist. They have treated the German poet with sympathy; they have tried painstakingly to understand the peculiar genius that was his chief claim to immortality; they have expressed their unbounded admirations for the artist; but only in rare instances has the poet succeeded in winning the unlimited and unqualified love and affection of his reviewers and critics.

The most important thing that Heine gets from the *Volkslied* is the peculiar ironic antithesis that so definitely marks, and mars, his work; and it is even this quality which has proved the great stumbling-block in the path of appreciative criticism of the poet's life and works. This *Stimmungsbrechung*, this

---

1. Pierre Gauthiez, *Henri Heine*, p. 54.

rapid and inexplicable changing from the sweet to the bitter, from the sublime to the ridiculous, proves for the most part too great a shock for the English temperament and results in the misunderstanding of a great many of the poet's works. Heine, as Immermann realized, had a peculiar horror of sentimentality that led him often to descend to the level of buffoonery, irreverence, and vulgarity in order to escape the charge of emotionalism.

It is this quality—the quality of belittling the important, the sacred—that proves most repulsive to English critics and prevents them from altogether loving the German poet. And yet, a few of the critics have scratched beneath the surface and found that Heine's satire, his irony, his antithetical moods and expressions, are, in reality, not the cheap, meaningless things they appear to be. There is an undercurrent of seriousness in all Heine's works, which a few of the English critics have been able to discern. As Heine himself says, "Witz in seiner Isolierung ist gar nichts wert, nur dann ist der Witz erträglich, wenn er auf einem ernsten Grunde ruht."[2]

Aside from the difficulty of Heine's wit, the critic encounters a still more formidable problem in the many-sidedness of the poet's nature. The constant pendulum-like swing from doubt to despair, the continual shifting of religious and political beliefs, the wavering between Hellenism and Hebraism, between Orientalism and Nationalism, between Romanticism and Realism, create considerable doubt in the critic's mind as to the true and genuine nature of the man and his work. Unlike Goethe and Shakespeare, Heine does not share the perfect harmony of nature and spirit. His is the genius that is associated with *Geist*, and despite wide differences, Heine as a "sentimental" poet is the heir of Schiller and the ancestor of Nietzsche and Thomas Mann.

That which distinguishes Heine from other German poets is the essentially human note of love and pain which sounds

---

2. Erich Eckertz, *Heine und sein Witz*, p. 7.

throughout his entire works. It is the second-rate artist who must fill his canvas with heroic life-sized figures and scenes of momentous import. The true genius can make a work of art out of the merest scrap of ordinary life. "So long as my heart is filled with love and my neighbor's head filled with folly, I shall never lack material to write on," writes Heine in the *Buch Le Grand*.[3] And Heine's poems are merely the notations of the vibrations of his own heart and of trivial bits from the life around him—all set down in the most unaffected, unadorned clarity and simplicity imaginable. "Ce que j'admire le plus en vous," said Grenier once to Heine, "c'est qu'après Goethe, le plus clair, le plus limpide de vos poètes, vous avez su donner à la poésie allemande cette même clarté, avec un air de négligence et de laisser-aller spirituel qu'elle ne connaissait pas encore. Vous avez fait en Allemagne à cet égard ce que Byron a fait en Angleterre et Musset en France."[4]

How easy it is to confuse simplicity in the treatment of commonplace things with a lack of depth and a want of power! The critic of Heine must avoid the pitfall of mistaking Heine's painstaking artistry for carelessness, and his familiarity of subject matter for mere banality. Some of the critics have succeeded unusually well in grasping the total significance of Heine while others have failed. The criticisms themselves begin nearly with the first publication of Heinrich Heine and continue almost uninterruptedly until the present time.

On the basis of the significance, influence, and popularity of the various criticisms, the critics themselves are here divided into major and minor groups. To make possible convenient reference and to facilitate tracing the general development of Heine criticism in England, each group is arranged in chronological order. The criticisms are, for the most part, to be found in English periodicals, although a few occur as individual pieces or as parts of separate volumes.

3. F. H. Wood, *Heine as Critic of His Own Works*, pp. 2-3.
4. Edward Grenier, *Souvenirs Littéraires*, p. 52.

Julian Fane (1827-1870).—An article on Heinrich Heine written in 1855 for the *Saturday Review* by Julian Fane is one of the earliest criticisms of the German poet published in England. Fane, a translator as well as critic,[5] makes some very sound comments on Heine's writings and reveals an astute appreciation of their merit. Serving as an introduction to his English versions of the German poet, the critical points of the article are based to a large extent upon the *Reisebilder* and the *Buch der Lieder*. The latter, in Fane's opinion, is truly a volume of and for all the people of Germany, for "the beauty of its inspiration was such as could be loved by the most unlettered, and understood by those who could give no reason for their admiration." Heine is compared to Wordsworth, Wilkie, and Byron; for, according to Julian Fane, his poems embodied the pathos of the first, the humor of the second, and the fierce fretfulness of the third. Unlike his successors, Fane does not write in so many words that Heine was a paradox, but his subtle contrasting of the many forces that combined to make up the personality that was Heine speaks for itself. Unaided by the perspective that succeeding writers possessed, Fane withal presents a keen and penetrating appraisal of the German poet.

George Eliot (1819-1880).—No other woman and but few men of nineteenth-century England were better prepared to write critically and authoritatively on Heinrich Heine than was Mary Ann Evans (George Eliot). Forced to leave school in 1835 at the age of sixteen, because of the illness of her mother who died in the following summer, George Eliot was hastened into maturity as the result of the charge of the household and farm which devolved upon her. Two or three years later found her buried in the serious studies which proved so beneficial in laying the foundation of her subsequent literary successes.

5. See section on Translation.

Endowed with a great passion for music, which undoubtedly led to her serious study of German and Italian, she entered upon the study of languages with the view in mind of acquiring a greater knowledge of world-music, and in an effort to round out her interrupted formal education. A Signor Brezzi was engaged to come from Coventry two or three times a week in order to tutor the eager, intelligent girl. In a letter to Miss Lewis on November 22, 1839, we find her writing, "I have just received my second lesson in German."[6] Her interest increased, and a year later—October 1, 1840—she wrote again to Miss Veronica Lewis: "I have made an alteration in my plans with Mr. Brezzi, and shall henceforward take Italian and German alternately, so that I shall not be liable to the consciousness of having imperative employment for every interstice of time. There seems a greater affinity between German and my mind than Italian, though less new to me, possesses."[7]

It would seem, from the remarks of Signor Brezzi, who often spoke of the great ease with which George Eliot learned the languages, and from the marvelous progress she herself made in her studies, that the English writer possessed an uncommon talent in linguistic matters although she spoke the languages with difficulty. Indeed, her progress in German was so rapid that in 1842 George Eliot volunteered to give instruction in the tongue. Shortly thereafter, she became a full-fledged tutor of German, teaching her little neighbor, Mary Cash, and a Coventry minister's daughter, Mary Sibree, and no doubt others. In 1843 she translated with unusual success the *Leben Jesu* of Strauss, and from that time on, every spare moment was filled with readings and translations of German authors too numerous to mention. In her journal for 1855 are listed copious readings from the German masters of letters among which is found Heine's *Geständnisse*, concerning which she says that she was "immensely amused with the wit of it in the first

---

6. J. W. Cross, *George Eliot's Life*, I, 49.   7. *Ibid.*, I, 58-59.

fifty pages, but afterwards it burns low, and the want of principle and purpose made it wearisome."[8]

The natural enthusiasm of George Eliot for things German was no doubt greatly increased by her numerous and prolonged visits to the country itself and through the efforts of her husband, George Henry Lewes, the English biographer of Goethe. Lewes shared no little of her unbounded enthusiasm for German literature, as the following statement made after an eight months' stay in Germany succeeding her marriage attests:

> They were very happy months . . . we spent at Berlin, in spite of the bitter cold which came on in January, and lasted almost till we left. How we used to rejoice in the idea of our warm room and coffee as we battled overway from dinner against the wind and snow! Then came the delightful long evenings, in which we read Shakespeare, Goethe, Heine, and Macaulay, with German *Pfefferkuchen* and *Semmels*. . . .[9]

The enthusiasm for Heine continued throughout her life; we find her writing to Mrs. Burne-Jones on March 23, 1878, of the enjoyment and delight experienced in reading the *Two Grenadiers*.[10]

It is particularly, however, in connection with her essay on the German poet with which we are here concerned. On November 29, 1855, George Eliot wrote to Miss Sarah Hennell: "I have just finished a long article on Heine for the 'Westminster Review,' which none of you will like."[11] The essay appeared in the periodical in January, 1856—several years in advance of the admirable study by Matthew Arnold. It was entitled "German Wit: Heinrich Heine," and proved to be one of the finest and most incisive bits of critical writing produced during the century.

Taking as a point of departure Goethe's statement that "Nothing is more significant of men's character than what they find laughable," George Eliot proceeds to what probably

8. *Ibid.*, I, 297.
9. Oscar Browning, *Life of George Eliot*, pp. 40-41.
10. J. W. Cross, *op. cit.*, III, 237-238.
11. *Ibid.*, II, 10.

amounts to the most brilliant brief treatise on the differences of wit and humor ever written. The niceties of distinction between the two great traits are set forth succinctly and with remarkably clear penetration, though the style is somewhat labored at times. As Haldane in his study of the writer points out: "The essay on Heine gives George Eliot a subject worthy of her steel. Satire, wit and humor were her favorite subjects at this time; and the contrast between the last two, their respective qualities and natures, is a topic on which she loved to dwell, and to which she applied all her powers."[12]

While she finds the German nation superior to many other countries in most fields, George Eliot finds no sense of measure or instinctive tact in the laborious, floundering, and clumsy antics of German wit and humor. Heinrich Heine, with an "*esprit* that would make him brilliant among the most brilliant of Frenchmen," she considers Germany's earnest of a worthy, future crop of wits and humorists.

The essay falls logically into three divisions: a discussion of wit and humor, a biographical account of Heinrich Heine, and an estimate of Heine the poet. The first section, which has been discussed briefly already, bears no great significance for our study. The second division is confined wholly to the general details of Heine's life. It is in this section, especially, that the sympathetic attitude of the English writer toward her German subject is manifested to the greatest degree. George Eliot's method here is a pictorial one. While the section dealing with Heine's life is extremely informative and unusually accurate, those details (cited directly from passages in Heine's autobiographical pieces) only are emphasized which put the poet in the most favorable light. Although the baser nature of Heine is by no means overlooked—indeed, she admits that "Heine's magnificent powers have often served only to give electric force to the expression of debased feeling, so that his works are no Phidian statue of gold, and ivory, and

12. F. S. Haldane, *George Eliot and Her Times*, p. 107.

gems, but have no little brass, and iron, and miry clay mingled with the precious metal"—it is nonetheless clear that George Eliot's purpose is to present to the English reading public the fairest possible picture of a poet who has been deeply wronged by unjust and unfortunate criticism. For the poet's vacillating political views, his unstable religious principles, and his general laxities in moral and social matters, she offers a stubborn and courageous defense. She excuses his many faults with the arguments that he is fundamentally a poet, and, as such, to demand of him that he be a hero, a patriot, or a solemn prophet, is a gross injustice: "Nature has not made him of sterner stuff—not of iron and adamant, but of pollen of flowers, and juice of the grape, and Puck's mischievous brain, plenteously mixing also the dews of kindly affection and the gold-dust of noble thoughts."

In her review of Heine the artist, she finds that Heine bears the closest affinity to Goethe. "Both have the same masterly finished simplicity and rhythmic grace; but there is more thought mingled with Goethe's feeling—his lyrical genius is a vessel that draws more water than Heine's, and though it seems to glide along with equal ease, we have a sense of greater weight and force accompanying the grace of its movement." Special praise is given to *Deutschland* as the most charming specimen of Heine's humorous poetry, and among the prose writings the *Reisebilder* is cited as possessing the greatest poetic and humorous merit.

Her total concept of Heine is summed up in a marvelous bit of writing:

But whatever else he may be, Heine is one of the most remarkable men of this age; no echo, but a real voice, and therefore, like all genuine things in this world, worth studying; a surpassing lyric poet, who has uttered our feelings for us in delicious song; a humorist who touches leaden folly with the magic wand of his fancy, and transmutes it into the fine gold of art—who sheds his sunny smile on human tears, and makes them a beauteous rainbow on the cloudy background of life;

a wit, who holds in his mighty hand the most scorching lightnings of satire; an artist in prose literature, who has shown even more completely than Goethe the possibilities of German prose; and—in spite of all charges against him, true as well as false—a lover of freedom, who has spoken wise and brave words on behalf of his fellow men.

Written in admirable style and revealing remarkable critical acumen, *German Wit: Heinrich Heine* probably did more than any other single work in introducing to English-speaking peoples the genius that was Heine.

Matthew Arnold (1822-1888).—Undoubtedly the greatest critical utterance on Heine to come from nineteenth-century England is that from the pen of Matthew Arnold. An omnivorous reader whose wide familiarity with German literature is not to be questioned, Matthew Arnold, as is true also of George Eliot, is to a great extent responsible for the popularity of Heinrich Heine in England. Through the medium of two essays "Pagan and Medieval Religious Sentiment"[13] and "Heinrich Heine,"[14] both published in 1865, he aided immeasurably in further establishing and spreading the fame of the great German poet.

Had Matthew Arnold persevered in his first impression of Heine, the result would have no doubt proved detrimental to the popularity of the poet in Britain. For Arnold, himself a Byron enthusiast and imitator in his earlier days, resented what he considered an affected Byronism in the young German poet. Writing to his mother on May 7, 1848, he expresses a hasty and crude verdict for which he later in his essays more than compensated: "I have just finished," he writes Mrs. Arnold, "a German book I brought with me here: a mixture of poems and travelling journal by Heinrich Heine, the most famous of the young German literary set. He has a good deal of power, though more trick; however, he has thoroughly disgusted me. The Byronism of a German, of a man trying to be gloomy, cynical, impassioned, moqueur, etc. all *à la fois*, with

13. *Essays in Criticism*, pp. 192-195.   14. *Ibid.*, pp. 140-173.

their honest bonhommistic language and total want of experience of the kind that Lord Byron, an English peer with access everywhere, possessed, is the most ridiculous thing in the world."[15] Fortunately, Matthew Arnold traveled soon and acquired a taste, at least, of Heine's "total want of experience" and a broader and more understanding outlook, which qualified him better to speak of the merits of such a man as Heine. Indeed, in a letter to Clough dated March 9, 1861, he recommends the works of Heine as being far more profitable studies than those of Tennyson; and more than one entry concerning Heine is found in the *Notebooks*.

"There is time neither for mourning nor for triumph. The trumpets sound again. The battle breaks out afresh. I am the Sword. I am the Flame." So wrote Heinrich Heine in 1830 while sojourning on the north coast of Germany and picturing himself surrounded by the corpses of his friends. This is the picture of Heine that Matthew Arnold presents in his admirable study, "Heinrich Heine." As the most important German successor of Goethe, as the author upon whom "incomparably the largest portion of Goethe's mantle fell," Matthew Arnold presents Heine to us as the greatest continuator of Goethe in that poet's most important line of activity —his work as "a brilliant, a most effective soldier in the war of liberation of humanity. . . . With that terrible modern weapon, the pen, in his hand, he passed the remainder of his life in one fierce battle. . . . It was a life and death battle with Philistinism."

It is here that Matthew Arnold introduces into English the term "Philistine," which he defines as "A strong, dogged, unenlightened opponent of the chosen people." It is here, too, that Arnold, with malicious pleasure, launches into a lengthy but interesting discussion of Heine's detestation for England as the land of the Philistines, and avails himself of more than

---

15. Hugh Kingsmill, *Life of Matthew Arnold*, p. 85.

a few instances to add malicious comments of his own. Arnold is mistaken, however, when he identifies the Teuton Philistinism attacked by Heine with the Goliath of his own abomination, as one critic has pointed out.

Now and then Arnold recovers from what Kingsmill is pleased to call his "dawnest trance" and pronounces upon Heine the poet. Delighted by the ease, power, and pathos of Heine's poetry, he quite accurately recognizes the fact that it is the wit and spirit of France combined with the culture, sentiment, and thought of Germany that gives the remarkable charm to Heine's poetical works. To Arnold, Heine is a combination of two elements—the Greek in the completeness of his form and in his love for clarity and beauty, and the Jew in his industry and his longing. The English critic is mistaken in thinking that Heine aped the classicism of Goethe, and carries his notion of the Greek in Heine to too great an extreme. There is but very little of the genuinely classical in Heine.

It is Heine's pathos that strikes the most responsive chord in Arnold—"Heine's sweetest note, his plaintive note, his notes of melancholy"—and Arnold in excellent bits of criticism calls attention to several of the author's works illustrating this trait. Of interest is the fact that in speaking of the *Romanzero*, Arnold calls it "A collection of poems written in the first years of his illness with his whole power and charm still in them." Heine himself, though, considered it an inferior work and expressed an opposite view of the volume in a letter to his mother dated December, 1851: "I assure you it is a very weak book—but nobody must say so. I wrote it with my powers broken."[16]

But even in his discussion of Heine's poetry, Arnold is engrossed with the idea of showing the poet's relation to the main currents of political and social ideas and ignores with comparative indifference the true soul of Heine, the source of both his poetry and his cynicism. As if conscious of his failure to

16. Embden, *Family Life*, Preface, p. xi.

support in the essay his concept of Heine as "a soldier in the liberation war of humanity," Arnold returns to the notion at the conclusion of his criticism:

> He died, and has left a blemished name; with his crying faults,—his intemperate susceptibility, his unscrupulousness in passion, his inconceivable attacks on his enemies, his still more inconceivable attacks on his friends, his want of generosity, his sensuality, his incessant mocking,—how could it be otherwise? Not only was he not one of Mr. Carlyle's "respectable" people, he was profoundly *dis*respectable; and not even the merit of not being a Philistine can make up for a man's not being that. To his intellectual deliverance there was an addition of something else wanting, and that something else was something immense; the old-fashioned, laborious, eternally needful moral deliverance. Goethe says that he was deficient in *love;* to me his weakness seems to be not so much a deficiency in love as a deficiency in self-respect, in true dignity of character. But on this negative side ... I for my part ... have no pleasure in dwelling. I prefer to say of Heine something positive. He is not an adequate interpreter of the modern world. He is only a brilliant soldier in the war of liberation of humanity.

Thus, in typically Arnoldian fashion, Arnold pronounces Heine's weakness to have been—not as Goethe said, deficiency in love (actually Goethe's statement was made not in reference to Heine at all but in speaking of Platen)—but want of moral balance and nobility of soul and character.

Richard Monckton Milnes (1809-1885).—Richard Monckton Milnes, Lord Houghton, in publishing in 1873 his essay, "The Last Days of Heinrich Heine,"[17] made one of his most enduring contributions in the field of literary endeavor. The essay, written during the year of the death of Heine, purports to be a character picture of the German Lazarus as he lay on his pitiful mattress-grave. In reality, Lord Houghton (who is discussed elsewhere in this study)[18] attempts, through the citing of anecdotes and facts from the entire life of Heine—concerning his Bonapartism, his hatred for England, his views on politics and religion, etc., to paint Heine's portrait against

---

17. *Monographs—Personal and Social.*
18. See sections on Translation and Informal Opinion.

the back-drop of European and world affairs. As in the case of Edward Dowden, Milnes feels that Heine's many-sided nature was both the glory and misfortune of the poet although Milnes is inclined to tend toward the idea that the contradictory nature of the poet is rather the result of unhappy circumstance than inherent make-up:

> Above all literary characters of our time, Heine had throughout the calamity of false position. With so acute a sense of classical forms and antique grace as to make him often well content to live "A Pagan in a creed outworn," he was regarded as a chief of the Romantic school; with a genial and pleasure-loving temperament, he was mortified by physical infirmity and moral disappointment into a harsh and sometimes cruel satirist; with a deep religious sentiment, and even narrow theological system, he was thrust into the chair of an apostle of scepticism; with no clear political convictions or care for theories of government, he had to bear all the pains and penalties of political exile, the exclusion from the commerce of the society he best enjoyed, and the inclusion among men from whom he shrank with an instinctive dislike.

Highly similar to Dowden's "A Centenary Retrospect" in pointing out and seeking to establish Heine in his relation to the religious, political, and social problems of the day, and like that essay in ignoring completely the question of Heine the poet, the essay of Milnes, though not nearly so brilliantly conceived and executed, attempts a composite picture of Heine the man. The actual "last days" are touched upon only in Lucie Duff Gordon's account, which Milnes quotes in full.

An interesting variant in the Milnes critical essay becomes apparent when the two versions of the study are examined. In the 1873 reprint in the *Monographs*, Milnes says in reference to Heine and his work: "These poems, this temperament of mind, even this noble endurance, must not be judged by a Christian standard. He remained essentially a Hebrew." In the original, appearing in the *Edinburgh Review* for 1856, we read: "It is a painful admission, that we must not, and indeed cannot, judge these poems by a Christian standard. He remained essentially a Jew."

Charles Grant (1841-1889).—In 1859, partly on the advice of the Reverend F. D. Maurice, Charles Grant went to Jena in Germany where he attended the university and managed to provide for his support through lecturing and teaching. It was at this time that he laid the foundations of a profound and intimate knowledge of German literature, which increased with his travels throughout the nation.

In September of the year 1880, Charles Grant contributed to the *Contemporary Review*[19] one of his most scholarly articles, entitled "Heinrich Heine." It is in this article that the English critic's wide and deep knowledge of German literature becomes most apparent. The piece is in the nature of a comparative study in which the author places Heine in his relationship to world literature and treats his similarities and differences to world figures in the field of letters.

Hailing Heine as the true successor of Goethe (although differences are pointed out between the two great poets), the German lyricist is compared with and contrasted to such eminent literary figures as Charles Lamb—in whom is found the same racy individual flavor and the same oddities of expression—Swift, Dryden, Pope, and Shelley. The comparison of Heine to Shelley is the finest of the lot and is elaborated upon at length to show the similarity of political ideals in the passionate love of freedom evinced in the two poets.

The chief claim of Heine (who is said by Grant to be after Goethe the only German man of letters to exercise a wide and direct influence on the literature of Europe) to immortality lies, according to the critic, in the fact that "in his work the whole spiritual life of his age is reflected and expressed"—the life of an age marked by problems of all sorts. "In a word, Heine was the poet of an age of doubt, of intellectual ferment, of rapid spiritual transitions, which at one moment clung lovingly and timorously to the breast of the past, and at the next cried passionately with outstretched hands for the baubles that

---

19. XXXVIII, 372-395.

gleamed through the half-closed fingers of the future—an age of infinite hope and infinite despair, when Germany—sated with her intellectual triumphs, yearned blindly, and as yet vainly, for the life of action which had hitherto been denied her."

In a most scholarly and able fashion, Charles Grant's "Heinrich Heine" correctly places the man Heine in his relationship to world events and world literature. Very little, except the praise of the later works of the poet, such as the *Romanzero, Atta Troll, Deutschland,* and the letters to the *Augsburg Gazette,* as exhibiting the finest and truest characteristics of the writer, is said concerning the literary work of the German author. All in all, though, the article by Grant is a marvelous bit of criticism and is hailed by no less an authority than John Snodgrass as "an admirable contribution towards an enlightened estimate of Heine's work."[20]

Coulson Kernahan (b. 1858).—In an article called "Some Aspects of Heine" appearing in the *Gentleman's Magazine*[21] during the year 1886, Coulson Kernahan, the brilliant and witty Victorian critic, has attempted, with much success, a character delineation of Heinrich Heine. Stressing the paradoxical nature of Heine,—"Creature of moods and moments. . . . He is by turns a Greek and a Jew, a German and a Frenchman, a moralist and a libertine, a poet and a politician, a sentimentalist and a satirist. He is tossed hither and thither by his passing moods, as withered leaves are tossed by autumn winds. In his gayest mirth we catch the glitter of tear-drops, in his loudest laughter we hear a wail of despair. . . ."—Kernahan presents one of the most sympathetic understanding character analyses ever made of the German poet.

Writing with the perspicacity of a true scholar and the grace and ease of the genuine artist, the English critic proclaims Heine's poems the most exquisitely beautiful and musical

20. *Heine's Religion and Philosophy in Germany,* pp. ix-x.
21. CCLXI, 233-253.

expressions of emotional feeling in the language—"full of the fragrance of June roses, his songs melodious with the moonlight thrillings of the nightingale."

The lines seem to drip blood as we read them, and a strange awe holds us spell-bound—when, suddenly, there flashes across the page, like a gleam of purple lightning, one of those deadly coruscations of wit with which Heine struck and stabbed at many a reputation. Hardly has the deep thunder-roll of savage laughter died away, before there rises again the wail and cry as of the death-agony of a lost soul; and then there is a sudden change in the music, and the lines skip and leap, ripple and run as if to the accompaniment of dancing feet. Now he holds us in awe solemn and silent as when we stand at twilight in the cool recesses of some dim-aisled minster, and listen to the dying cadences of the organ song; now there rises in the silence which he himself has created a wild burst of mocking and ribald laughter.

In one of the finest comparisons of the relative merits of Goethe and Heine in the English language, Kernahan maintains:

Goethe and Heine had little in common except that they were both poets. Over Goethe's grave rests the serene afterglow as of the setting of a placid, clear-shining planet; the spot where Heine lies is marked only by the wild meteoric trailing of some fallen star. . . . Goethe is self-poised, self-centered and self-contained. . . . Heine is a prodigal and a spendthrift. He lives upon his principal. . . . Goethe's voice is the voice of an infinitely wise man, his poems are beautiful as diamonds cut and polished in myriad facets, and set in chastest gold; but Heine is the living voice of Nature herself, and his songs touch and thrill us like the carol of the lark, or the perfume of the first rose.

Kernahan, another Alexander Pope uttering "Whate'er was done but ne'er so well expressed," cannot lay claim to a great deal of originality in "Some Aspects of Heine," but does deserve unrestrained praise for having written the old, familiar ideas in such a vital and artistic manner. The biographical material used in the article is obviously drawn from Stigand's longer account; and in the critical matter, Kernahan relies to large extent upon his predecessors in the field—notably upon the views of Nina H. Kennard and Matthew Arnold.

With Kennard, he feels that the odd, evil twist in Heine's nature is directly traceable to the poet's long endured disease; with Arnold, he proclaims the chief deficiency of Heine to be a lack of moral balance:

To the thoughtful minds there is something inexpressibly mournful in his story. It is the story of what should have been a great and noble soul, a soul in which there existed grand intellectual and spiritual possibilities—all alas! irretrievably dwarfed and perverted by the lack of moral principle; that all-important element without which none can be truly and really great.

Declaring instability and lack of earnestness the dominant traits of Heine's character, Kernahan finds:

The great secret of the failure and misery of Heine's life, however, is that he was a *moral coward;* a man who wilfully and despicably chose the ignoble part because he had not the manliness to suffer for the right; a man who habitually shrank from the task which duty imposed when it clashed with his own personal inclinations; a man who persistently listened to the promptings of his own evil passions, rather than to the voice of his truer and loftier nature. "Alas! mental torture is easier to be endured," he says, "than physical pain; and were I offered the alternative between a bad conscience and an aching tooth, I should prefer the former."

To anyone who wishes a brief yet thorough, graceful yet fundamentally sound analysis and appreciation of the character that was Heine, the article by Kernahan is heartily recommended.

Edward Dowden (1843-1913).—The first mention of Heinrich Heine by the well-known English critic, Edward Dowden, is found in a letter written by the latter and dated October 9, 1872:

Heine at one time had a great or at least a very decided and peculiar charm for me. After an interval, I returned to him, and never was more disenchanted. The aroma and piquancy had evaporated and what remained was unsatisfactory enough. Perhaps it is because I don't know German rightly, but I certainly was alienated from much of its lyrical poetry by the facile run of the verse, and I must confess to the heresy of finding a great deal of delicate and rich music in French verse. But I am sure our own English is incomparably greater than either.[22]

Three years later, Dowden's distaste for Heine's poetry had increased to the point that he considered the poetical works far inferior to the German's prose. Writing on August 27, 1875, he states in connection with the prose of Heine:

> ... A good share of it is well worth reading, far better, I think, than his verse. He is a heathen and anxious to restore the religion of pleasure in place of the religion of sorrow, but with this the deep and tender fibres of Judaism and Jehovah-worship mingle curiously. Of his poetry some, of course, is really of the truest and most abiding preciousness, but of much that is generally admired I find the bouquet pass off marvelously quickly, and sometimes an unwholesome sour wine is left behind.[23]

On the same day he expresses the purpose of translating a bit from Heine's study of Portia and Shylock, which, it would seem, had revolutionized Dowden's original concept of *The Merchant of Venice*.[24] Further interest in Heine was awakened in Dowden by his chance discovery of Stigand's *Life of Heinrich Heine* during December of 1875,[25] and in the following month in a letter to Miss West (January 6, 1876) he states that he was at the time busily engaged in the reading of the new biography.[26]

Despite Dowden's disillusionment in re-reading the poems of Heine, his antipathy did not go to the extreme that he could not pronounce one of the most lucid judgments in English upon the poet. In "A Centenary Retrospect," Dowden has given perhaps the most enlightened general appreciation ever written by an English critic. "My name is Legion for we are many." With this as a text, Dowden proceeds to elaborate upon the multifariousness of the character that was

22. *Fragments from Old Letters*, I, 35.
23. *Ibid.*, I, 139.
24. *Ibid.*, I, 138-139.
25. *Ibid.*, Letter to Miss West, II, 102.
26. *Ibid.*, II, 103.

Major Critics

Heine—tracing his development from the deepest things within him (the inheritance of race and the unquenchable thirst for life, and the insatiable appetite for pleasure inherited from his father), through Heine's militant Hellenism, his half-understood Hegelian philosophy, and his various religious and political concepts, to the ultimate return of the poor sick Jew to the beliefs and traits of his ancestors.

Heine, to Dowden, is a diamond the many facets of which but reflect a multitude of contradictions; and this diversity of personality is to him Heine's chief trait:

> To be born with diverse souls is embarrassing, but it was Heine's distinction. It signifies that life is to be no steadfast progress, directed by some guiding light, but a wavering advance through a countless series of attractions passing into repulsions, and of repulsions transformed into attractions. To belong to the past and to the future, to be romanticist and realist, to mingle Mephistopheles with Faust, to be an aristocrat and a revolutionary, to be of a tribe and of a nation, to be a patriot and cosmopolitan, to be a monotheist through the emotions, a polytheist through the imagination, a pantheist through the intellect, to see Jerusalem through the atmosphere of Hamburg, to sit at the feet of Moses and of Aristophanes, to reckon Brother Martin Luther and the Patriarch Voltaire among one's ancestry—all this makes fidelity to one's true self a difficult and intricate affair.[27]

In no other critical work is there a finer general appreciation of Heine in his relationship to religious, political, and social matters than in Dowden's "A Centenary Retrospect." Written in an extremely interesting, vital, and facile style, the essay cannot be overpraised. Unfortunately, no attempt is made to pronounce upon the merits or faults of Heine as poet, but it is nonetheless gratifying to read the pronouncements of Dowden upon Heine the man.

27. *Essays, Modern and Elizabethan*, p. 61.

IV. *Minor Critics*

Edinburgh Review, 1832.—There appeared in the *Edinburgh Review* for October, 1832, an anonymous criticism of Heine's *Reisebilder*.[1] Aside from the fact that the article contains some pointed criticism on Heine, its prime significance lies in the fact that it was published almost a quarter of a century before George Eliot wrote the criticism of Heine which has usually been credited as being the first to be put before the English public. The anonymous critic showed no hesitancy in voicing his candid opinion of the German poet and criticized him rather severely in some instances. Heine's political sympathies evidently disgusted the writer, as well as the political principles in Germany that inspired them. The writer suggested in this connection that Heine's association with Börne and "other literary bravoes of Germany" was responsible for the degeneration of his literary merit:

The facts of the association seem to have been anything but favourable either to his morality or his intellect. One by one his imagination, his humour, possessed in a high degree, seem to be taking leave of him; till at last, in his latest work [*Nachträge zu den Reisebildern*, "Supplement to the Travelling Sketches"] his originality of speculation has degenerated into mere paradox or audacious impiety, his strength and freshness of style into a prolonged whine, his humour into a convulsive and almost demoniacal grimace. . . .

The author, however, conceded that prior to his "political pollution," Heine showed extraordinary literary potentialities. But even here, the writer condemned Heine for occasional lapses of good taste and general lack of finish; he says that

[1]. "Recent German Lyrical Poetry," LVI, 37-51.

"even in his best works there is a want of finish, and often of taste, but these are generally redeemed by a quick sensibility, a rapid and powerful style of sketching, and that air of nature and truth in the whole, which reconcile us to so many defects of detail."

Without qualification of any sort, the critic heartily admired Heine's ability to depict feeling and emotion, as well as his success in creating pictures of the simpler life: "the life of the cottage, the forest, and the mountain. . . . Give him some little section of the panorama of life to depict, some passing emotion, the memory of some almost forgotten feeling to call up, and it is wonderful with what brevity, and what truth, he places it before us." By this early critic, Heine is credited with a light steady hand, a simple style, and an "artless movement of versification."

This anonymous critic who, as we have noted, came many years before George Eliot, showed a remarkable perception of Heine's works and the influences that played upon them. The obvious disapproval of Heine's political views, and the appreciation of Heine's ability when untouched by them, show that the writer was at pains in appraising Heine as accurately as he could.

Fraser's Magazine, 1842.—Although in 1842 Heine was not well known in England, he was evidently deemed noteworthy enough to warrant a character sketch in *Fraser's Magazine* for December of that year.[2] Whether or not the anonymous writer intended that the article serve as an introduction of Heine to English readers or merely to show his appreciation of the man, is not known, but he does offer a thorough analysis of Heine the man. The author met Heine in Paris and evidently developed a degree of intimacy with him, for he wrote a great deal about his personal mannerisms and idiosyncrasies as well as about the more general aspects of the man. He characterized Heine as more French than German in tempera-

2. "Reminiscences of Men and Things," XXVI, 733, 736.

ment, and compared him with Talleyrand to whom he was similar in character. The critic's personal enthusiasm for Heine made his article perhaps somewhat biased, but the picture created is clear. That Heine was at the time not so well known in England is evidenced by the concluding sentences: "Reader have you ever heard of him before? Perhaps not. Then more's the pity."

Tait's Edinburgh Magazine, 1851.—According to an anonymous critic writing in *Tait's Edinburgh Magazine* in 1851,[3] Henry Heine was one of the last of a group of writers who tried to cure Germany of her ills. In an article essentially biographical, the critic emphasized the fact that Heine was a poet as well as a political philosopher, and that his worth as a poet was more enduring. In this instance the author was somewhat hampered by the fact that he was writing of a man who was then living and consequently could not achieve a proper perspective of his contributions. For, whereas the writer felt that the German revolution of 1848 had lessened the value of Heine's political writings, the fact is that through the skillful manipulations of Heine's publisher, Julius Campe, the revolution proved a boon to Heine's works. Of Heine's poetry the author was more sanguine, for he compared it to the ancient national poetry of Germany and declared some of the poetry "chips from the old block of the German *Volkslied*." As in the case of the author of the anonymous article in the *Edinburgh Review*,[4] the writer felt that Heine's best medium was that of the people, the humble folk.

The writer said a great deal about Heine's life, emphasizing the early influences, many of which, he felt, accounted for the sorrow and melancholy of his later years. In discussing the facts of the poet's early life, the author did, however, miss the implication of Heine's renunciation of his Jewish faith. Heine assumed the Christian faith in order to pursue

3. "Heine, His Works and Times," XVIII, N.S., 618-622 and 679-683.
4. 1832.

the law course at Göttingen, and not, as the writer intimated, because he was ashamed of his descent. Beyond the material indicated, the article contained merely factual matter in regard to Heine's life.

Sharpe's London Magazine, 1852.—It is indeed unfortunate that the article on Heinrich Heine published in *Sharpe's London Magazine* in 1852[5] was unsigned. Had the author but signed his name, he would have been ranked with the better-known critics of Heine, for he showed a thorough knowledge and understanding of Heine's life and works, as is evidenced by the many quotations and references he employs. In defiance of other critics, this one ousted the terms sensuality and spirituality as related to Heine and insisted that humor, on the contrary, characterized his writings. Heine's gift for satire, which was described as a perverted form of love, taking root in Heine's childhood, and his capacity for deep sorrow and melancholy were also touched upon. The *Intermezzo* was cited as typical of the latter—reflecting an incomparable sadness and melancholy. That Heine was to publish *Letzte Gedichte und Nachlese* could not have been foreseen by this critic who thought that Heine's work was done at the time the article was written. However, he would, no doubt, have appraised the last volume with the same precision that distinguished his criticism of the others.

Edinburgh Review, 1856.—The same year that George Eliot published her criticism of Heine, a criticism of two translations of Heine's works appeared in the *Edinburgh Review*.[6] The translators were Julian Fane and John E. Wallis, who respectively offered a miscellaneous collection of poems by Heine and the *Book of Songs* to the British public. The reviewer offered a decidedly sketchy account of Heine's views on religious and political affairs after having indicated at the outset that Heine's death demanded an adjustment of the mis-

---

5. "The Life and Writings of Heinrich Heine," XVI, 291-298 and 362-369.
6. "Heinrich Heine," CIV, 192-209.

understandings and misinterpretations of the German writer. Of the individual works, note was made of *Deutschland*, characterized as an example of the coarsest satire; and brief reference to some few other works appeared in the review. Julian Fane's facility in translating some of the most difficult of the poet's works was ascribed to his exactness and scholarliness while Wallis's translations were deemed less accurate but more pleasing in the general effect. The critic made a significant comparison of Heine to Keats, declaring that both "attest the power of the appeal which Grecian glories made once and forever to the sensuous imaginations of mankind and which all the influences of our position and demure civilization protest against in vain."

Colburn's New Monthly Magazine, 1859.—An article designated as "The Last Days of a Poet" appeared in *Colburn's New Monthly Magazine* in 1859.[7] The poet was Heine, and the account gave a rapid summary of Heine's life with emphasis on the last days during which Heine suffered so intensely. The material is purely factual, offering no criticism of the man or his works.

Dublin University Magazine, 1859.—Although some of the earlier critics of Heinrich Heine were hampered because they lacked a sufficient perspective of the poet, the author of the article on Heine's works which appeared in the *Dublin University Magazine* for November, 1859,[8] seemed to have no difficulty in estimating the poet's writings. In an authoritative manner, Heine's likeness to Aristophanes, Rabelais, Cervantes, Burns, Sterne, Jean Paul Richter, Swift, Voltaire, Byron, and Béranger was suggested, with a more prolonged comparison made of Heine to Rabelais and Burns. The essential difference between Voltaire and Heine was described as earnestness in atheism on Voltaire's part, earnestness in nothing on Heine's. A warped mind, developed from childhood, was held account-

7. CXVII, 363-370.   8. LIV, 590-598.

able for the perverted aspects of his nature—his cynicism, skepticism, and mockery.

The *Book of Songs* was highly praised for its imagination and its warm passion which would appeal to youth. Love and frustration are embodied in many of the poems, and these elements, too, appeal to the reader. Of *Atta Troll* the critic said that here more conflicting elements were embodied than one would be likely to find in any other one poem. Humor, imagination, pictorial power, wit, knowledge of the world, a terrible sarcasm, a sense of physical beauty—all played their part in the poem. Evidently well acquainted with all of Heine's works, the critic referred to Heine's two dramas, *Almansor* and *Ratcliff*, as failures, and to Heine's *History of Modern German Literature* as the most important of the German's prose works.

According to the author of this article, Heine was not well known in England in 1859 because no complete translation of his works had been available prior to that year. At the time the article was written, however, E. A. Bowring had just completed a translation of all the poems. Possibly Bowring's publication prompted the writing of the criticism.

Edgar A. Bowring (1826-1911).—Edgar A. Bowring prefaces his translation of *Poems of Heine* (1861) with a biographical sketch which offers but few departures from those considered previously. In character it strongly resembles those composed by Kate Kroeker, Thomas Evans, and other translators for use in their volumes. In his biographical sketch of Heine, he says that the *Book of Songs* most truly "exhibits the whole nature of Heine free from all disguise." A brief elaboration of the idea follows and represents the only effort on Bowring's part to penetrate the character of Heine. The facts of the poet's life and a list of his works are faithfully recounted.

Cornhill Magazine, 1863.—In an article rather colloquially entitled "Sharpshooters of the Press in England, France and

Germany" published by the *Cornhill Magazine* in 1863,⁹ we find another biographical account of Heinrich Heine. Preeminently the aim of the article was to give a faithful account of the activities and events which comprised the life of the poet. There are, however, some references to the man's character and many to his spiritual point of view. In reference to the latter it was pointed out that Heine was, from youth, a Napoleonist, developing logically into a revolutionist, and ultimately becoming a devotee of Saint-Simonism. Heine's leaning toward atheism and Catholicism are likewise touched upon.

Robert Buchanan (1841-1901).—Robert Buchanan, one of the best-known figures in Victorian criticism, has devoted considerable attention to Heinrich Heine in four of his principal works, *David Gray and Other Essays, Chiefly on Poetry* (1868); *A Look Round Literature* (1887); *Master Spirits* (1873); and *A Poet's Sketch Book* (1883). The volume *Master Spirits* contains two short notices of Heine, the first being a brief and ineffectual consideration of the manner in which women are treated in the poetry of Tennyson, Alfred de Musset, and Heine.¹⁰ The second notice, equally brief and nearly as ineffectual, is a literary tid-bit of purely biographical nature, describing the sufferings of Heine in the throes of his final agony.¹¹ One or two critical comments are brought in, in purely incidental fashion, chief among which are the trite remark that, after Goethe, Heine is undoubtedly Germany's greatest bard, and the odd, exaggerated praise of the dull fragment, *Ratcliff*, as the most dreadfully realistic poem of modern times. The short notice in *David Gray* is merely concerned with recounting the familiar Heine-Hegel anecdote about the stars—"the brilliant leprosy in heaven's face."¹²

The only significant critical utterance of Buchanan on the

9. VII, 246-251.
10. "Tennyson, Heine, and DeMusset," *Master Spirits*, pp. 54-87.
11. Ibid. *A Poet's Sketch Book* contains this same notice.
12. Pp. 271-272.

Minor Critics

poet Heine is to be found in the little article "Heine in a Court Suit."[13] Heine, hailed as the "Gnome of impudence and infidelity capable of the most maudlin Wertherism" and "equally matter of fact in singing of Herodias with John the Baptist's head under her arm and of Hortense dying in a Parisian hospital," is to Robert Buchanan a truly fascinating subject—fascinating primarily because of the German lyricist's unfathomable contrariety of mood. The article, however, is in reality one of Buchanan's typical mendacious diatribes; and, in this instance, it is Sir Theodore Martin, the famous translator of the German poet, who is subjected to Buchanan's lash of scorn. In almost as bitter an attack as that upon poor Dante Gabriel Rossetti in the brilliant if erring *Fleshly School of Poetry*, Buchanan flays Sir Theodore Martin for his presumption and inability to clothe the lyrics of Heine in English dress.

In typically Buchanan fashion, the English critic caustically concludes the article with the statement (which in reality is the core of the entire attack):

That cadence and that theme are not for Mr. Theodore Martin. They belong to the wild heart and the wild mood; their region is the lonely greenwood and the dreary sea; and they are not to be "adapted" to the Court or the drawing room. He who translates Heine must possess something of Heine's nature—free, wild, wicked even, and overbold. Heine himself carried his wickedness to the extent of hating England and Englishmen with all his heart. His cup of hate would have been full, if he had lived to read Mr. Martin's translation.

Despite the bitter prejudices of criticism for which Buchanan is notorious, the review of Martin's translations is more than a little just.[14]

J. D. Lester.—A purely biographical account of Heine, based on the work of Strodtmann, was written for the *Fortnightly Review* by J. D. Lester.[15] In only one respect does Lester veer away from the stereotyped account of Heine: he

---
13. In *A Look Round Literature*, pp. 210-217.
14. See Sir Theodore Martin in section on Translation.
15. XII (1869), 287-303.

says that the *Romanzero* represents the most sustained power that Heine achieved. Usually, the *Book of Songs* in general, or the *Intermezzo* in particular, is given most applause. As ever, Heine's nature of many contrasts is emphasized. A quotation from the *Revue des deux Mondes* for July, 1848, is included which summarizes these contrasts: "Ce n'est pas un vain cliquetis d'antithèses de dire littérairement d'Henri Heine qu'il est cruel et tendre, naïf et perfide, sceptique et crédule, lyrique et prosaïque, sentimental et railleur, passionné et glacial, spirituel et pittoresque, antique et moderne, moyen-âge et révolutionnaire."

Robert, Earl of Lytton [Owen Meredith] *(1831-1891)*.— A criticism of Heine's "Last Poems and Thoughts," which appeared anonymously in *The Fortnightly Review* in 1870,[16] offered an excellent commentary on the aim of poetry as exemplified by the works of Heine. Quite obviously, the critic, who has been identified as Robert, Earl of Lytton, was a Heine enthusiast; yet he was by no means impervious to what he called the obscenity, the grossness, of the German poet. Nor was he unaware of the beauty, the delicacy, and grace that Heine could reflect in his poetry, for he repeatedly referred to these *Last Poems* as pearls worthy of a rosary, as glittering gems to be preserved. Yet he called Heine a poet of the "profane vulgar" and justified the vulgarities with a philosophy that maintained that the poet should not only represent humanity, but should represent to mankind the realities of his nature, even those realities which mankind must "blush to recognize." And although Heine's lack of taste proved most offensive in many instances, the reader is reminded that obscenity, for Heine, was merely an aspect of his constant sense of mockery. *Bimini* was used here to show how Heine embodied tenderness, mockery, bitterness, satire, beauty, and wit in one poem. Of other individual works nothing was said.

E. B. Shuldham.—That creative literature is closely allied

---

16. "Heinrich Heine's Last Poems and Thoughts," XIII, 257-277.

to creative art is strongly emphasized by E. B. Shuldham, noted translator and critic, in the article "Heine as an Impressionist," published in the *Temple Bar* magazine.[17] Taking as the main theme "impressionism in art," Shuldham elaborates on the principles and aims of the impressionist and relates them to Heine's writings. The introduction to the article reveals the chief premise:

In literature as in pictorial art a new tendency has of late years been at work. In art it has been called impressionism. I see no reason why the same term may not be equally suitable in literature.

This impressionism in art may be, after all, nay it is, only a new way of looking at nature, and of interpreting the mental impression to which this observation gives rise.

We are speedily assured that impressionism does not mean sketchiness, or a lavish use of garish colors as opposed to a restrained handling of solid and more somber colors, but that "impressionism demands as much serious thought for its execution as do the literary impressions of the best modern work." In literature, impressionism is like any other style, insists Shuldham; it assumes its character through the writer—*Le style c'est l'homme*, he reminds us. And thus, the literary artist, in order to use impressionism well, must be educated to it. "Impressionistic work in literature depends for its excellence on the keenness of the writer's observation and on his literary technique in recording his observations. The writer's individuality plays the great part." From this statement on, Shuldham confines himself to Heine and his peculiar genius, which he identified as impressionism. Emphasizing Heine's individuality of style, his freshness of phrase, his knack for words, Shuldham well illustrates his point.

In extending the comparison of Heine to a painter, the writer expresses the view that the poet did not have a landscape touch. In painting his pictures, Heine showed a strong tendency to suggest, rather than to elaborate. Like the painter

17. CXXI (1900), 420-430.

Corot, and unlike the poet Keats, Heine shied away from detail or the specific. He might mention a tree, Shuldham tells us, but quite probably he would fail to indicate the kind of a tree: "Heine loved his flowers and his moonlight skies, his forests dark and mysterious in a broad, general literary sort of way: he sang of the rose, but not of one special kind, such as the tea rose with its cool perfume; he sang of the woodlands but of no special tree."

Had Heine confined himself to nature, his significance might have been lessened; but as Shuldham points out, he had "books, pictures, music, theatres, restaurants . . . heroes to worship, rivals to satirize, Prussia to belittle, professors to picture forth. . . ." And all this was more than enough material for Heine's impressionism. Yet, though his nature poems were lacking in the detail and depth that were prevalent in the poems of, say Wordsworth or Keats, they represented great beauty and delicacy of thought.

Shuldham's viewpoint is original and unusual. The early part of the article, in which the introduction and vigorous development of the premise are found, is excellent in its treatment. Toward the middle, however, the author's logic is somewhat disturbed in sequence when he makes references to Keats and Wordsworth. Digressions from this point on are frequent, and although the general idea is sustained, the earlier unity of ideas is considerably weakened.

Shuldham, in 1900 (at the time of the appearance of this article), had long been a critic and commentator of Heine. In 1870, he contributed an account of Heine's life and works to the *Temple Bar* magazine which merits note here. Though based to a large extent on Strodtmann's biography, the article reveals that Shuldham was well informed on the life of the poet. The references to Heine's works are mostly to the prose, but the poems and the several references to the poetry included show a discriminating sense. The article first considered, when taken in conjunction with this earlier article, makes us realize that Shuldham was not only a scholarly critic but an imaginative writer as well.

Joseph Gostwick (1814-1887).—Few writers denied themselves the privilege of offering reasons for the bitter and cynical nature that was Heine's. Heine was always puzzled by the "riddle of the world"; critics of Heine are ever puzzled by the "riddle of Heine." Joseph Gostwick, in his *German Poets* (1874),[18] writes that there are two solutions to the problem of Heine's "polemic, satirical and negative writings." One is the fact that Heine had an inborn "love of negation." The second, rather vaguely stated, is that Heine's bitter irony "was an indirect confession of belief." The author elaborates on these two solutions, but fails to clarify them to any great degree. He seems to lean toward the negation of Heine rather than to the other theory, for he identifies all the disciples of "Young Germany" as assertors of the negative. The account is, in general, more biographical than otherwise and not particularly able.

Kate Hillard (1839-1915).—Even were the name of the writer not signed to the article on Heinrich Heine which appeared in the *Victoria Magazine*,[19] one might easily surmise that the author was a woman. For Kate Hillard, in characteristically feminine manner, reveals Heine in a romanticized, rosy light. Ascribing his distorted and perverted outlook not to the man's own lower nature, nor to the spirit of the age, but to some influence that touched him at birth, Kate Hillard likens Heine's bitterness and cynicism to a blight on a blossom. And carrying her parallel further, she writes that just as an insect preys on a bud, eventually destroying the exquisite blossom, so a mental illness, born with Heine, ultimately ate away his body and his soul.

In an attempt to substantiate her premise, Kate Hillard traces through Heine's letters references to severe headaches

---

18. Pp. 245-265.
19. "Heinrich Heine," XXII (1874), 501-515.

and to his unusually embittered reaction toward an unrequited love. Early physical discomfort and emotional turmoil are evidently the bases of Kate Hillard's assumption that Heine suffered a mental disorder. Rather naïvely ignoring the fact that everyone suffers disillusionment, the writer partially accounts for Heine's viewpoint by ascribing it to his recoil from the world: "The first contact of a poetic nature with the world must inevitably produce a recoil: it is only the older and experienced mind that learns to see the real poetry, the tremendous tragedies that lie beneath the commonplace surface of everyday life."

Kate Hillard speaks mostly of the beauty of Heine, comparing him with Byron (who is less sweet than Heine, she feels), to Tennyson (whose musical qualities Heine possessed), and to Goethe. Heine's works reveal a "divine incompleteness" to the writer whereas even the shortest poem of Goethe "contains a fully rounded thought, complete and perfect from all sides. It is finished, and there is nothing for the most daring or restless fancy to add or alter...."

To this writer, Heine's greatest fault was his tendency to attack his contemporaries: "The worst trait in Heine's character was his savage way of tearing people to pieces. Nothing in the way of personal abuse was too coarse or too severe when the fit was upon him." However, this was but one aspect of a character of which the subtleties and variations were many. Kate Hillard well defines it thus:

Imagine a nature with all the Hebraic inheritance of pride, intensity and stubborn devotion of the idea, power and sadness as of the sea; endow it with Hellenic susceptibility to beauty and to love, with ardent passions and tender susceptibilities; add to these the German dreaminess and quiet humor, simplicity and tenderness, through which play swift gleams of truly French wit and enthusiasm; and then in this wonderfully organized brain, this instrument that should be capable of producing the strangest and sweetest of earthly harmonies, implant a fatal disease that gradually tightens its hold till life itself is stifled in its terrible grasp.

Matthew Arnold felt that the one element lacking in Heine's life was moral balance; some thought it was love he missed; Kate Hillard felt that a healthy brain was his loss. Yet all granted that his was a great genius.

Charles Beard (1827-1888).—Charles Beard, editor of the *Theological Review* from 1864 to 1879, published during his term of editorship, in January, 1876, an article, "Heinrich Heine,"[20] based on the biographies of Stigand and Strodtmann. The rather lengthy article represents the views of Beard on the character of Heine the man. A great deal of the criticism is of the stock variety although here and there are interspersed a few fairly original ideas.

Chief among these is Beard's attempt to account for what he considers a lack of popularity on Heine's part in England. "To English readers, Heinrich Heine is little more than a name, the mention of which recalls certain lyrics of a strangely delicate grace and sweetness, which amateurs in verse are always trying to translate, though usually with very scant success. He would commonly be put down among the minor poets of Germany—Körner, Uhland, Rückert, Freiligrath—with a vague feeling perhaps that in his snatches of song was an intense and peculiar individuality, and that his reader must always be prepared for stumbling on the improper." Beard accounts for the general misunderstanding of Heine's genius on the part of the English public by the inability of the English to appreciate and understand Heine's peculiar brand of humor.

The usual general account of Heine's Napoleonism, his religious views, his political attitudes, and like matters is likewise included in the article. Beard finds the dominant note of his poetry to be love, a love which is in reality a passion perishing in its own gratification, and not the deeper, if less intense, affection which attaches itself to whatever is loveable in

20. XIII, 174-201.

human character in general, believing always in good and hoping for the best.

William Stigand (1825-1915).—William Stigand wrote, in 1876, a comprehensive summary of his *Life, Work and Opinions of Heinrich Heine* to serve as an introduction to his translations from the German poet. Stigand's essay contains fundamentally the same material found in his biography of Heine, which appeared in two volumes in 1875 and is the first complete English *Life* of the poet. Since the biography is well known to all Heine enthusiasts, no attempt to discuss the resumé contained in the 1876 essay should be necessary here.

Henry G. Hewlett (d. 1897).—"A more fascinating subject for portraiture has seldom offered itself to the literary artist than the life and character of Heine," writes Henry G. Hewlett in his review[21] of Stigand's *Life of Heine*. In a conventional account of the poet's life and the singular influence in it, his works and his philosophy, Hewlett makes few original observations. He does mention *Songs of Creation* as exemplary of Heine's mockery—in this case unredeemed even by wit. Heine's cynicism, as evidenced in these poems, as in others, is ascribed by the critic to the persecutions the German writer suffered. Unlike many writers, Hewlett credits Mathilde Heine with rescuing her husband from vicious habits and being responsible for the happiest period in Heine's life.

Calling attention to the grave social disadvantages of the English Byron and the German Heine, Hewlett proceeds to an admirable comparison of the two men. Both were handicapped severely—the one by race, the other by physical defect. Both were bitter, both rejected love, and both were endowed with a vigorous, albeit coarse, humor of which Heine's was the more grotesque. The remainder of Hewlett's article is sound though rather stereotyped in treatment.

L. A. Montefiore (1853-1879).—In an excellently written

---

21. "Heinrich Heine's Life and Works," *Fraser's Magazine*, XCIV (1876), 600-623.

article on Heinrich Heine, whom he calls the "hot volcano of enthusiasm, over which there would fall occasionally a snow avalanche of laughter," L. A. Montefiore reviews and analyzes the poet's religious and political beliefs.[22]

The author points out that Heine never believed in Judaism, but he always loved its custom; that although he hated Christianity, he admired the Roman Catholic Church. He despised public worship, the paid clergy, and the fact that no orthodox religion gave a satisfactory answer "as to why things are." Heine, according to Montefiore, admired the Greek Church and advocated the philosophies of Spinoza and Luther. His creed, gathered from these three sources, is stated by the author: "There is a Divine Being, and He is present in all things. But this must, of course, be construed differently from the meaning the words would bear in the mouth of a believer in revealed religion. Further, he insisted on the necessity and beauty of maintaining the family tie, and recognized the value of the feasts and festivals of religion, although he denied that Divine inspiration belonged exclusively to any one book."

Discussing Heine's political views, Montefiore reiterates the poet's appreciation of Napoleon and the French Revolution. His political creed also included an intense hatred of the nobility, the members of which, Heine declared, used kings for their own purposes just as priests used the God they pretended to serve. Particularly vehement against English politics, Heine expressed real hatred for Wellington.

The article, unusually concrete, well written, and specific in its aim, concludes with a tribute to Heine: "The supreme greatness of Heine springs from the completeness of his humanity. . . . Heine shall be recognized as the Human, and find in one word the fittest and highest fame."

Blackwood's Magazine, 1877.—In 1877, *Blackwood's*

22. "Heinrich Heine in Relation to Religion and Politics," *Fortnightly Review*, XXVIII (1877), 325-339.

Magazine[23] published an anonymous biographical account of Heine, notable because it recounts the poet's life in terms of the influences that played upon it. Like Strodtmann, the anonymous writer cites Heine's association with Le Grand as basis for his Napoleonism, his bitterness against the persecutions and humiliations that the Jews suffered in Germany as accountable for his harsh sarcasm and irony, and his unrequited love for Amalie Heine as further reason for a perverted, distorted outlook. References to Heine's works are scant in this article that shows a genuine understanding and appreciation of the poet, and which was written with a penetration that gives the material both weight and depth.

Havelock Ellis (1859-1939).—Havelock Ellis, whose familiarity with Heine is discussed elsewhere,[24] is not only a translator of Heine but a critic of the German poet as well. In the *Notes*, consisting of short paragraphs set down in the form of a diary of ideas during the year 1878, Havelock Ellis first pronounces critically upon the merits and faults of Heinrich Heine:

> He is no Goethe, no demi-God. Indeed, a man, "cradled into poetry by wrong." The cries of a soul grievously crushed in life's wine press by the feet of sorrow and error and sin. And, therefore,—yes therefore so full of divine meaning, of sweetness, of infinite pathos, so full, to him whose own soul teaches him to see it, of love. This man truly is the brother of Sappho and Catullus and Villon, and Burns and Shelley and De Musset and Leopardi, youngest born among these glorious ones, not assuredly least.[25]

In 1880, Havelock Ellis completed his first formal prose article, which was printed two years later in *Modern Thought* under the title, "The Two Worlds!" These two worlds are the ideal and the real, and Heinrich Heine is selected as an exponent of both types. More than a poet, a man striving for freedom and a thinker striving for thought, Heine, according to Ellis, wrote poetry embodying two spirits: "the sweet

---

23. CXXII, 75-89.
24. See section on Translation.   25. Goldberg, *op. cit.*, p. 70.

ethereal spirit of the ideal world and the straight-forward, matter-of-fact, sometimes coarse, spirit of the real world."[26] The irony in Heine is accounted for by the poet's inability to harmonize these two worlds.

In 1889, Ellis completed an article on Heine, which was first published as an introduction to the Camelot volume of Heine's prose (which he edited) and was later, in 1892, included as a chapter in his *The New Spirit*.[27] The article, primarily biographical, presents Heine as a poet, an artist, a dreamer, a perpetual child. To Ellis:

He [Heine] represents our period of transition; he gazed, from what seemed the vulgar Pisgah of his day, behind on an Eden that was forever closed, before on a promised land he should never enter. While with clear sight he announced things to come, the music of the past floated up to him; he brooded wistfully over the vision of the old Olympian gods, dying, amid faint music of cymbals and flutes, forsaken, in the medieval wilderness; he heard strange sounds of psaltries and harps, the psalms of Israel, the voice of Princess Sabboth, across the waters of Babylon.

Regarding Heine fundamentally as a true descendant of the tribe of Israel, Ellis gives a most sympathetic treatment of "this defender of the inalienable rights of the spirit," this odd creature "with the face of Mephistopheles made radiant by the smile of Christ."

A. H. Japp (1839-1905).—One of Heine's most capable English critics was A. H. Japp, a writer whose perceptive and analytical powers, to say nothing of his interpretative ability, where Heine was concerned, were masterly. His article in the *British Quarterly Review* in 1881,[28] for example, dealing with the character and personality as well as the life of Heine, is a most notable essay. Here he leaves nothing to be desired, for he defines the German poet in terms of his likeness to other writers and his relation to the times, as well as in accordance with his peculiar genius and temperament.

26. *Ibid.* 27. Pp. 68-88.
28. "Heinrich Heine," LXXIII-LXXIV, 137-154.

Fundamentally Heine was, in Japp's as in the opinion of others, a paradox of no few complexities. Even his ideals lacked a "oneness" of purpose. His ideal of love, writes Japp, had "feet of clay" but the "forehead of beaten gold and the breast of silver, set with gems that glittered like the breastplate of the Jewish high priest." His whole being represented just such contrasts:

Lyrical sweetness, depth of sentiment, captivating grace, and piercing subtlety of expression, passionate yearning after lofty ideals together with deliberate coarseness and the most profound scorn and irony—an irony that literally seemed to run riot in throwing ridicule over the very beauty that he had but a moment before brought into being.

Japp quotes from another critic who wrote:

Never was a nature composed of elements more contrasted than that of Henri Heine. He was at the same time gay and sorrowful, sceptical and believing, tender and cruel, sentimental and satirical, classical and romantic, German and French, delicate and cynical, enthusiastic and full of cold blood; he had everything except ennui.

Japp reminds us that Heine himself spoke of the world's heart as being "cleft in twain," and insisted that since the poet is in a central position to the world, he must experience and reflect both pain and sorrow as well as other opposed emotions. Heine, according to Japp, justified the rupture between the ideal and the real; in so doing he was strongly suggestive of Byron. They differed in that Heine achieved a unity from a moral ideal whereas Byron never bridged the gap between the real and the ideal. Both have been accused of deficiency in mental chastity, but Japp insists that whereas that may be justly said of Byron, it cannot in all fairness be said of Heine.

Much of the bitterness against Heine was based on his renunciation of the Jewish faith. Japp devotes a great deal of time to the religious convictions of the poet, emphasizing the fact that it was the eternal aspect of Judaism that he condemned and not pure Mosaism. Heine declared himself a pure Hellenist; yet he loved Christ and the Bible. To substantiate

Minor Critics 143

these statements Japp gives fully satisfactory excerpts from Heine's works as evidence.

In Japp's opinion, Heine, though well known for many years in England as a lyrico-satirical poet, was never, until the publication of Snodgrass's *Wit, Wisdom and Pathos from the Writings of Heine*, adequately interpreted. And though Japp's article was ready for publication before the appearance of the book, the Snodgrass volume stands as the first of the criticisms of Heine's more serious aspects. In further development of his own excellently prepared article, Japp writes a synopsis of Heine's life, includes a number of quotations from his prose and poetic works, and offers a summary of the whole. That Japp was a scholar is indisputable in the light of his handling of the article. His statements are in no wise speculative—all are ably substantiated by quotations or references.

In a later article, "Recurrent Ideas in Heine,"[29] Japp elaborates on the idea that so few—if any—ideas are original, and that although Heine was less imitative of other poets than many writers, he was wont to reiterate his own ideas. Japp cites the motifs of the sea and soul, and love and solitude as most recurrent in his works. Poems, an anecdote, and prose references are included to demonstrate the points. Here again, Japp shows a thorough knowledge and appreciation of the writings of Heine. Although this article demanded far less scholarly treatment than the first, it is interesting, informative, and accurately prepared.

Nina H. Kennard.—Nina Kennard, in an article for the *Contemporary Review*, writes a vivid and intimate account of Heine's family life. Her article, "A Family Portrait,"[30] gathers most of its facts from a little volume by Maria Embden Heine, the poet's niece. Through letters, many of which contained amusing and interesting anecdotes, Nina Kennard builds up for us a picture of the close and loving home life that was

29. *Gentleman's Magazine*, CCLII, 71-78.
30. XLI (1882), 981-983.

Heine's. His letters to his sister, his brothers, and his mother all reveal the affection that Heine had for his family. Later letters reflect his marital happiness and tell much of his love for Mathilde. The childhood pictures constitute the most enjoyable reading in the article though the whole is of sustained interest.

London Quarterly Review, 1882.—In 1882, the July issue of the *London Quarterly Review* carried an anonymously written article on Heinrich Heine.[31] The avowed purpose of the article was to introduce to the English public a poet who was little known but who maintained a prominent place in literature after the death of Goethe. The criticism, frankly based on the material of Strodtmann, Stigand, Martin, and Snodgrass, deals primarily with the life of Heine, although some time is devoted to a critical survey of the poems and the style Heine employed. Of the latter, the critic wrote ". . . His touch is light as the beat of a bird's wing, and yet as sure; and no matter what the subject that occupies him, his treatment is sure to be at once both bold and skilful. Certainly the possibilities of the much abused German language can scarcely be understood until he has been studied. . . ."

Here again, Heine's flexibility of religious point of view was cited: "At one time he apparently speaks and thinks in pure Paganism; at another time he is a Hellene, beauty loving and sensuous, who verges on Neo-Platonism, again he is a Hebrew who forgets his baptism, and exults in the permanence of his race. . . . Now he speaks under the spirit of the Napoleonic idea; again as a disciple of St. Simon, Lassalle and a Democrat." There are references to but few works, emphasis having been laid on the life and character of Heine.

Athenaeum, 1883.—Although the reviewer of Heine's *Reisebilder* writing in the *Athenaeum*, 1883,[32] stated that he could not, with a safe conscience, recommend Heine to all

---

31. "Life and Works of Heinrich Heine," LVIII, 411-438.
32. "Heine's Reisebilder," pp. 115-116.

German scholars, he did concede the poet a large measure of original wit and intellectual power. Heine, unknown to the British public, was characterized as "a cosmopolite and . . . a votary of liberty, a despiser of patriotism and a worshipper of Bonaparte" as well as a cynic and an unbeliever. Of the works, more references are made to Heine's political writings than to his poetry, and the writer admitted failure in his attempt to present some of the poems representative of Heine's "minstrel powers."

Walter S. Sichel (b. 1855).—Walter S. Sichel's article, based on the letters of Heine, published in the *Nineteenth Century Magazine*,[33] reveals that the author possessed a wealth of facts about German and English literature which he was anxious to share with the public. His many facts, however, proved a handicap, for the article is, as a result, very confusing.

Beginning with the thought that Heine was never truly known to England because of the various incomplete and untrue pictures painted of him, Sichel's aim, presumably, is to present here a lucid interpretation of the poet. But he immediately digresses and rather disconcertingly launches into a comparison of Byron and Heine. "Both," he says, "were reputed libertines, both enthusiasts for liberty, both passionate admirers of the sea, in the souls of both raged a conflict between a higher and lower self." Further he says that there were differences in the two men—Byron "was devoured by the idea of national freedom . . . he exhibited the true Christian spirit of international self-sacrifice." But, on the other hand, he writes that Heine lacked the power of such loving. He sought "love in every thoroughfare" and his was a pagan ideal. And in another contrast, "Byron was a stubborn protest against his age, Heine its most sensitive mirror. Bryon was a pessimist, Heine an optimist," and so the likening of the two men goes.

To Sichel's mind the answer to the riddle of Heine lay in the fact that, by his own admission, he had a soul. "I am

33. "The Letters of Heinrich Heine," XVI (1884), 118-133.

positive that I have a soul," wrote Heine; and this statement, when taken into consideration with his awareness of his position outwardly as a product of a transitional age, and inwardly as a creature of contradictions makes Heine seem to Sichel the aeolian harp upon which played the "sweeping blasts of the century." The English writer's only other reference to Heine was made in connection with a short incident based upon the immortal *Lorelei*.[34]

Thomas Wiltberger Evans (1823-1897).—Thomas Wiltberger Evans, a translator of Heine's memoirs, writes, in the introduction to one of his volumes, an appreciative tribute to the poet.[35] Heine, he says, was no model of virtue, but he was no more faulty than many men who were so credited. And further, that as the most influential poet who followed Goethe, he exercised a great influence in German literature. Evans offers a rather stirring challenge to the critics of Heine:

Those who read Heine's writings from beginning to end, who are broad enough not to be scandalized by his allies, who are generous enough to pardon his faults, and intelligent enough to perceive the undercurrent of his thoughts must come to the conclusion that he was not only a brilliant writer but also a man endowed with a most noble soul, inspired by the most lofty feelings and always wishing for the highest and the best; in short a man, who, though he often went astray in his search after truth, never relaxed in his efforts to find it, and remained faithful to himself even to the very brink of the grave.

Kate Freiligrath Kroeker (1845-1904).—In an introduction to her *Poems Selected from Heinrich Heine* (1887), Kate Freiligrath Kroeker writes a conventional account of the poet's life with a record of his publications. Emphasis is laid on Heine's place in literature, which is designated as the last in the German Romantic School. Kate Kroeker, whose significance as a translator has been estimated, gives special emphasis to the *Book of Songs*, the beauty and worth of which she strongly acclaims.

34. Walter Sichel, *Types and Characters*, pp. 285-287.
35. *Memoirs of Heinrich Heine* (1884), Preface.

Spectator, 1887.—Francis Storr's translation of Heine's *Reisebilder* provoked a rather unfavorable response from a critic who reviewed the work in the *Spectator* (January 15, 1887).[36] Expressing a full appreciation of Heine's composition which he deemed most brilliant and "unsurpassed by literature in any country," the critic flayed the translation of Storr, pointing out innumerable errors, and, worse, suggesting that the author had plagiarized the work of the American translator Leland. Interesting is Storr's letter of justification and reply to these criticisms, also published in the *Spectator*.[37]

Garnet Smith (b. 1862).—A companion piece to Franklin Peterson's "Heine on Music and Musicians"[38] is Garnet Smith's "Heine as an Art Critic," which appeared in the *Magazine of Art* in 1887.[39] Heine, here, is not credited with any great knowledge of art. In fact, had his name not been affixed to the letters sent to the *Allgemeine Zeitung* (upon which this article is based), there would have been no record of Heine's informal, witty, and altogether unconventional reaction to the arts. Heine called himself a supernaturalist and believed that the artist "cannot find all his types in nature, but rather that the most remarkable types spring immediately from his consciousness as symbols of his innate ideas." His greatest enthusiasm was for Robert, Descamps, Scheffer, Delaroche, and Vernet. Although Heine dealt with the problems of art with a light touch and frequently strayed from his topic, Smith points out that his style was of such charm and brilliance that the reader's interest is sustained throughout.

Thomas Pryde.—The *National Review* published, in 1887, Thomas Pryde's article on "Heine's Visit to London."[40] The essay is difficult to evaluate from the standpoint of utility because it is too short to give a comprehensive account of the trip to London and too general to give one any specific details or

36. "Heine's 'Reisebilder,' " LX, 77-78.
37. *Ibid.*
38. *Fortnightly Review*, C (August, 1913), 296-313.
39. X, 402-404.   40. X, 542-548.

point of view. The style is sketchy, and the material does not include a single reference to Heine's reactions to or his opinion of anything he saw in England. The article hardly merits notice.

Lady Magnus (d. 1924).—In her article entitled "Heinrich Heine, A Plea," Lady Magnus, writing in *Jewish Portraits* (1888),[41] reveals a vague, haphazard, and uninteresting literary style. This lack of technique combined with a failure to produce new facts makes a rather dull and worthless article. No references are made to Heine's personality, his religion, or even his works. Lady Magnus managed to cover forty pages, but that is her only achievement.

Westminster Review, 1888.—The aim of the article which appeared in the *Westminster Review* in April, 1888,[42] was to give only the most salient facts of the life of Heine—the "grandson of Goethe and Voltaire." Evidently greatly admired by the writer, Heine was credited with writings which resembled "a flash of Oriental perfumes, choice and strong." The article cannot boast of breadth. The facts are not elaborated upon sufficiently, and there is a deplorable lack of unity. To one not familiar with Heine's life, the article would do little toward giving a satisfactory picture of it.

Quarterly Review, 1889.—Although Heine was not well known in England for some years, he had many staunch admirers as, for example, the critic who christened Heine "the child of the age and its embodiment." In a contribution to the October, 1889, issue of the *Quarterly Review*,[43] this writer made a singularly keen analysis of Heine. A strangely varied character was the poet, for he was a "Hebrew by his pathos and energy, a German by his dreamy Pantheistic speculation, a Rhinelander by the one grain of sentiment which even cynical Paris could not quite neutralize in him and, above all, the singer of the 'Lyrical Intermezzo,' with its wild passion and

---

41. Pp. 45-81.
42. "Heinrich Heine," CXXIX, 426-441.
43. "Heinrich Heine," CXLIX, 399-430.

its unaffected simplicity." Heine, like Byron, lived a life that "was a battle and a march," for he, too, was famous for his championship of new ideas.

Heine, though declared comparable to Victor Hugo in his reflection of the ideas of an age, went to the root of situations while Hugo was more superficial. Though influenced by Hegel, Heine commanded a great measure of "naïve and plastic" symbolisms directly opposed to the dry scholasticism of that philosopher. Heine, unlike most poets in the critic's opinion, was original to an unusually great degree; his writings sparkled with unique wit and charm.

In the earlier part of his life, Heine stood for revolt. "His very striving after the Greek clearness, the blithe classic temper, are conceived in the spirit of revolt." But further along the critic writes: "It was Heine's endeavor, during the second part of his life, to propagate self-indulgence as a religious creed, and he did so vehemently . . . until he was stricken down with disease . . . last sufferings of which he has sung in his gloomy 'Last Poems' with heart-rending pathos and self-contempt. The whole reads like a modern version of Prometheus. . . ." The writer assumed a rather moral attitude toward Heine's perversion, his sensuality, calling him a "blackamoor whom no washing, seven times repeated, would make white." Later he said that "for the abuse of his transcendent gifts he must answer a higher judgment-seat than man's."

Alice G. Royston.—Based primarily on Heine's *Book of Ideas*, Alice G. Royston's article bearing the same caption, does, however, digress a bit and gives a few observations on Heine's poetry.[44] Miss Royston's general comments on Heine cannot be disregarded. Evidently a keen admirer of Heine—for she writes: "Inconsistent, irreverent, capricious, ungrateful, he with subtle touch shows us such a wealth of tenderness, such infinite capacity for good, such wilful persistence in evil, and withal so living, so true, that one closes the book feeling the author has

44. "The Book of Ideas," *Universal Review*, VII (1890), 437-452.

but thought aloud, and that unconsciously his own head has withdrawn the veil from the sanctuary of his inner life"—Alice Royston reveals a sensitivity to Heine's finest and most beautiful qualities though she is fully cognizant of his faults. She regards him as a master of simplicity, whose works showed in some instances a likeness to those of Rousseau. Although the article reveals strong admiration on the part of the author, there is an honest, impersonal element in the writing which places it beyond and above the realm of the "feminine essays."

Lady Duff Gordon (1821-1869).—In *Murray's Magazine* for 1891 occurs an article[45] devoted to the relations of Lady Lucie Duff Gordon to the German poet, Heinrich Heine. The article, written by Lady Duff Gordon's daughter, Janet Ross, is essentially the same as her excellent description of the friendship between the English gentlewoman and the poet Heine found in the author's admirable volume *Three Generations of Englishwomen*. As the entire episode is discussed elsewhere,[46] the account of the relationship need not be repeated.

Included in the article are the translations from Heine attempted by Lady Lucie Duff Gordon, which we shall not attempt to evaluate here but just say that they are quite a deal better than the average run of Heine versions in England. Indeed, Lady Duff Gordon brought to her work in this respect a wealth of experience in the art of translation; for not only was her familiarity with German language and literature of unusual proportion as a result of her study and life in the country itself, but she had rendered several German works in English prior to her attempts in Heine. Her English versions of Heine were declared by John Addington Symonds too good to be lost.

R. McLintock.—The translation of *The Works of Heinrich Heine* by Charles Godfrey Leland drew a most pointed

---

45. Janet Ross, "Some Translations of Heine by Lucie Duff Gordon," IX, 769-776.
46. See section on Informal Opinion.

criticism from R. McLintock.[47] Expressing keen disappointment over Leland's work, McLintock writes that the translator's failure lay in his faulty German and his careless English. He even goes so far as to say that the work lacked maturity and suggested "some Heine struck youth."

McLintock also criticizes Leland's translation in an article which he wrote on Von Embden's *Heinrich Heine's Family Life*.[48] In this article, although he writes primarily of the unimportance of Von Embden's work, he takes another opportunity to condemn Leland's ability to render Heine's poems in English. It must be said of McLintock, however, that in his comments on the Heine literature and his own pronouncements in German, he seems well qualified to make authoritative criticism. As a translator, he is known for his version of the *Buch Le Grand* of Heine's *Reisebilder*.

Spectator, 1892.—Charles G. Leland's translation of the works of Heinrich Heine was considered by a literary critic writing for the *Spectator* (1892)[49] as superior to any of the translations made by Englishmen up to that time. That certain of Heine's writings should be expurgated before presentation to the English public was a strong contention of the critic. The obscenities, the vulgarities, and the petty attacks on persons who did not merit Heine's vicious onslaughts of wit and satire were held as of no interest to the English reader. Leland was commended for his discrimination though held up to a rather searching criticism of his failure to make sufficient notations and his inaccuracies in translating. Although several faulty versions are cited, the writer insists that many more could have been recounted; and he warns the would-be translator of the difficulties that Heine's works present.

New Review, 1893.—The nephew of Heinrich Heine, Baron von Embden, edited a great deal of the correspondence

---

47. "The Works of Heinrich Heine, tr. by C. G. Leland," *Academy*, XL (1891), 256-257.
48. *Academy*, XLIII, 364-365.
49. "Heine's Works in English," LXVIII, 92-93.

of his uncle, publishing it as *Some Unpublished Letters of Heine*. A review of the letters appeared in the February issue of the *New Review* in 1893.[50] The letters were compiled with the hope of establishing a veracious picture of Heine's family life. Those to his mother and sister revealed the greatest depth of feeling while those to the brothers were of a superficial nature. The letters in the volume are linked with biographical notes and brief statements introducing the occasion of their composition.

Mrs. E. M. Davy.—Although women are said to have a finer capacity for translating the poems of Heine, they do not, in every instance, reveal an equal effectiveness in reviewing and analyzing the life of the poet. Mrs. E. M. Davy, in an article called "Some Passages in the Life of Heine,"[51] is typical of the feminine, fluttery type of writer one finds periodically. Her article makes no pretense at scholarship; her style can be defined only as sketchy and gossipy. A number of anecdotes are loosely strung together with little purpose, and the writer's observations and comments are childishly conceived and set forth. The whole is neither significant nor worthy of serious consideration.

Academy, 1897.—The centenary of the birth of Heinrich Heine saw the publication of numerous criticisms, reviews, and translations of Heine's works as well as studies of the man himself. The *Academy*[52] published a rather comprehensive interpretation of Heine's philosophy and attempted to account for his attitudes in terms of his life experiences. That Heine appeals to his readers in diverse ways is emphasized again—"to some he [Heine] is a silver-tongued poet . . . to others the incarnation of lust and discord. . . ." And of the works it is said that "glowing passion and delicate fancy intertwine with coarse sensuality and brutal directness. Flashing wit and

---

50. "Some Unpublished Letters of Heine," VIII, 139-150.
51. *Belgravia*, LXXXIII (1894), 291-299.
52. "The Centenary of the Birth of Heine," LII, 576-577.

dainty humor alternate with dirty buffoonery and impish spitefulness. . . ."

Heine's realization of life's manifold incongruities accounts, in large measure, for his mocking, cynical attitude. His cynicism was not actually mocking but took root in his attempt to find truth, to "reach the kernel of life's philosophy." Heine was endowed with a prosaic life and a poetic soul. Hence the constant antagonism within himself, the dualism of his nature. The first half of the article, as may be seen by the foregoing statements, dealt generally with Heine and his character. The latter half gave an interpretation of "Heine, the Singer." Here, only Heine's beauty and lyricism are emphasized, with numerous references to his poems. The whole article is good in its concreteness and its definiteness of purpose and point of view.

Athenaeum, 1897.—In October, 1897, the *Athenaeum*[53] published a review of J. W. Oddie's *Choice Poems of Heinrich Heine*. The critic dealt entirely with Oddie's success and failure in translating Heine, his style, and his aim in presenting the poems. No criticism of Heine's original works is included.

Dr. Buchheim.—The October 2, 1897, issue of the *Athenaeum*[54] carried an article, "Heine's Centenary," which was contributed by one Dr. Buchheim from King's College. The article deals almost exclusively with that controversial issue, the date of Heine's birth. In view of the fact that as many admirers believe one date as the other, quite obviously celebrations of Heine's birth are somewhat less effectual than they would be were all agreed on the date. In speaking of Heine's numerous devotees, the writer says that "England has good humoredly long forgotten his sallies against her, and there is no country where his poems have found so many admirers." No attempt is made here to settle the question of the date of Heine's birth; the problem is simply stated.

Edmund Gosse (1849-1928).—Somewhat in contrast to

53. No. 3649, p. 453.   54. No. 3660, p. 856.

the usual account of Heine's distaste for England, is the article by Edmund Gosse, written for the *Saturday Review*,[55] which deals with England's distaste for Heine. In the Mid-Victorian period, England harbored a bitter prejudice against Heine mainly because he offered so violent a contrast to the temperate countrymen to whom they were accustomed. In addition to his abhorrent literary productions, Heine stood for other detestable standards in English eyes—chiefly political and religious. "He was a Jew, and a Pagan and a sceptic, a compound of all that was least in keeping with the sobriety of the Anglican Communion. He was busied in creating an idolatrous Napoleon—just at the moment when the Napoleonic phantom seemed comfortably laid at last." "Mephistopheles proposing to succeed Faust as king of 'das junge Deutschland,'" was certainly a thing hardly to be relished by Victorian England.

It was not until Heine gave voice to his lyric power that England allowed herself a receptive attitude toward the poet. And even then her enthusiasm was perforce modified because the poems of Wordsworth and Keats, for example, had attuned their ears to a different type of lyric poem. In time, however, his works were more fully understood and appreciated, and the antagonism wore away. And so we come to the time when an Englishman can concede not only merit to Heine's poems, but also a debt of gratitude to Heine:

We owe to him . . . all that is most original, least servile, and most sensitive in the European arts of today. We owe, no less, what seems to us chaotic and anarchistic in the principles of those arts. Some Frenchman has said of a writer of his own country that "his tears became projectiles"; the phrase might singularly well be applied to Heine, whose very powerlessness and faint, ineffectual beatings against the prison bars of life, have helped, more than all the guns and clubs, to break down the Bastille of conventionality.

As a final expression of his appreciation of Heine the artist, Gosse writes:

55. "The Centenary of Heine," LXXXIV (1897), 705-706.

It is precisely the mystery of Heine, his enigmatic smile, his want of a definite outline, which, combined with the pure flame of his personal talent, have given to his arrogance and irony, his pity and indignation, his romantic melody and his capricious wit their triumphant charm. Wherever a new vision of beauty rises, wherever an outworn shell is broken down, wherever the false is mocked at and the true encouraged, wherever the conception of a young enthusiasm disturbs the comfortable inactivity of the elderly,—there Heine is present in spirit, there "the strange guest sparkles."

Academy, 1898.—The *Academy* for October 23, 1898, published a little article called simply "Heine's Mouche."[56] This account of Camille Selden, who was responsible for the last lovely little poems of Heine, is purely biographical. As far as the facts of Miss Selden's life are known, the article is fairly adequate. There are but brief references to the fact that "La Mouche" really represented Heine's last love, and was thus quite significant in a consideration of the poet's final days.

Quarterly Review, 1899.—"Heinrich Heine was the spoiled child of misfortune. This troubadour errant of irony, this aristocrat of Democracy, this prodigal son of religion, proved in his lifetime the petted and persecuted sport of that Time Spirit which stimulated and tortured him. A true patriot, who was branded a renegade; a profound thinker, he was hailed as esprit moqueur. His deeper meanings and feelings were misjudged or mangled; his lighter sallies and arabesques have been . . . applauded." Thus wrote, in the *Quarterly Review*, 1899, an anonymous critic, who believed that seldom in England had Heine been rightly criticized.[57] In deliberate contrast to the attitude commonly assumed by English critics—that of condemnation of Heine's "want of moral balance"—this writer indicated that his objective was to consider Heine as a moral and intellectual force. The objective was to be achieved through a study of the prose works of the German author.

56. LV, 110-111.
57. "The Ideals of Heinrich Heine," CLXXXIX, 424-452.

Of the man Heine, much is said in a general fashion. The influences of Napoleon and Goethe as well as those of the French Revolution upon him are reviewed; and his cosmopolitanism, his credo of freedom, and his likeness to Byron are all recounted in some detail. In a final comparison, Heine is called the founder of "Young Germany" very much as the man who, ten years later, was destined to become the founder of "Young England," Disraeli. In general, the material is sketchy and little adaptable to our purpose because of its direct connection with Heine's prose rather than with his poetic works.

Temple Bar, 1900.—Many commentators of Heine have said that the one thing the great poet lacked was love. These critics disregard Heine's wife, cataloguing her significance as physical only. Yet, according to the author of an article called "Heine's Frau Matilde,"[58] Heine did as a number of men do—voluntarily chose his opposite rather than his counterpart for a life-mate. That she was common, ignorant, coarse, shallow, and extravagant was nothing to Heine, who loved her for her gaiety, her charm, her beauty, and her devotion to him. The writer paints Frau Heine in honest, unbiased colors and evidently feels that Heine was happy with her, some of his comments notwithstanding.

William E. Henley (1849-1903).—William E. Henley,[59] writing in the same vein as Robert Buchanan in that critic's essay "Heine in a Court Suit," decries wholeheartedly the futile efforts to translate the poems of Heinrich Heine, in a short essay, written about 1900, "The Villainy of Translation."[60] "Heine," says Henley, "had a light hand with the branding-iron, and worked his subjects not more neatly than indelibly. And really he alone was capable of dealing adequate vengeance upon his translators. His verse has only violent lovers or violent foes; indifference is impossible. Once read

---

58. *Temple Bar,* CXX, 395-405.
59. See also section on Influence.   60. *Works,* V, 94-98.

Minor Critics 157

as it deserves, it becomes one of our spiritual acquisitions. We hate to see it tampered with; we are on thorns as the translator approaches, and we resent his operations as an individual hurt, a personal affront." Henley says a little later, "To give an adequate idea of an artist's work a man must be himself an artist of equal force and versatility with his original," and the English critic finds that, for the most part, the many writers who have attempted to translate the immortal works of the artist Heine have failed utterly because of the want of kindred spirit. In the many English versions of Heine, "the man is gone, and only an awkward, angular, clumsily articulated, entirely preposterous clay-figure remains to show that the translator has been by."

Jaye Garry.—There were many Englishmen who were sorely offended at Heine's unfavorable opinion of their homeland. Heine's dislike of England was and is notorious, but as Jaye Garry remarked in his article, "Heine in London,"[61] Heine's criticisms of England were usually fair. Although he heartily disliked England, he was careful always to modify his remarks. They were never so bitter as they might have been, coming from Heine. Seemingly, Heine's only favorable opinion of England and English institutions was in connection with the debates in Parliament. He attended them constantly and gave them "ungrudging approval."

Garry conceded Heine's distaste for England but partially excused it thus: "It was the first country he had seen outside his own and he brought with him all those poetic rose coloured illusions which the untravelled cherish concerning foreign lands; and one by one, as he trod the streets of the mightiest city in the world, they were torn away. . . ." Jaye Garry was unusually generous in his appreciation of the bases for Heine's feelings, and took no personal offense at the poet's dislike for England.

William Francis Barry (1849-1930).—William Francis

---

61. *Gentleman's Magazine*, CCXCV (1903), 231-243.

Barry, Protonotary Apostolic, Canon of St. Charles, Birmingham, and Rector of St. Peters, Leamington, wrote an article on Heine which appeared originally in the *Quarterly Review* and later in *Heralds of Revolt*.[62] Based to some extent on the Strodtmann biography, the article represents an interesting survey of Heine and his works in general, with an emphasis on Heine's "better side." Though sympathetic to him, the writer does not completely ignore the baser aspects of Heine's writings. Barry accounts for much of Heine's bitterness by his lack of genuine hope. " 'This world,' says Carlyle in a well-known passage, 'is properly defined as a place of hope; without hope we cannot live.' But that was the chord on which Heine never struck, which would yield him no music. He merely professed to hope; it was the flesh with its vices and concupiscences that was made to be immortal."

Barry makes strong favorable criticism of the *Reisebilder* and the *Buch der Lieder;* their merit, in his estimation, was never surpassed. In further consideration of the works, Heine is compared to Leopardi and likened to Sterne. Leopardi and Heine differed because the former was possessed of deep melancholy plus "a variety of tones and a sense of colour." Like Sterne, Heine was a "child of the tragic muse" with a capacity for mirth, tragedy, sorrow, music, and comedy. The article is extremely well written and reflects the author's familiarity with many notable literary characters.

James Henderson.—It is gratifying to Heine enthusiasts that he, though he despised England, was not petty enough to be insensible to its great men of letters. James Henderson, in an article published in *Temple Bar* in 1904,[63] writes of Heine's intense admiration of Sir Walter Scott. Many references were made to the English writer in Heine's letters; and, although there were many dissimilarities between the two, Scott was always openly admired by the German. At only one

---

62. *Heralds of Revolt* (1904), pp. 120-157.
63. "Heine and Sir Walter Scott," CXXIX, 284-290.

period did Heine's enthusiasm waver, and that was when Scott wrote disparagingly of Napoleon. Heine was incensed; but, as time went on, he recovered his equanimity and was, as of old, an ardent admirer of Sir Walter Scott.

Athenaeum, 1904.—The American translator of Heine, Charles G. Leland, having died before completing his task, Margaret Armour and Thomas Brooksbank assumed the job of finishing the English version. A brief and rather succinct review of the work of the collaborators appeared in the *Athenaeum* in 1904.[64] Miss Armour is credited with a better and more pleasing transcription of Heine's poems while Brooksbank's lack of the lyric gift is deplored. The review deals with the exactness, the precision, and the lyric quality with which the translations are achieved.

Henry W. Nevinson (b. 1866).—The author of *Goethe the Man and Poet* and *The Life of Schiller*, Henry W. Nevinson, wrote also a volume called *Books and Personalities*, published in 1905, which includes an essay on Heinrich Heine.[65] In treatment it is chiefly biographical and analytical. In his consideration of the poet's personality, Nevinson credits him with originality and independence of style. Heine "refused to imitate the so-called nature poets in their easy-going rhymes on the beauties of creation, and the gratitude due to God, following the common prescription for German song—take Sonne and Wonne, add Schmerz and Herz and stir up with a little Wehmut. At the bottom of his wildest and sweetest dreams, his nightingale songs, his daunted moonlight, his Indian visions, there lurks the modern thought, the heart and brain of Heine himself, a man of the nineteenth century, quite alive to the time of day." Nevinson charges that Englishmen should be especially fond of Heine, for he possessed the two qualities that Englishmen demand from a lyric poet—the qualities of brevity and reality. Of his other characteristics, "lyrical irony" may be noted, and within the essay are examples of it. Bio-

---

64. No. 4019, p. 617.   65. Pp. 1-34.

graphical facts and analyses of some works constitute the bulk of the essay. Frequent references to Heine occur in other of the critic's works.[66]

James Baker (1847-1920).—In a review of *The Memoirs of Heinrich Heine,* written about 1905, James Baker evidently did not have in mind presenting more to the public than a summary of the poet's life.[67] No critical estimate of the works and but slight appraisal of the poet's character are included. Memoirs of Heine began to appear in the *Gartenlaube* in 1884, according to Baker, which were thoroughly genuine in content. There are but two notations to be made of this article: first, Heine is here compared with Hood in that they both suffered severe physical illness and "struggled with marvellous brilliancy of intellect and tenderness of mind"; and second, we find here Baker's translation of "Du bist wie eine Blume," which is deemed a fair piece of work.

Horace Barnett Samuel.—One of the best reviews of the early part of our century is that of Horace Barnett Samuel,[68] noted translator and editor. The essay is composed of two rather distinct parts, the one concerned with the period in which Heine lived, the other with the life of the poet. The latter section, though well done, is of less significance than the first, for in his evaluation of the age which produced Heine, Samuel makes some notable observations. The years in which Heine lived, according to the critic, were transition years—"disturbed, unsettled and paradoxical." The elements of which those years were compounded include the Revolution and the Reaction, Romanticism and Hellenism, materialism and mysticism, democracy and aristocracy, poetry and science. And in the midst of it all, Heine represented the clash between the illusions and disillusions of the age. Therefore, Samuel writes, we must regard the main currents—the Revolution, the

---

66. See *Changes and Chances* and *Running Accompaniments.*
67. *Literary and Biographical Studies* (1908), pp. 104-123.
68. "Heinrich Heine," *Fortnightly Review,* LXXXV (1906), 854-870.

Reaction, the literary movements of Romanticism and Aestheticism—in order to understand the poet truly.

The author's grasp of the history of the period reveals itself in his definite and authoritative summary of the trends noted. In a rapid summary of the effect of the Revolution on Romanticism and the ultimate effect on Heine, continuing to a brief account of Hellenism and its effect on him, the writer builds up the stage on which the German writer appeared.

The account of Heine's life is written with the idea of showing primarily the part that race, environment, and parentage played in Heine's life. Though naturally less creative than the earlier part of the review, this section is carefully developed. Samuel's desire to interpret Heine in the light of his time and background is, in the main, fulfilled. Had he elaborated on his material a trifle more, he might have made his article more enlightening.

Edinburgh Review, 1908.—In an exceptionally well-written article displaying keen and penetrating critical acumen, the anonymous author of "Heinrich Heine: Emotion and Irony"[69] has endeavored, with marked success, to trace the development of Heine's art through the varied influences and sundry events that played so formidable a part in shaping Heine the man. Although the author, comparatively speaking, has generally ignored discussions of Heine's political, social, philosophical, and religious tendencies, he, nevertheless, has analyzed accurately and adequately in so short a space the psychological, emotional, and real influences that contributed to the development of a style which veered "from an art dictated almost solely by the incited fantasies of imagination to an art coloured, if not moulded, by a keen apprehension of reality born of intimate contact with men and women."

It is the author's conviction and prophecy that the foreigner will ever cherish the aesthetic Heine—"not the author of 'Atta Troll,' 'Deutschland' or the shorter satirical poems, but

69. *Edinburgh Review*, CCVII, 151-177.

the poet of the inimitable and untranslatable love-lyrics, the ironic-sentimentalist of the 'Intermezzo,' and 'Heimkehr,' and the 'Nordsee' cycles, the ballad-writer of the 'Romanzen' and the tragic mocker, lover, and mourner of 'Lazarus' and the 'Letzte Gedichte.' . . ." Such a prediction is, of course, in itself of none too great originality or consequence, but the manner in which the unknown critic supports his thesis through the skilful interweaving of those details contributory to the emotion and irony of the aesthetic Heine makes of the article an extremely readable, interesting, and informative account.

The critic pictures vividly a Heine strewing "the sandy and parched thoroughfares of desert places with the 'rot und blaue Blumen' which the reaper casts away as useless, but with which the little country girl—the winder of garlands—wreathes her head as she hurries to dance with her lover where the music sounds," and finds:

Aesthetically Heine's poems remain a typical example of the literary expression of emotionalism—an emotionalism of sense, imagination and sentiment, to which an acute intellectuality gave the edge of a knife. Few writers have impregnated their work more deeply with the idiosyncrasies of personality and whether narrative, descriptive, pictorial, reflective, or purely lyrical, the profoundly mournful pessimism of the poet's outlook is stamped on every page. From first to last his verse writings are one long confession of defeat, a reiterated assertion that

> "Das ist das Los
> Das Menschenlos: — was gut und gross
> Und schön, das nimmt ein schlechtes Ende."

His songs are one long cry of distress, broken with anger, vibrating with mockery; they are threaded with a hopelessness that takes refuge in levity and a passion, which, as if ashamed of its barren impotence, puts on the ribald cap and bells of the professed wit and licensed humorist.

Arthur Ransom.—In what amounts to a quite general and none too brilliant appeal for the increased popularity of Heine among English readers, Arthur Ransom, in an article called simply "About Heine,"[70] accounts for Heine's want of popularity in England on the following grounds: first, that "much of his work deals with subjects that are purely German, or at best Continental, subjects that interest historical and political specialists rather than the 'general reader' "; second, his writings are "provokingly fragmentary"; third, the "reckless audacity of his satire, especially when that satire is directed against things very dear to the average Briton" alienates the affection of the English reading public; and last, but far from least, Ransom feels that "the great barrier to his success among us is to be found in the impossibility of translating him."

The major portion of the article is concerned with the impossibility of rendering in English "the most difficult of all modern writers to translate." Ransom finds that not only is the task of translating Heine's poetry an insurmountable one, but that of translating his prose presents equal difficulties; for, in both instances: "The outstanding characteristics of Heine's writings are just those which offer the greatest difficulties to the translator." The article concludes with a plea for a "thoroughly good English Life of him, a book that might stand in our shelves by the side of Lewes' 'Life of Goethe' and Carlyle's 'Life of Schiller,' " and an appeal to the English reader to forget, or at least forgive, the many faults of Heine in an effort to view him fairly and objectively.

Franklin Peterson.—What Garnet Smith attempted in the field of art in his article published in 1887, "Heine as an Art Critic," Franklin Peterson tries in the field of music in the article, "Heine on Music and Musicians."[71] In a rather poor article, written in a choppy, sketchy manner and building to no unified point, Peterson gives merely, in random notes, a few of Heine's "thumb-nail sketches" illustrating the German poet's familiarity with musicians in particular and music in general. Heine's praise of Donizetti, his likening of Rossini

---

70. *Westminster Review,* CLXXV (1911), 62-68, 149-155.
71. *Fortnightly Review,* C (1913), 296-312.

to Vesuvius pouring forth brilliant flowers, his comparing of Berlioz with a colossal nightingale are all cited, together with references found in the works to Chopin, Beethoven, Spontini, Meyerbeer, etc. Peterson accords Heine no special ability in music and admits freely that "his knowledge of music ... was on a par with his knowledge of one hundred other things, and is often broader than it is deep."

Count de Soissons (b. 1860).—In "The Jews as a Revolutionary Leaven,"[72] the Count de Soissons, a Parisian critic by rights, draws an interesting comparison of Heine and Alexander Herzen, the "forerunner of the Russian Revolution." Among other points of likeness, the author finds a marked similarity in the mental development, views, and lives of Heine and Herzen. Both had a pagan and sensual way of thinking antagonistic to Christian spiritualism; both were revolutionists; both derived their revolutionary principles from Saint-Simon and Hegel.

In a rather thorough analytical interpretation, the Count de Soissons treats the views and tenets of Saint-Simon, Spinoza, and Hegel; and proceeds to point out the similarity of Heine's *History of Religion and Philosophy in Germany* and Herzen's *Letters on Dilettantism in Learning*, finding that the fundamental difference between the two authors lies in their moral attitudes:

Heine is a worshipper of matter and an apostle of a new religious doctrine which is based on Saint-Simonism and, being the negation of Christianity, could only be built on its ruins. On the other hand, Herzen was dazzled neither by the fallacious happiness of sensual pleasure, nor by the desire for boundless freedom in that respect. He appreciated Saint-Simon, not as a writer whose aim was the production of a new spiritual power and a new religion, but as a man who wished to improve the lot of those who were slighted.

In a further elaboration on the same idea, the critic continues:

72. *Quarterly Review*, CCXXXIII (1920), 172-187.

Herzen is morally superior to Heine, who found in opposition to Christianity his own ideal of mankind—an ideal of pleasures, dances, and feasts of unbridled sensuality. On one side he was prompted by the hatred of the Jew for Christianity in which he saw the source of his humiliations; on the other, by the proneness of the Semite to fleshly pleasures.

Herzen could not be satisfied with that aim. He was a foe not only of the ideals which produced contemporary culture but also of all negations of the ideals approved by the Revolution. He was absorbed by the dream of a world of absolute good, embodying the truth which he knew through Hegel, and was aware that he would be unable to see that world here below. Since he disbelieved in life hereafter, in despair he announced death to the people as "good news." That longing for the Absolute made him morally superior to Heine.

The last part of the article is concerned with Heine's spiritual affinity with Marx and Lassalle, and with Heine's "prophetic vision" of the Russian Revolution. Although the article as a whole bears no outward earmarks of scholarship in the form of footnotes and the like, there is an abundance of evidence on the part of the Count de Soisson of thorough, interpretative scholarly insight and literary ability.

Kenneth Hayens (b. 1891).—In a scholarly article,[73] Kenneth Cochrane Hayens shows conclusively the indebtedness of Heine, the critic, in *Shakespeares Mädchen und Frauen* to the earlier work of Hazlitt in *Characters of Shakespeare's Plays* and to that of Mrs. Jameson in *Shakespeare's Heroines*. Hayens carries out in more detail work along the line done by Ernst August Schalles in a dissertation, *Heines Verhältnis zu Shakespeare*, published in Berlin, in 1904. Hayens gives a sufficient number of quotations and examples from the work of Heine and that of the earlier English writers to offset any charge of coincidence or fortuitousness in the matter of selection—and the reader must conclude with him that Heine "benefitted markedly by the work of Hazlitt and Mrs. Jameson."

73. "Heine, Hazlitt and Mrs. Jameson," *Modern Language Review*, XVII (1922), 42-49.

E. M. Butler.—In an article published in 1923,[74] Eliza Marion Butler treats Heine's relationship to the doctrines of Saint-Simon, a subject on which the author elaborated three years later in her book called *The Saint Simonian Religion in Germany*. The article is, in reality, a double one, the first part of which deals with Heine's Saint-Simonism, and the second with the date of the letters from Heligoland. In the first section, the critic, in brief, points out the fact that Heine's adoption of the Saint-Simonian religion served fundamentally to clarify, synthesize, and harmonize his chaotic and contradictory religious views and resulted in a greater hopefulness of tone in the poet's works—a hopefulness which later gave way to pessimism when Heine discarded the doctrines of his newly-found religion. The second section, displaying soundness and thoroughness of scholarship, presents some interesting theories on the dating, alteration, and genuineness of the letters from Heligoland.

Orlo Williams (b. 1883).—

... I sometimes wonder whether we have any impression of Heine that resembles reality.... He seems a disembodied spirit.... And, at best, if with a little more knowledge and sympathy we mentally embody the poet after the song is over, it is as the German youth who lost his heart "in the lovely month of May," whose dearest images were roses and violets, lilies and nightingales, and who, having buried "the old bad songs," in a coffin as big as the Heidelberg tun, wandered enthusiastically over the Harz, listening to the fairy tales of miners' little daughters or sat upon the beach at Norderney singing love-songs to pretty fisher maidens.

So begins Orlo Williams, after a brief and insignificant portrait of Heine, in his comparatively recent article, "The Heine of the Harzreise,"[75] in which the English author attempts to impute to the neurotic and oversensitive Heine—"a man divided against his time and against himself"—a solidity

---

74. "Heine and the Saint Simonians," *Modern Language Review*, XVIII, 68-86.

75. *Cornhill Magazine*, LIX (1925), 207-422.

with which he is rarely credited. It is in the young Heine, the Heine of the *Harzreise,* says Williams that we find, not our "disembodied spirit," but a typical German student, a "jovial, poetical, simple and sensuous creature" who discusses at length "green-parsley soup, violet cabbage, Kalbsbraten, smoked herring, the simplicity of the people of Klausthal, etc. ...." "The solid German Heine, now tender, now boisterous, was not extinguished all at once. We find him again in the poems and prose written at Norderney and in many pages of childhood's reminiscence which come into that strange mixture of genuine beauty and artificial wit called 'Das Buch Le Grand.'"

The "solidity" of which the English critic speaks, we gather, is more or less confined to the writings of the *Harzreise* period and disappeared forever when the years of ill-health, conflict, and irritation hardened and sharpened the spirit of "the jovial student," forcing him to lay aside "the lyre of Apollo to take up those other weapons of the God of poetry, the bows and arrows."

Samuel Gordon.—In a flat and pointless essay, "Heine, the German and the Jew,"[76] Samuel Gordon proclaims Heine's genius "encyclopaedic and kaleidoscopic," crediting him almost as the *"dernier cri* of literary versatility" although he insists "his reputation rests most firmly on his fame as lyric poet." In an attempt to explain why this "Teuton St. Simon Stylites" became the mental hypochondriac we know, Gordon gives us the following causes: his volatile temperament, his unhappy attachment to Amalie, his self-expatriation, and, chiefly, his apostasy. The critic attributes Heine's success as an immortal and unforgettable singer not to the fact that Heine was a Jew, but to the fact that he was a German with the German's nature "of tripartite composition, the three ingredients being war, philosophy and song." After expressing a rather unorthodox preference for Heine's dramatic poems, and after drawing a weak and ineffectual comparison of Heine and Disraeli, the

---

76. *Contemporary Review,* CXXVII (1925), 230-236.

author expresses his doubts as to whether there will ever be another Heine.

Not only is the essay planless, haphazard, and abrupt in its awkward bounds from one point to another, but no effort is made to advance any particular notion. In fact, the title itself goes unsupported, for in a surprising close, and one for which we find no justification in the article, the English critic practically declares Heine "neither a German nor a Jew—but a Greek *plus* something else."

G. A. Black.—In a scholarly article[77] dealing with James Thomson's translations of Heine, G. A. Black comments upon and gives excerpts from James Thomson's contributions on Heine in the Victorian weekly, the *Secularist*. The article sheds light on Thomson's little-known articles on Heine, which were made available to the author through the kindness of Bertram Dobell's son. Since Thomson's connections with Heine are treated elsewhere in this study,[78] and since there is no attempt to give the author's own opinion of Heine, mention of the publication should be sufficient here.

Spectator, 1936.—An anonymous author, writing in the *Spectator* for February 21, 1936, contributed a one-column notice on the occasion of the eightieth anniversary of Heine's burial in the Parisian cemetery of Montmartre.[79] The notice, which includes a brief and very general survey of Heine's life and works, is written entirely in German and is of little or no significance. In no way does the author exceed his purpose, namely, to call attention, in the nature of a commemoration notice, to the burial of the German poet four score years prior to the time of his article.

77. "James Thomson: His translations of Heine," *Modern Language Review*, XXXI (1936), 48-54.
78. See section on Influence.
79. "Heine," CLVI, 299.

3.

Heine

IN ENGLISH INFORMAL OPINION

---

v. *Letters, Diaries, Notes, Conversation*

ASIDE FROM the numerous translators and critics of Heine's works, who, by virtue of their efforts alone, attest the popularity and significance of the German poet in England, there appear many others who show the tremendous familiarity of Heinrich Heine to the English reading public. In letters, diaries, notes, papers, biographies, commentaries, and miscellaneous works, there is a wealth of material, found for the most part in scattered and isolated bits, which further strengthens the notion of the German poet's prevailing influence on England and Englishmen. These scattered and isolated scraps viewed as a whole throw light upon the opinion held by Englishmen on the work and character of Heine. The collected materials fall logically into four large and distinct classes and represent four distinct camps of opinion in regard to Heine. There are many prominent Englishmen who have merely mentioned Heinrich Heine in passing—those to whom the German poet's name is known, but who have been at no pains to discover anything concerning him that was not known to the general public; there are a few who cannot abide the mention of the poet's name, and who see nothing in him but an ugly and repulsive person who offends good taste; there are many whose enthusiasm for the poet knows no limitations—those who would rank Heine with the great immortals; and, finally, there is an extremely limited circle of Heine's English acquaintances who can boast an intimate and personal contact with the poet.

Even those who have but mentioned Heine in passing have contributed to the general notion of the poet's popularity in England; for merely the calling of a person's name, if done frequently enough, is evidence in itself that the person is alive in the minds of the public and is significant for some definite reason. Because of the fact that the references to Heine made by those who but barely mention the poet and his work are of such an isolated nature, no particular conclusions as to point of view can be drawn. It can only be hoped that the evidence through its mere preponderance will enhance, to some extent at least, the idea of Heine's significance for and familiarity to English letters.

The Honorable Henry J. Coke (1827-1916) twice mentions Heine in his *Tracks of a Rolling Stone*,[1] quoting from the German poet in each case. Stephen Allard refers but once to Heine, who as "The singer of the 'Buch der Lieder,' Heine the godlike, the devilish, found no solace in his many tears, nor in his 'world-shattering' irony."[2] In the letters of Gerald Manley Hopkins (1844-1889) and Robert Bridges (1844-1930), there is evidence to show that the two manifested an interest in Heine.[3] The German poet is also mentioned by James Lindsay (1852-1923) in connection with that writer's work on *Faust*.[4] The former editor of the *Free Review* and the *National Reformer*, John M. Robertson (1856-1933), makes frequent reference to Heinrich Heine in his *Essays*

---

1. Pp. 136 and 373.
2. Garnet Smith, *The Melancholy of Stephen Allard*, p. 44.
3. *The Letters of Gerald Manley Hopkins to Robert Bridges*, ed. by C. A. Abbott, I, 31.
4. *Essays Literary and Philosophical*.

Heine in Letters, Diaries, Notes

Towards a Critical Method.[5] In the letters of Charles Sorley (1895-1915) occur several references indicating that Heine's poems were read with interest.[6] Thomas Wright of Olney (1859-1936) likewise makes frequent reference to Heine.[7] The most extensive, impartial mention of Heine is that recounted by Madame Horschelt and ascribed to her father, Charles Boner, whose knowledge of German letters was quite broad. As the reference is mentioned in connection with the views of Carlyle, it will not be presented here.[8]

Among others who would appear to have had a definite interest in Heine are Richard Middleton,[9] Joseph Skipsey (1845-1903),[10] Mark Rutherford (William Hale White, 1831-1913),[11] Edward Thomas (1878-1917),[12] Arnold Bennett (1867-1931),[13] Edward V. Lucas (1868-1938),[14] D. H. Lawrence (1885-1930),[15] Canon Patrick A. Sheehan (1852-1913),[16] Sir Walter A. Raleigh (1861-1922),[17] and "Beachcomber" (John B. Morton, 1893-   ).[18]

Surprisingly few are the unfavorable reactions to Heinrich Heine; yet some of England's greatest literary figures display strong antipathy towards the magnificent German singer. The antipathies evidenced toward Heine find their bases in a number of causes. In some instances, they are based upon the religious, political, and philosophical views held by the poet, in others the question resolves itself into one of stubborn English misunderstanding of what Heine attempted to accomplish,

---

5. Pp. 35, 79, 104.
6. *The Letters of Charles Sorley*, ed. by W. R. Sorley, pp. 77, 79, 90.
7. See views of John Payne in sections on Translation and Informal Opinion.
8. See Thomas Carlyle in this section.
9. Henry Savage, *Richard Middleton*, pp. 27, 149.
10. B. Ifor Evans, *English Poetry in the Later 19th Century*, p. 347.
11. W. Robertson Nicoll, *A Bookman's Letters*.
12. R. P. Eckert, *Edward Thomas*, p. 67.
13. *Journal*, p. 854.
14. *Reading, Writing and Remembering*, p. 47.
15. Hugh Kingsmill, *The Life of D. H. Lawrence*, p. 149.
16. *Parerga*, pp. 130, 349.
17. *A Selection from the Letters of Sir Walter Raleigh* (1880-1922), ed. by Lady Raleigh, p. 178.
18. "Beachcomber," *By the Way*, p. 179.

and in one or two cases the basis of the antipathy seems rooted in racial prejudice.

Among those whose dislike of the poet is based upon religious, political, or philosophical grounds are George Birkbeck Hill, Lady de Rothschild, and the Earl of Lytton. The three named would seem to bear no particular malice to the poet in general, but have fastened upon one or two elements in Heine which prove to be, in their case, a source of irritation.

It must be borne in mind that Heine is not a philosopher in any meaning of the word. It is true that his work shows the influences of the philosophies prevalent at the time in which he lived, but only as the main currents of any given generation are reflected in the artistic works of that period. A sensitive, impressionable soul, exposed to the lectures of August Wilhelm Schlegel, the philosophy of Hegel, and the views of Germany's leading thinkers in general, could scarcely have avoided a philosophical bent in original work. Heine is merely the mirror in which the various philosophies he encountered are reflected—and none too clearly reflected at that. In no instance does he purport to be a philosopher in his own right, and George Birkbeck Hill (1835-1903), who has confessed a disappointment in the emptiness and confusion of what he terms "moonshine" and "rubbish" (in speaking of Heine's *Religion and Philosophy in Germany*)[19] has failed to realize that here was no Kant, Fichte, Schelling, or Hegel, but fundamentally only a singer of divinely inspired songs.

One of the elements in Heine's works most distasteful to the respectable Englishman or Englishwoman is the poet's seeming lack of reverence and respect for God and religion. It is this element, especially, that accounts for the publication of so many "Bowdlerized" editions of the poet's work in respectable Victorian England. Translators, critics, and biographers have in some instances glossed over or omitted entirely those details of disrespectful and blasphemous nature which are

---

19. *Letters of George Birkbeck Hill*, ed. by Lucy Crump, pp. 204-205.

so offensive to English taste. It is surprising, then, to note the lenience and tolerance with which nineteenth-century England politely ignored and smiled away the religious failings of Heine. It is nearly with a sigh of relief that we encounter such a woman as Lady de Rothschild (1821-1910), who, in righteous English indignation, voices what must have been a widespread distaste of Heine's cynical and irreverential attitude toward things sacred. Writing as early as 1847, Lady de Rothschild says: "I am reading Heine's 'Allemagne.' It is extremely witty and amusing, but I cannot regard with anything but deep aversion his Pantheistic doctrines and the slighting, mocking way he speaks of what is to many most sacred."[20] Years later, after having read Heine's life, in 1876, Lady de Rothschild, while sympathizing utterly with the terrific agony of the poet's last years, implies that just this agony was needed to bring the poet back into the fold: "to give him those feelings, which he had not before—faith in God and Immortality."[21]

Robert, first Earl of Lytton (Owen Meredith, 1831-1891), whose interest in and knowledge of German literature came probably as the result of his study and travels in Germany, can hardly be considered a great disparager of Heine's genius. Considering Heine as a mere dwarf beside Goethe and Schiller,[22] he finds the poet, as an interpreter of his age, inferior to Elizabeth Barrett Browning, the author of the admirable *Aurora Leigh*.[23] Lytton's views on Heine are extremely sound and without prejudice of any sort. His sympathy toward Heine's shortcomings is unquestioned in every respect but one. As in the case of the poet's own countrymen, Lytton, it would seem, is unable to forgive what many consider a political *faux pas*—namely, Heine's application for a pension which he in no wise deserved. In a letter to his father, written

20. Lucy Cohen, *Lady de Rothschild and Her Daughters*, p. 27.
21. *Ibid.*, p. 28.
22. *Personal and Literary Letters of Robert, First Earl of Lytton*, ed. by Lady Betty Balfour, I, 133.
23. *Letters from Owen Meredith to Robert and Elizabeth Barrett Browning*, ed. by A. B. Harlan, p. 130.

March 10, 1856, shortly after the death of Heinrich Heine, Lytton says: "... Poor Heine is dead. That is a great light gone out. A great light once, but of late only the stink and grease of it were observable.... I forgive him all, but asking for a pension from Russia which I hear he did before his death."[24]

Reginald, Viscount Esher (1852-1930) is one of the few English writers to find but scanty satisfaction and pleasure in reading the works of Heine. In an entry made in 1876 found in *Ionicus*, Esher declares that there is not much else to be found in Heine's "scraps" but a bitter wit.[25] Esher's criticism, however, must be taken with the proverbial "grain of salt," for the English writer's knowledge of the German language is highly doubtful—indeed, from his own statements concerning the language, it is extremely questionable as to whether he was able to read Heine in the original.

In one of his famous conversations with Eckermann, Goethe once made the statement: "Wie hat Carlyle uns Deutsche studiert! Er ist in unsrer Literatur fast besser zu Hause als wir selbst; — zum wenigsten können wir mit ihm in unsern Bemühungen um das Englische nicht wetteifern."[26] Thomas Carlyle (1795-1881) is, indeed, the Mogul of German culture in nineteenth-century England, and his remarks on Heine should be of utmost significance. There is actually no little similarity between the two men in their railings, their singularity, and their unhappy later lives. There is, too, no little similarity between the German poet and the English prose master as thinkers and artists. Of the two, Heine is probably the clearer thinker. Both attacked "humbugs," and both loathed essentially the same thing—Heine, his "philistinism," and Carlyle, his "respectability." Heine, however, took himself far less seriously than did Carlyle.

"To ignore Heine and Schopenhauer," says Oliver Elton,

24. Balfour, ed., *op. cit.*, I, 75.   25. P. 103.
26. H. Kraeger, "Carlyles Stellung zur deutschen Sprache und Literatur," *Anglia*, XXII (1899), 155.

Heine in Letters, Diaries, Notes

"was as bad an omission as any of those for which Carlyle castigated Taylor."[27] How odd it is that critics have repeatedly referred to Carlyle's total indifference to Heine! How often we read that, "that blackguard Heine" was Thomas Carlyle's sole reference to the German poet! It is true that the great English writer is by no means generous in the number of his references to Heinrich Heine, but it is equally true that Carlyle says enough of the poet to enable us to determine his true attitude and to stamp him as Heine's greatest foe in England.

Perhaps the earliest reference to Heine made by Carlyle is that found in a letter to Heine's lifelong friend, Varnhagen von Ense, with whom Carlyle also was acquainted. The letter was written as early as November 7, 1840, and contains the statement:

. . . I read few German works at present; know almost nothing of what you are doing. Indeed, except your own writings there turns up little which a lover of German literature, as I have understood the word in old years, would not as soon avoid as seek. In these days I have read a new volume of Heine's with a strange mixture of feelings. *Heine über Börne*—it is to me the most portentous amalgam of *sunbeams* and brutal *mud* that I have met with for a long while.[28]

Carlyle, who is moved to a large extent in his antipathy for Heine by the matter of race prejudice, attempts, somewhat in the manner of the truculent Bartels, to separate Heine the Jew from Heine the German. As an entry for April, 1862, in the *Notes* of Charles Boner there is the following description of a conversation between that writer and Carlyle:

He [Carlyle] said that when a young man he had great hopes for German literature, but they had been deceived, or rather disappointed. All was going and had gone downwards. There was a sort of Socialism rampant everywhere. All had degenerated into newspapers and parliaments. The aristocratic spirit which showed so prominently in Goethe was no longer to be found. Spoke of Heine. One thing he thought he discovered in him, a stern, grim sort of humor, but still,

27. *A Survey of English Literature 1830-1880*, I, 11.
28. *The Last Words of Thomas Carlyle*, pp. 277-278.

more than he had seen generally in Germans. A Jew, he said, never laughed a hearty, outbursting laugh. I told him Mrs. Austin once met Heine at Boulogne when she was a child, and he said, "Now you can say that you have seen Heinrich Heine!" She said, "Who is Heinrich Heine?" which seemed to amuse him greatly, for he burst out into a hearty laugh; showing that, at all events, he was no Jew.[29]

Indeed, we may well believe that the matter of the racial element in Heine intrigued Carlyle to no little extent, for the English author probed thoroughly the ancestry of the German poet and discovered, to his own satisfaction at least, on going into the matter that Heine's parentage was Jewish only on one side.[30]

Carlyle's dislike for Heine continued as time went on. His disgust of the German poet increased with the years, and his antipathy is expressed in ever-increasing expressions of inexplainable bitterness—bitterness of the type of which only Carlyle was capable. In 1865, about the time that Matthew Arnold was boosting the fame of the German poet primarily through the medium of his excellent critical study, Carlyle became infuriated and "tore up" Arnold himself for regarding Heine as the natural continuator of the great Goethe, and added that, in his opinion, Heine was a "filthy, foetid sausage of spoiled victuals."[31]

Five years later, on a Sunday afternoon in October, 1870, Althaus paid a visit to Thomas Carlyle, and the two men sat before the drawing-room fire and discussed the past and future of German literature. The conversation led quite naturally to the merits of Goethe, of whom Carlyle was particularly fond. With deep regret the great English writer lamented the fact that for a long time he had not seen a single essay or new book on Goethe, and added that on the contrary he had heard a great deal about a "dirty, blaspheming Jew, Heinrich Heine"

---

29. R. M. Kettle, *Memoirs and Letters of Charles Boner*, II, 9-10.
30. R. H. Shepherd, *Memoirs of the Life and Writings of Thomas Carlyle*, II, 277.
31. D. A. Wilson and D. W. MacArthur, *Carlyle in Old Age*, p. 23.

who had "wit of a sort," but concluded that "it would be shameful to put him in front of Goethe."[32]

A nearly similar experience was enjoyed by William Black, the popular Scottish novelist, who, on July 24, 1875, secured through William Allingham an appointment with Carlyle. As before, the conversation centered on Germany, and after a while the name of Heine was introduced. According to Black, "for the next quarter of an hour, poor Heine had a bad time of it," and the whole Jewish race was thoroughly scourged and proclaimed a race "fit only to eat sausages made of toads."[33]

The views of Coventry Patmore (1823-1896) are highly similar to those of Carlyle. In a letter to his wife, written toward the end of 1874, Patmore says of Carlyle: "I believe he is the only man living, besides myself, who dares to think, much less speak, evil of Heine."[34] In answer to the question "who is Heine?," Charles Kingsley's (1819-1875) sole comment on the German writer was, "A bad man, my dear, a bad man!"[35]

William Allingham, the Victorian Boswell, was probably incited to a study of German literature through the efforts of Thomas Carlyle with whom he spent many pleasant hours chatting about the relative merits of Goethe, Schiller, and other great masters of German letters. His knowledge of German literature and art, however, can by no means be proclaimed one derived entirely from secondary sources, for Allingham had traveled extensively in Germany, and his familiarity with the language made it possible for him to read his favorite authors in the original. Indeed, so great was his familiarity with German that no less a personage than Carlyle suggested that he translate the *Nibelungenlied* into English, and promised, if he did so, it would prove a lasting work.[36] While

32. *Ibid.*, p. 218.   33. *Ibid.*, p. 358.
34. Basil Champneys, *Memoirs and Correspondence of Coventry Patmore*, I, 281.
35. Gosse, *loc. cit.*, *Saturday Review*, LXXXIV, 705.
36. William Allingham, *A Diary*, p. 231.

Allingham has but little to say of Heinrich Heine, we can easily infer his high regard for the German poet through his opinion of Baudelaire, who, he thinks, is not worth naming in the same day with the great German master.[37]

The Scottish writer, Robert Pearce Gillies, the founder of the *Foreign Quarterly Review*, ranks as a minor Carlyle in his attempts to make England conscious of the glories of German letters. The first to introduce to the English reading public the German *Schicksal* drama through his translations of Müllner's *Schuld* and Grillparzer's *Ahnfrau*, Gillies, through innumerable other translations, through articles, studies, and interpretations, sought to transplant German letters in English soil. Indeed, he is one of the first in England to recognize the worth of a great many German writers, including Heinrich Heine. Sympathetically, Gillies excuses the faults and grossness of the German poet, calling attention to the beauty and power of his lively, conversational style. Long before the fame of Heine was firmly established, Gillies recognized the genius of the man and predicted that his would be no insignificant rôle in the world of letters.[38]

John Payne, a prolific translator from the German,[39] is primarily known in connection with his efforts to spread the fame of Richard Wagner in England. Although he was one of the minor figures of the period, his work in the field of German literature and music makes him of significance in this study. Heinrich Heine, to John Payne, was representative of the highest form of literature, and the peculiar flavor of that author's work was, to the English writer, essentially masculine. In connection with the poems written by Heine upon his deathbed, which Payne considered his finest efforts, Payne declared: "Heine is the first poet of Germany. His only rival is Goethe. No woman could appreciate Heine. Indeed

---

37. William Allingham, *Varieties in Prose*, III, 339-340.
38. Sibilla Pfeiffer, *George Eliots Beziehungen zu Deutschland*, pp. 29-31.
39. See also section on Translation.

Heine in Letters, Diaries, Notes

you would not like her if she could. Heine is thoroughly spontaneous."[40]

Luther's motto in translating the Bible, "No day without a line," would seem to have been George Gissing's creed in his intense study of German. Gissing, who as a youth studied and taught at a German university, displays almost fanatical interest in all things German. His letters of the 1880's to his sister and brother are filled with pleas and requests that they begin at once to enter upon a scientific study of German, and admonitions that, under no conditions, must they neglect their studies of the language and literature of the land in which he was so interested. It is interesting to note that in listing the truly great men of world letters, the German writers who are declared by Gissing to be indispensable are Goethe, Jean Paul, and Heine.[41] Of the works of Heine, Gissing appears to have been particularly impressed with the *Buch der Lieder*, which, in a letter to his sister Ellen on December 16, 1886, he describes as "the beginning of an epoch of intellectual life."[42] In another letter written twelve days later he says: ". . . I sent you Heine's *Buch der Lieder*, one of my most precious possessions. Poor Heine! I made a pilgrimage to his grave in Paris. In all literature he is one of the men most akin to me. But you will not understand him till you have read his prose as well as verse."[43] Although Gissing's interest in Heine seems to have been at its highest during the decade 1880-1890, actually it had been awakened some years earlier; for, when still a month under nineteen, we find him writing to his brother William from America, on October 5, 1876, and advising him to read the *Buch der Lieder* which he promises will prove "simple and very delightful."[44]

Among the letters of Maurice Hewlett is found one to Mrs. Leaf, written in January, 1919, expressing that writer's deep regard for Heinrich Heine:

---

40. Thomas Wright, *Life of John Payne*, p. 23.
41. A. and E. Gissing, *Letters of George Gissing*, pp. 160-161.
42. *Ibid.*, p. 187.   43. *Ibid.*, p. 188.   44. *Ibid.*, p. 14.

MY DEAR LOTTA:

You take my strictures very generously. I feel horrid when I write them because it is quite obvious that your heart is in your verses—but Art is a hard master and won't accept, or look at intentions. Performance is all he cares about. You can't have a better example of how to do the thing than Heine—he is in most respects the best Lyric poet in the world's history, if not in all respects. But how entirely impossible to imitate, or even to realize! I think that if I could be sure I had done one lyric, or one lyric passage, as good as Heine I would let everything else I have done go to the devil.[45]

That Olive Schreiner, of South-African fame, should be listed among the most fervent of Heine's many English admirers is unquestioned. Hers was an affection of long standing, and one that was rooted, in a typically feminine way, in a sympathy for the tragic figure that was Heine the man, rather than in extreme love of Heine the poet. As early as 1884 we find her writing to Havelock Ellis:

. . . I love Shelley, and there is another man I love in that same impersonal way, Heinrich Heine. I know how and why he wrote every line that he did write. There is more depth and passion in one of his sneers, more quivering tenderness veiled under it, than in the outcries of half the world. I feel that I owe a debt of personal gratitude to the girl who comforted him in his "mattress grave."[46]

Other letters of the same period to Havelock Ellis[47] speak of her sympathy for Heine's attitude toward Wellington, her readings in Heine, and her desire that Ellis send her a copy of Heine's poems.

Still further letters, addressed to Mrs. Francis Smith and written in the early part of the present century, reveal Olive Schreiner's admiration for Heine's style and manner of writing.[48] The following letter gives, perhaps, the most comprehensive statement of her attitude toward the German poet:

---

45. *The Letters of Maurice Hewlett*, ed. by Lawrence Binyon, p. 201.
46. *The Letters of Olive Schreiner 1876-1920*, ed. by S. C. Cromwright Schreiner, p. 16.
47. *Ibid.*, pp. 23, 35, 124.   48. *Ibid.*, p. 282.

Heine in Letters, Diaries, Notes 181

SEPTEMBER, [c. 1906]

... Many people have been surprised that I said Heine's grave was the most sacred spot to me in Europe. I don't say he was the greatest man; he has never helped me nor modified my life as Mill did. But that seven years on the mattress-grave, that beautiful joy-loving soul dying away by inches and fighting to the end. If only I could have been that woman who went to him at the end and cheered and comforted him. The very name of the Rue d'Amsterdam is to me sacred because he lay there. I know that other men have suffered but not just so, because he was in a way alone to the end. If anyone showed me a lock of hair and said "That is Wordsworth's," I should look at it and pass on; if they said it is Shakespeare's or Shelley's, I should stroke it and if it was Shelley's kiss it, but I should lock it up in a drawer; but if it was Heine's I should carry it about with me wherever I went. I don't know why I love him so.[49]

Rather sentimentally, Frank Harris stated once that he entered the world in the same month that Heine left it,[50] and it would seem that he regarded that circumstance as symbolical of the forces which shaped his entire life, for of all men who have yet lived, Frank Harris felt himself most closely akin to his spiritual brother, Heinrich Heine. Among the accounts of his readings, Heine is listed as one who helped most in moulding his thought,[51] and his writings include frequent reference to the German poet. In the original copy of his autobiography was included what Harris considered one of his best bits of writing, a chapter on Heine.[52] Although he had "remonstrated with Carlyle for wasting a dozen years on Frederick the Great, instead of painting his contemporaries," among whom Heine was listed,[53] Harris himself declined to accede to the hope of Hugh Kingsmill (expressed in a letter of 1911) "that he would do for Heine what he had done for Shakespeare" on the grounds that "he felt too intensely about Heine ... to wish to write about him in an English paper."

49. *Ibid.*, pp. 254-255.
50. A. I. Topin and E. Gertz, *Frank Harris: A Study in Black and White*, p. 21.
51. Hugh Kingsmill, *Frank Harris*, p. 56.
52. Topin and Gertz, *op. cit.*, p. 3.   53. Kingsmill, *op. cit.*, p. 189.

That Harris had contemplated writing a life of Heine, however, is indicated extensively in his *Jahre der Reife*. According to the account, which is too long to quote, Frank Harris tells us of mentioning once to H. S. H. Princess Alice of Monaco (the grandniece of Heine, with whom he was quite intimate, and with whom he chanced to be in Claridge about 1899) that he would like very much to visit Germany in order to obtain from Heine's sister, still living, some intimate details concerning Heine's earlier and later years, which might throw new light on the life and works of the poet. When asked by the Princess why he had not written a biography of Heine, Harris replied that the project would cost him five thousand pounds, a sum he could not afford. The Princess volunteered to supply the amount, but unfortunately nothing came of the venture, and when, shortly afterward, Harris learned of the death of Heine's sister, the possibility of a new biography along the lines proposed ceased to exist. It is regrettable that the work was not undertaken, for Harris tells us that he would have much preferred writing the life of Heine to that of Oscar Wilde; and there is no doubt but that the undertaking would have been an interesting as well as significant one.

Still another class of Heine admirers in England comprises a relatively small circle of the German poet's English acquaintances and friends. The very limited extent to which Heine himself was familiar with contemporary English men of letters is quite remarkable. Of Shakespeare, Byron, and others who preceded him, the poet expresses a profound admiration, but the great figures of Victorian letters are for the most part ignored. But then, Heine had a genuine dislike for all things British of his own time. Did he not write after visiting England for the first time—in a fit of spleen it is true: "The mass of them, the stockish English—God forgive me—do offend me to my inmost soul and sometimes I cannot regard them as my fellow men, but as lamentable automatic machines, whose mainspring is egoism."⁵⁴ Even eight years later, when Heine, admitting that he had brought with him to England a good stock of ill-temper, wrote of the country, it was still with certain bitterness and want of sympathy.⁵⁵

In consideration of Heine's views toward England and her sons, it is little wonder, then, that he speaks so little of his English contemporaries and fellow-craftsmen. Browning, Tennyson, and others of the first water are completely ignored. Edward Fitzgerald is mentioned but once and then by name only. Disraeli received a favorable review of his *Contarini Fleming* of which Heine wrote: "Modern English Letters have given us no offspring equal to *Contarini Fleming*."⁵⁶ Of all the Victorian writers, Charles Dickens seems to have been Heine's favorite. His letters to his mother⁵⁷ show keen delight in and wide familiarity with the works of the great novelist.

Only three English writers of the period can rightfully lay claim to Heine's personal friendship—Charles Wentworth Dilke (1789-1864), Richard Monckton Milnes (1809-1885), and Lady Lucie Duff Gordon (1821-1869). Of the three, Dilke, former editor and proprietor of the *Athenaeum* and a man frequently mentioned by Keats, Hood, Lady Morgan and others for the solidity of his judgment, is the only one of whom Heine himself gives us no record. In the memoir of the English author written by his grandson, however, we have it on fairly reliable authority that Heine was reckoned among Dilke's best friends abroad.⁵⁸ Richard Monckton Milnes (Lord Houghton), who is discussed elsewhere in this study,⁵⁹ was first introduced to Heine by Lady Duff Gordon, and formed a lasting attachment for the German writer.

Heine's most intimate English friendship was that with

54. Karpeles, *Heines Memoirs*, II, 728-729.
55. *Ibid.*, I, 198.
56. Wilfred Maynell, *Benjamin Disraeli*, p. 30.
57. See *Gesammelte Werke*, ed. by Karpeles, IX, 356, 357.
58. C. W. Dilke, *The Papers of a Critic*, I, 24.
59. See sections on Criticism, Translation, and Influence.

Lady Lucie Duff Gordon, of which both writers have left ample accounts. In August of the year 1833, Heinrich Heine was in Boulogne, and at the *table d'hôte* sat next to a pretty little girl of twelve years with long plaits of hair down her back. Heine chanced to hear the little girl, Lucie Austin, who later became Lady Duff Gordon, address a few words to her mother in German, and ventured to speak to both mother and child. The friendship between the great poet and the little girl began with Heine's saying that when she returned to England she could tell all her friends that she had seen Heinrich Heine, whereupon she asked, "And who is Heinrich Heine?" which amused the poet greatly.

The poet and the child passed long hours together lounging on the pier while the little girl sang old English ballads which delighted Heine, who repaid his little friend by recounting to her fantastic tales of watersprites, mermaids, and fish, in which an old French fiddler and a black poodle were inevitably concerned. Heine remained at Boulogne a month or two, and the friendship between the poet and the child increased daily. Indeed, one of Heine's finest lyrics was written for the little friend whose "braune Augen" he never forgot:

> Wenn ich an deinem Hause
> Des Morgens vorüber geh',
> So freut's mich, du liebe Kleine,
> Wenn ich dich am Fenster seh'.
>
> Mit deinen schwarzbraunen Augen
> Siehst du mich forschend an:
> "Wer bist du, und was fehlt dir,
> Du kranker, fremder Mann?"
>
> Ich bin ein deutscher Dichter,
> Bekannt im deutschen Land;
> Nennt man die besten Namen,
> So wird auch der meine genannt.
>
> Und was mir fehlt, du Kleine,
> Fehlt manchem im deutschen Land,

Nennt man die schlimmsten Schmerzen,
So wird auch der meine genannt.
(Die Heimkehr)

Eighteen years passed before they met again. In 1851, Lady Duff Gordon and her husband accepted the kind invitation of Barthelmy St. Hilaire to use his apartment in Paris. Quite by chance they learned that Heine lived not far away in the Rue Amsterdam, that he was poor and dying. Lady Duff Gordon sent to ask if the great poet remembered the little girl to whom he had told fairy tales at Boulogne several years ago and requested an opportunity to see him. Heine sent for her immediately, and the two renewed the friendship begun so long ago. Each little incident at Boulogne was recalled, and Heine spoke particularly of a ballad the little girl had sung to him— a ballad which recounted the tragical fate of Ladye Alice and her humble lover Giles Collins, and ended by Ladye Alice taking but one spoonful of gruel, "with sugar and spices so sweet," while, after her death, "the parson licked up the rest." The incident delighted Heine, who asked directly after the parson who drank the gruel.

The ravages of time and disease had played havoc with the physical appearance of Heinrich Heine in the interim, and Lady Duff Gordon, who still held in her heart the picture of the dapper comrade at Boulogne, was shocked at the change:

I, for my part, could scarcely speak to him so shocked was I by his appearance. He lay on a pile of mattresses, his body wasted so that it seemed no bigger than a child under the sheet that covered him, the eyes closed and the face altogether like the most painful and wasted *Ecce Homo* ever painted by some old German painter. His voice was very weak, and I was astonished at the animation with which he talked; evidently his mind had wholly survived his body. He raised his powerless eyelids with his thin white fingers and exclaimed, "Gott! die kleine Lucie ist gross geworden, und hat einen Mann; das ist eigen!" He then earnestly asked if I was happy and contented, and begged me to bring my husband to see him. He said again he hoped I was happy now, as I had always been such a merry child. I answered that I was no longer so merry as "die kleine Lucie" had been, but very happy and contented; and he said "Das ist schön; es bekommt Einem gut eine Frau zu sehen, die kein wundes Herz herum trägt, um es von allerlei Männern ausbessern zu lassen, wie die Weiber hier zu Lande, die es am Ende nicht merken, dass was ihnen eigentlich fehlt ist gerade, dass sie gar keine Herzen haben." I took my husband to see him, and we bid him goodbye. He said that he hoped to see me again; ill as he was, he should not yet die.[60]

In September of 1854, Lady Duff Gordon was in Paris again and found the poet removed and living in the same street in which she resided, the Champs Elysées. She sent him word of her arrival and received directly the following note written painfully by him in pencil:

HOCHGEEHRTE, GROSSBRITANNISCHE GÖTTIN LUCIE!
Ich liess durch den Bedienten zurückmelden, dass ich, mit Ausnahme des letzten Mittwochs, alle Tage und zu jeder beliebigen Stunde bereit sei, *your Godship* bei mir zu empfangen. Aber ich habe bis heute vergebens auf solche himmlische Erscheinung gewartet. *Ne tardez plus de venir! Venez aujourd'hui, venez demain,* venez souvent. Vous demeurez si près de moi, dem armen Schatten in den Elysäischen Feldern! Lassen Sie mich nicht zu lange warten. Anbei schicke Ihnen die vier ersten Bände der französischen Ausgabe meiner unglückseligen Werke. Unterdessen verharre ich Ihrer Göttlichkeit
Unterthänigster und ergebenster Anbeter

H. HEINE

P.S. The parson drank the gruel water.[61]

Lady Duff Gordon went immediately to see Heine and found him on the same pile of mattresses, looking more dead than alive. He welcomed her saying, "Ich habe jetzt mit der ganzen Welt Frieden gemacht, und endlich auch mit dem lieben Gott, der schickt mir dich nun als schöner Todesengel: gewiss sterbe ich bald" to which she replied, "Armer Dichter, bleiben Ihnen doch immer so viele herrliche Illusionen, dass Sie eine reisende Engländerin für Asrael ansehen können?" Heine, delighted with seeing her once more, spoke affection-

---

60. Janet Ross, *op. cit.*, p. 474.
61. *Gesammelte Werke*, ed. by Karpeles, IX, 507.

Heine in Letters, Diaries, Notes

ately of his good English friends—Lady Duff Gordon herself and the good Milnes. The conversation turned to the poet's works. M. Leon de Wailly had told him of Lady Duff Gordon's admirable translation of his novel *Stella and Vanessa*, and Heine, anxious to be well translated into English, offered her *carte blanche* to undertake his own works in English. After talking at length on politics, religion, and the little intimacies of their early acquaintance in Boulogne, the visit was terminated; and Lady Duff Gordon left with a last lingering and never-to-be-forgotten glance at the sad, pale face of the dying Heine.[62]

The last class of Heine's English admirers comprises a group of poets who, in their enthusiasm for the genius of the German writer, have dedicated to him eulogistic poems of their own making. With the exception of *Heine's Grave* by Matthew Arnold, most of these poems are comparatively unknown to the English reading public, and for that reason, as well as for the intrinsic value and interest of the poems themselves, they are given here. The poems are relatively simple and tell their stories far better than critical interpretation or incidental remark could hope to do.

Henry Crossley Irwin, discussed also as translator of Heine, has dedicated the following poem to the German poet:

HEINE

Sound sleep the dead who lie in German earth:
So saidst thou, but O Heine, not for thee
Such sleep as theirs. Save love for Germany
Little in thee was German. At thy birth
Large wealth of scorn, unconquerable mirth,
A heart untameable and savage wit,
Blent with a strain of pathos infinite
The gods vouchsafed thee, and what these were worth
Thou taughtest all men from thy mattress tomb.
Child of the Revolution wert thou, yea,

---

62. For a full account of Lady Duff Gordon's relationship with Heine see *Murray's Magazine*, IX (Jan.-June, 1891), 769-776 and Janet Ross, *op. cit.*, pp. 472-476.

> Revolt incarnate; and its meetest home
> Thine aweless spirit in its brightest day
> In that bright city found where now, thy doom,
> Of strife fulfilled, thou restest from the fray.[63]

One of the earliest of the poems addressed to Heine is that of Clement Mansfield Ingleby (1823-1866), written April 1, 1865, about the time that Arnold was doing so much to spread the fame of Heine in England:

EPIGRAM ON HEINRICH HEINE
(By the ghost of Dryden)

> Three Lyric Poets, in three generations
> Were born and flourished in three rival nations.
> The first in mockery and wit surpassed:
> The next in intellect: in both the last.
> Spent Nature rested when she'd made the pair,
> Then Heine formed from Byron and Voltaire.[64]

Among the poems of Edward Cracroft Lefroy (1855-1891) is found one which, in all probability, is addressed to Heinrich Heine. There is no concrete evidence to support the theory that the piece is in honor of the German poet, but because of the fact that Heine was definitely "in the air" in late nineteenth-century England, and because of the fact that the content of the poem is so appropriate to Heine himself, there appears some little justification in supposing that the poet in the poem is actually Heinrich Heine. Then, too, Lefroy's poem, published posthumously in 1897, the year of Heine's centenary, and entitled *On Reading a Poet's Life*, probably received its impetus from the newly published biographies of Stigand (1875) and William Sharp (1888).

ON READING A POET'S LIFE

> Because he sang of pleasant paths and roses,
> You thought that summer joys were all his care.
> "The only wisdom," so you cried, "he knows is
> How much delight one crowded day can bear:

---

63. H. C. Irwin, *op. cit.*, p. 63.   64. *Poems and Epigrams*, p. 48.

The reason why his verse uniquely flows is
That he alone has wealth of bliss to spare:
In Tempe's vale for life he gathered posies,
And flings the few he doth not keep to wear."
The veil is lifted now. Behold your singer,—
A sick poor man, despised, and barely sane,
Who strove awhile to shape with palsied finger
The hard-wrung produce of a sleepless brain,
Rich but in throes,—till Death, the great balm bringer,
Stooped to kiss him through the deeps of pain.[65]

Walter Herries Pollock (1850-1926), former editor of the *Saturday Review of Politics, Literature, Science and Art*, published, in 1890, the following poem on Heine:

HEINRICH HEINE

There was a singer, a poet bold,
Compact of Fire and Rainbow Gold:
Compact of Rainbow Gold and of Fire,
Of sorrow and sin and of heart's desire—
Of good and of evil and things unknown,
A merciless poet who cut to the bone.
He sounded the depths of our grief and our gladness,
He laughed at our mirth and he wept at our madness;
He knew all the joy of the world, all the strife,
He knew, and he knew not, the meaning of life.[66]

In a similar vein, Horace B. Samuel, discussed among the critics of Heinrich Heine, points out the conflicting natures that went to make up the personality and genius of the German writer:

Life has two faces Janus-like, the one
Grim, old, grotesque; a foul and dark wound sears
Its riven visage, and a grin it wears
Alaughs its own grotesqueness; dauntless, lone
It stares the void, but worst all undergone,
How dead this cold security from fears;
Yet ever and anon, life's mortal tears
Roll slowly down, each as a silent stone.

---

65. Wilfred Austin, *Edward C. Lefroy: Life and Poems*, p. 124.
66. *Old and New*, p. 46.

The other smooth and young and all afire
With the live and light and laughter of the earth,
Bright as the golden chords of a mystic lyre
Singing a sweet ineffable refrain,
A faery fantasy of delicate mirth:
And thou, oh Heine, art Life's faces twain.[67]

Serving as an introduction to his translations from the German poet, Rennell Rodd (b. 1858),[68] has the following short piece in which he attempts to catch the spirit of Heine the pure lyric poet:

Faint echoes of a voice that sung
The song of every day,
With music on the bitter tongue
That took the sting away:
For sweeter singer never smote
On such a simple lyre,
Nor stayed on such a tender note
The fugitive desire.
The voice is hushed that battled long
With passion and with pain,
But from the fount of living song
The echoes rise again.[69]

In similar wise, Emily Pfeiffer (1827-1890), one of the major English translators of Heine, prefaces her versions of the German poet with the following envoy:

O shade of Heine, if I dare
Apostrophise that spirit bright,
That lucent spirit, keen and rare,
By other name than that of Light!

Forgive that from your amber verse
I take your tears and make them mine,
And in my ruder speech rehearse
What in your own is so divine.

---

67. *Fortnightly Review*, LXXXV (January, 1906), 854.
68. See section on Translation.   69. *Unknown Madonna*, p. 75.

Heine in Letters, Diaries, Notes

Your thoughts I folded to my breast,
I took your words upon my tongue;
Your thoughts rose up in sweet unrest,
Your words were clamorous to be sung;

I caught your breath and gave them forth,
But wintry currents changed to sleet
Your burning sighs, your airy mirth;—
And thus I rain them at your feet.[70]

The following poem by Robert Buchanan (1841-1901), who is treated at length as a critic of Heine, prefaces his short sketch, "On a Passage in Heine," in *David Gray:*[71]

I am a pilgrim on the quest
For the City of the Blest;
Free from sin and free from pain,
When shall I that city gain?

When suns no longer set and rise,
When bishops' mitres star the skies,
When alms are dropt in all earth's streets,
And angels nod upon their seats,

O pilgrim, thou shalt take thy stand
Within the City yet unplann'd,
And see beneath, with sleepy shrug,
The draff within the Pit undug.

When, shortly after the death of Dante Gabriel Rossetti, Hall Caine and Theodore Watts-Dunton stood at the grave of their beloved friend, the mind of the former reverted to a touching sonnet which the friend at his side had just printed, and Caine was forcibly impressed with the applicability of the piece to him who lay in death. The sonnet, written by Theodore Watts-Dunton (1832-1914), had been addressed in its printed form to Heinrich Heine and ran:

Thou know'st that island far away and lone
Whose shores are as a harp, where billows break
In spray of music and the breezes shake
O'er spicy seas a woof of color and tone,

---

70. *Quarterman's Grace*, pp. 117-118.   71. P. 270.

While that sweet music echoes like a moan
In the island's heart, and sighs around the lake
Where, watching fearfully a watchful snake,
A damsel weeps upon her emerald throne.
Life's ocean, breaking round thy sense's shore,
Struck golden song as from the strand of day:
For us the joy, for thee the fell foe lay—
Pain's blinking snake around the fair isle's core,
Turning to sighs the enchanted sounds that play
Around thy lovely island evermore.

"How strangely appropriate it is," said Caine, "to Rossetti, and now I remember how deeply he was moved on reading it." Whereupon Theodore Watts-Dunton admitted that, in reality, the sonnet was intended for the dead Rossetti. "He guessed its secret," said Watts-Dunton referring to Dante Gabriel, "I addressed it, for disguise, to Heine, to whom it was sadly inapplicable. I meant it for *him*."[72]

The most famous English poem, and perhaps the most famous poem of world literature commemorating Heine, is that of Matthew Arnold (1822-1888) entitled *Heine's Grave*. The length of the poem forbids quotation here.[73] Arnold, through his famous essay on Heine and this equally famous commemorative poem, has probably done more than any other English writer to spread the fame and increase the popularity of the "German Byron" among English speaking peoples. For that reason, if not for the intrinsic value of the poem itself, special attention should be warranted in considering *Heine's Grave*.

"It is a curious and significant fact," writes Stuart P. Sherman, "that Arnold is most bracing when he stands by a grave; his most inspiring lines are his commemorative poems: the prayer at the end of 'Heine's Grave'; the 'Memorial Verses' for Wordsworth; 'Westminster Abbey' written in commemoration of Dean Stanley; 'A Southern Night,' occasioned by

---

72. Hall Caine, *Recollections of Rossetti*, p. 297.
73. See Appendix.

the death of a brother; and above all 'Rugby Chapel,' in which he pays to his father's memory an almost religious veneration."[74] Sherman, indeed, is right; and the poem at hand, *Heine's Grave*, is one of the finest of the lot, despite Monahan's assertion that the poem, "egregiously over-praised," is for the most part merely "a disjointed prose homily."[75]

It is true that the piece is faulty in spots. Arnold's digressions scarcely add to the central idea; but who would sacrifice what is perhaps his most decided political outburst in verse—the marvelous, if despondent, picture of England, the "weary Titan" staggering on to her goal—an utterance which springs spontaneously and naturally from the chief subject, merely for the sake of an artificial coherence. Arnold, too, errs in thinking it Heine to whom apply the famous words of Goethe, "He had every other gift but wanted love." It was, as has been noted before in this study, Platen of whom Goethe spoke.

"What are we all but a mood," asks Arnold, "a single mood of that great spirit, one of whose moods, bitter and strange, was the life of Heine?" The epigram is, as Edward Dowden says, a "graceful fantasy but no true criticism,"[76] for Heine's was no single mood. His nature is one of complexities, and his moods are as changeable as fickle winds in April. If anything, Heine represents a composite of all moods, all passions, all ideas. That is his chief characteristic, and no one mood can be singled out as a dominating trait. Despite trivial and perhaps inconsequential faults, *Heine's Grave* remains essentially a fine piece of work.

When Heine lay on his mattress-grave in the last throes of his long protracted agony, Frederick Locker-Lampson (1821-1895) made a visit to Paris and had hoped, while there, to form, among other acquaintances, an acquaintance with Heine.[77] We

74. *Matthew Arnold: How to Know Him*, p. 88.
75. M. Monahan, *Heinrich Heine: Romance and Tragedy of the Poet's Life*, p. 172.
76. Loc. cit., *A Centenary Retrospect*, p. 61.
77. Frederick Locker-Lampson, *My Confidences*, p. 157.

learn, unfortunately, that the meeting between the two men never materialized. That Locker-Lampson was familiar, however, with the life and works of the German writer is attested by the following poem written in 1876:

>HEINE TO HIS MISTRESS
>
>What do the violets ail;
>So wan, so shy?
>Why are the roses pale?
>Oh why? Oh why?
>
>The lark sad music makes
>To sullen skies;
>From yonder flowery brakes
>Dead odours rise.
>
>Why is the sun's new birth
>A Dawn of gloom?
>Oh why is this fair earth
>My joyless tomb?
>
>I wait apart and sigh
>I call to thee;
>Why, Heart's-beloved, why
>Didst thou leave me?[78]

On January 11, 1911, John Payne (1842-1916)[79] wrote to Thomas Wright of Olney in reference to a proposed work on Heine: "Heine . . . is being launched, but it will depend upon subscriptions . . . whether it will be printed."[80] By the end of the same year, according to Wright, the *Heine* "was in the hands of the subscribers" and "was prefaced by the poem entitled 'A grave at Montmartre,' which had first appeared in the selection called *The Descent of the Dove*."[81] Because of the fact that the volume and poem mentioned were unable to be found, we must rely on Wright's account of the piece: "In this powerful original poem Payne represents a staid and un-

78. *Poems*, p. 231.   79. See also section on Translation.
80. Wright, *Life of John Payne*, p. 233.
81. *Ibid.*, pp. 234-235.

usually phlegmatic Englishman shaking his head at such productions as Heine's:

> "Heine's not the man," you say, "for me,
> Tennyson or Kipling is my poet.
> If I must be plagued with poetry
> Let me have it as at home they grow it.
>
> . . . .
>
> "Something sapid, cut and come again,
> On the tickled palate such as lingers;
> Not like Heine, jam who gives you, then
> Raps you with the spoon upon the fingers;
>
> "Verse *(sec.me)* should be a proper guest
> For the table of the virtuous thickhead;
> Heine's muse was mostly half-undrest,
> Seldom sober, generally wicked."

"Turning upon the good dullard Payne admits that Heine,

> Was a tropic weed, whose flaming blooms
> Now rose-fragrant were, now henbane-sickly;
> In accordance with life's lights and glooms,
> Lily-soft it showed or aloe-prickly.

"But the rose is a foul-feeder, lilies spring from the moorish mud, and the sea in which we dive for pearls and coral is astir with monsters. Nature's fashions were good enough for him. So for ending,

> Here he lies, her singer every inch:
> See, the very blossoms seem to know it.
> Go thy ways, du dummer dicker Mensch!
> What hast thou to do with flowers or poet?"

Alfred Noyes (b. 1880), the eminent contemporary English writer, included among his poems the following piece on Heine:

HEINE'S DREAM

> In dreams my false love comes to me,
> In dreams, in dreams by night;
> But her kiss is a yearning agony,
> Her face is wrung and white.

> I feel the cold and quivering mouth
> Cleave as in long past years;
> But oh, the sufferings and the drouth,
> And the salt strange tears!
>
> Come no more, come no more,
> Often I wake and moan,
> While the heart of the sea, on the distant shore
> Breaks in the dark, alone.
>
> Why wilt thou tear the deep old wound
> Open in sleep anew,
> Oh lips that I have kissed and found
> So sweet and so untrue?
>
> Nay come, love, come in dreams to me,
> I turn and weep again;
> Thy far-off world misuseth thee!
> Thou art in pain, in pain![82]

Humbert Wolfe (b. 1886),[83] who, in his anarchical tendencies and stylistic traits, has often been compared with Heine, is an ardent admirer of that poet and has written possibly more poems in his honor than has any other English writer. The longest of the poems to Heine appears in two of Humbert Wolfe's many volumes[84] and is called *Heine's Last Song:*

> Life's a blonde of whom I'm tired
> Being fair is just a knack
> Women learn to be desired
> By a Jew—who answers back:
>
> "Blonde, oh blonde, ye lost princesses
> With the shadow in your eyes
> As of bodiless caresses
> Known ere birth in Paradise.
>
> Little ears of alabaster,
> Where like ocean in a shell
> Gentle murmurs drown the vaster
> Voice of rapture or of Hell.

---

82. *Poems*, pp. 8-9.   83. See also section on Translation.
84. *Shylock Reasons with Mr. Chesterton*, pp. 37-38 and *Early Poems*, pp. 88-90.

Tender bodies—ah too tender
To be given or be lent
Unto love the money-lender,
Who demands his cent per cent.

Thus you took a man and tricked him,
Life and ladies, to a will
In your favour, but the victim
Cheats you with a codicil.

All I had, you thought, was given—
Life and ladies, you were wrong:
In a poet's secret heaven
There is always one last song.

Even he is half afraid of,
Even he but hears in part,
For the stuff that it is made of,
Ladies, is the poet's heart.

Not for you, oh blonde princesses
Is that final tune, but I
Sing it drowning in the tresses
Of a darker Lorelei.

For her hair than yours is stranger;
Wilder lights are lost in hers
Where the heart's immortal danger,
That you cannot know of, stirs.

Life and ladies, it is over:
Blonde asks all, gives nothing back;
You must find another lover,
For the poet chooses black.

Where death's raven marriage blossom
Falls in clouds about her breast,
On his dark beloved's bosom
Heinrich Heine is at rest.

In the little poem called simply *Heine*, Humbert Wolfe has endeavored to capture some of the fleeting moods of Heine as expressed in his popular lyrics:

I thought of Heine, and of your sea-thrilled hair,
and of that least small movement of your mouth,
when the Northern words you speak come through the air,
steadily beating to the heart's dim South;

and how he cried that the beloved was too fair,
too lily-cold for love, too white to guess it,
and how he would have laid his hands on her hair
gently, as I do now on your hair, to bless it.[85]

The last poem of Humbert Wolfe to Heine consists merely of a quatrain:

It is enough to carve upon this stone:
"The poet Heinrich Heine lies below.
When what was hidden in all hearts is known,
his secret he will neither tell nor know."[86]

85. *This Blind Rose*, p. 29.   86. *Snow*, p. 55.

4.

Heine

IN ENGLISH POETRY

―――・・―――

VI. *Major Influence*

ONE OF THE MOST important and most interesting spheres in which influence is exerted by one writer upon another is that of the formulation and reflection of ideas, concepts, and attitudes. A good poet is like a sensitive instrument which responds to the slightest impulse of the time and to life in general. Each individual note struck can be detected in itself, but, in the general effect, it is subordinated usually in a totalitarian scheme. The greatest poets of all nations react to changes of all sorts, but there is, nevertheless, a dominant strain that runs through their thoughts and feelings on the problems of life and death. This strain may be one of doubt, hope, despair, or belief; but whatever its nature, it takes precedence over the remaining conflicting notions.

In this regard, Heinrich Heine remains a unique exception. There are few writers, indeed, that are more consistently inconsistent than the great German poet and prose master. No single idea, philosophy, or concept, can we fix upon as Heine's own, for he runs the gamut of all thoughts and feelings and does not linger long enough in any attitude for us to determine definitely his position. On the two great problems of his day, religion and politics in the broad sense of the terms, his is a stand of paradoxical indefinite definiteness. For us, this is, to be sure, unfortunate, for it excludes nearly entirely the possibility of saying with confident authority that this or that idea is derived directly from Heine.

In the sphere of religion alone, for example, Heine embraced nearly every creed, at one time or another, and was in every instance both true and false to each concept. Beginning with Judaism, which he both revered and mocked, he bought his entrance into European circles of culture by conversion to Christianity. Although his conversion was one primarily of mere expediency, Heine found in his newly acquired religion certain advantages over that of his fathers—advantages which he later repudiated. From a religion of fundamental democratic principles, Christianity became later in his mind a code of repression consecrating injustice and intolerance. Christ he admired and respected as the symbol of freedom and equality; yet he mocked and ridiculed Him and disdained scornfully the New Testament "weil es noch nicht ganz klar geworden sei."

Simultaneously with his interest in Christianity, the Hegelian philosophy began to take hold of Heinrich Heine, in all probability because the Hegelian idea that the individual on earth was actually God flattered Heine's vanity. Later, when he realized that "the thinnest soup of Christian charity must be more life-giving than the grey mass of cobwebs of Hegelian dialectics," he dropped the study of Hegel for that of the eminent social philosopher, Saint-Simon. In 1831 Heine was not in Paris twenty-four hours before he affiliated himself with the branch of the Saint-Simonian religion headed by Enfantin. His *Zur Geschichte der Religion und Philosophie in Deutschland* attests his fervent belief in the newly organized cult, but already in *Lutetia* he assumed an ironical attitude and spoke of it in a far from complimentary tone as a *pantheistische Genussreligion*.

Moving through Pantheism, through Deism ("die Reli-

Major Influence

gion für Knechte, für Kinder, für Genfer, für Uhrmacher"), through Atheism, Heine came to his mattress-grave in the realization that all had failed him. Even the Hellenism of which he had boasted so strongly seemed of little significance. From the mattress-grave came the confession:

... I am no longer a divine biped; I am no longer the "freest German since Goethe," as Ruge called me in more healthy days; I am no longer the Great Heathen No. II, whom one compared with the vine-wreathed Dionysius, while one granted my colleague, No. I, the title of grand-ducal, Weimarian Jupiter; I am no longer a joyous, somewhat big-paunched Hellene who smiled down upon melancholy Nazarenes—I am now only a poor, death-sick Jew, a distorted picture of grief, an unhappy man.[1]

The dying Heine made his peace with man and God, and in his last days returned again to the belief in a personal God—the God of Israel—even though he condemned the Jews as "an accursed race who came from Egypt, the land of crocodiles and priestcraft, and brought with them, besides certain skin-diseases and the vessels of gold and silver that they stole, a so-called positive religion and a so-called church."[2] In his will, Heine rejected the last rites of all creeds, blamed the spirit of his age for his transgressions, and declared in conclusion, "I die believing in the One and Eternal God, Creator of the world, whose mercy I entreat for my immortal soul."[3] In the course of his religious vacillation, Heine never completely abandoned the old or adopted the new. With each change to a new creed clung the vestiges of the old. He himself has said, "On ne change pas de religion. On en quitte une qu'on n'a plus pour une autre qu'on n'aura jamais. Je suis *baptisé* mais je ne suis pas converti."[4]

In politics, in the broad sense of the word, Heine is equally vacillating and equally difficult to fathom. Lichtenberger has

1. Wood, *Heine as a Critic of His Own Works*, p. 152.
2. Monahan, *Heinrich Heine*, p. 127.
3. Embden, *The Family Life of Heinrich Heine*, pp. 355-356.
4. Alexandre Weill, *Souvenirs Intimes de Henri Heine*, p. 17.

traced admirably the stages of the poet's political and social ideas. Heine at first appeared as a narrow, romantic Germanomaniac who became in 1821 a liberal, in 1826 a radical, in 1828 a conservative, in 1831 a Saint-Simonian, in the middle period of his life a cosmopolitan, in 1842 a violent and truculent reactionary, and in 1845 a disillusioned pessimist.[5]

By his enemies, the German poet was accused throughout his life of having deserted his fatherland and of espousing the cause of the French. This, Heine strongly repudiated, saying, "It would be both mad and ridiculous for me to say about myself, 'I am a German poet, and I am also a naturalized Frenchman.' I should appear to be something horrible, like those freaks with two heads exhibited at side-shows. . . . When the stone-mason carves the inscription on my last refuge he will not be contradicted when he incises these words: 'Here lies a German poet.' "[6] By his principles, his birth, and his genius, Heine was the enemy of the social and political state; but there is no doubt but that he revered the spiritual Germany with its resplendent history, its traditions, and its romantic legends.

Circumstances have forced the Jew to become a cosmopolite and subsequently an apostle of freedom; and if there is any one consistent trait in Heine, it is his love for freedom, for liberty. It is the one thing for which Heine fought—the one thing that entitles him to be numbered among the soldiers in the liberation war of humanity. And yet, even in his battle for freedom, which he undoubtedly cherished, there occurs the vacillation and indecisiveness so typical of him. He was not to be trusted, for he was not a consistent fighter. Börne accused him of admitting, "er würde gegen seine Überzeugung ganz so gut schreiben wie mit ihr."[7] Friedrich Kummer states the matter succinctly:

---

5. J. A. Hess, *Heine's Views on German Traits of Character*, pp. 5-6.
6. Louis Untermeyer, *Heinrich Heine: Paradox and Poet*, p. 329.
7. Hess, *op. cit.*, p. 148.

Man weiss bei Heine, dem Virtuosen, nie, wo man ihm trauen darf und wo nicht . . . er kämpfte oft nicht um der Sache willen, sondern mehr aus der Freude am Kampf, am Klirren und Schwirren der blitzenden Degen, er kämpfte oft mehr um des Sieges seiner Eitelkeit, mehr um des erhöhten Gefühls seiner Persönlichkeit als um der reinen Sache willen. . . . Ihn reisst, sobald ihn die Kampflust ergreift, der Wunsch, den Gegner zu treffen, besinnungslos hin.[8]

In Frau Hindermann's dame-school, Heine was the only boy in a class of girls. Sitting in front of the class which she ruled with an iron hand and a convenient birch rod, Frau Hindermann herself used to mete out punishment for offenders in the school. Carrying out his first vendetta, Heine once filled her snuffbox with sand; and when asked why he did such a thing, he replied in words that were to become his motto in all his later controversies: "Because I hate you."[9]

In stylistic matters, Heine's dominant notes are far more easily discernible and are, for the most part, consistent throughout his work. James Alburn Chiles, in his thesis, *Über den Gebrauch des Beiwortes in Heines Gedichten,* and Artur Weckmüller, in *Heines Stil,* have both given excellent analyses of the stylistic characteristics of Heine's poetry. Without repeating, unnecessarily, details, examples, and explanations which are treated fully and accurately in these two works, the characteristics themselves might be stated briefly: repetition of epithets, symmetry and parallelism of structure, antithetical construction of verse and stanzas, use of the device of contrast, use of epizeuxis and polysyndeton, and peculiarities of rhythm and form.

"In der Kunst," said Heine, "ist die Form alles, der Stoff gilt nichts." This formula he followed assiduously throughout his life. He was a master craftsman and wrote with painstaking care—or as one author has put it, "with a sieve in his ear, which will not let anything bad pass."[10] Heine himself wrote, "Ich selbst bin wirklich immer sehr gewissenhaft im

---

8. *Ibid.,* p. 149.
9. Marcuse, *op. cit.,* p. 29.   10. Marcuse, *op. cit.,* p. 70.

Arbeiten gewesen, ich habe gearbeitet, ordentlich gearbeitet an meinen Versen."[11] Heine employs many forms in his poetry which, while they show careful and brilliant execution, are unfortunately not entirely original with him. He is a master of the technique of the folk-song, but Heine's manner of treatment is essentially that of his predecessors, Müller and Tieck.

It is fundamentally in Heine's *Weltschmerz*, his treatment of love, his passion for the sea, his epigrammatic style, his use of *Stimmungsbrechung* and ironic antithesis, and in the flavor and aroma and mood of his shorter lyrics that we find the chief sources of his influence in English poetry. Heine is no philosopher, no prophet, no teacher, and no interpreter; he is a singer of beautiful songs, and it is as such—as a gifted singer, as a poet of mood and sentiment—that he exercises the greatest influence.

James Thomson (1834-1882).—If it is impossible to call James Thomson ("B. V.") an imitator of any previous writer, as is undoubtedly true (for Thomson is essentially an original poet with a style of his very own, and his obstinate individuality of thought assures his independence), it can nonetheless be said in great truth that his literary development can be traced step by step in the light of the influences shed upon his work by Matthew Arnold, DeQuincey, the earlier Thomson, Shelley, Leopardi, Dante, Novalis, and Heine. Among the English writers, Shelley, perhaps, plays the greatest rôle in the development of Thomson as a poet. The chief influences upon the great pessimist, however, are fundamentally the Italian and German rather than the English.

Next to Dante and Leopardi, Thomson shows greatest kinship to Heinrich Heine, of whom he wrote in words oddly appropriate and applicable to himself:

In all moods, tender, imaginative, fantastic, humorous, ironical, cynical; in anguish and horror, in weariness and revulsion, longing backward to enjoyment, and longing forward to painless rest; through the doleful

---

11. Chiles, *op. cit.*, p. 3.

days, and the dreadful immeasurable sleepless nights, this intense and luminous spirit was enchained and constrained to look down into the vast black void which undermines our seemingly solid existence. . . . And the power of the spell on him, as the power of his spell on us, is increased by the fact that he, thus in Death-in-Life brooding on Death and Life, was no ascetic spiritualist, no self-torturing eremite or hypochondriac monk, but by nature a joyous heathen of richest blood, a Greek, a Persian, as he often proudly proclaimed, a lusty lover of this world and life, an enthusiastic apostle of the rehabilitation of the flesh.[12]

As Heine's pieces, the poems of James Thomson indicate the author's ability to enjoy the fullness and richness of life despite the dominant note of pessimism which runs throughout. As Heine, Thomson shows a fondness for the oriental, and particularly for the oriental love of repose. In politics, Thomson reveals himself as a soldier in the liberation war of humanity and as a champion of the oppressed. But here the generalizations cease, for Thomson does not remain the thoroughly joyous heathen; he is fundamentally no apostle of orientalism; he becomes a weary, battle-scarred veteran in his fight for progress and justice, and turns from them as from vain illusions; and with a shrug of the shoulders he dismisses the ideals of art, literature, and human progress with the scorn of the utter disbeliever.

Generalities of comparison wane, but specific instances of likeness and influence remain still constant. This is true in Thomson's wide use of Heine's favorite figures—the rose, the wine-cup, fragrant breezes, the nightingale, the sea, the sky, and still others. It is true in such an isolated case as that of *Weddah and Om-El-Bonain,* which depicts with Heine's *Der Asra* "the people who die when they love." Both works, incidentally, are supposedly from the same original source, although Thomson knew Heine's poem. A similarity, too, is evident to some extent in satirical approach. The ridicule of *The Naked Goddess* is, in a general fashion, in Heine's manner. Unquestionably in Heine's manner are both the satire and

12. H. S. Salt, *The Life of James Thomson,* p. 153.

philosophy of "L'Ancien Régime" which declares love, justice, truth and loyalty unfit gifts for the King, and which would suggest, as appropriate offerings, the courtier's servility, the soldier's brutal war, the harlot's flesh and lust, and the priest's scheming and lies.

The healthy poet of the poem "Art" with its *Lebenslust*, with its declaration that if the artist were in a position to make passionate love to his beautiful subject, there would be little time indeed wasted upon artistic creation, is the replica of the Great Heathen No. II, the German poet in whose verse *niedrige Minne* plays no small part. "The poor sick Jew" on his mattress-grave scribbling painfully the *Letzte Gedichte* is more than a little akin to the sleepless hypochondriac of that poignant bit of personal suffering, "Insomnia," and of the gloomy "opium poem," *The City of Dreadful Night*. Thomson's declaration that life is but a tortured Death-in-Life is the repetition of a term he derived from Heine's *Geständnisse*.

Vane's Story shows to the greatest extent the influence of Heine upon James Thomson. In a general sort of statement, William Maccall, in his essay *A Nirvana Trilogy*, once said: "Leopardi and Heine are the two men with whom James Thomson acknowledged most of his spiritual kindredness. His conscious or unconscious brotherhood with Leopardi exalted Thomson, that with Heine dragged him down."[13] In the same spirit, Arthur Lyttleton, in speaking of the Heinesque bitterness and irony interposed in *Vane's Story*, declares more specifically that the rather lengthy English poem "is almost utterly defaced by the incongruous mixture of grave and gay, the gay being both bitter and vulgar."[14] That Thomson is but following the model of Heine in injecting into the poem unexpected and, perhaps, unwarranted bits of irony is an acknowledged fact. That the poem is undoubtedly marred by the incongruity and impropriety of such passages is equally true. However, it is

---

13. Josefine Weissel, *James Thomson der Jüngere*, p. 146.
14. A. T. Lyttleton, *Modern Poets of Faith, Doubt and Paganism and Other Essays*, p. 241.

Major Influence

all too often overlooked that it is this very blemish which gives the English poem (as it gives the poems of Heine) distinctiveness.

When the speaker in *Vane's Story* tells the rather vague Mr. Brown that the female vision that has accompanied him to the ball is a creature from a foreign land, Mr. Brown is determined to speak to her and, in so doing, wishes to employ French, feeling that of all tongues, the vision will surely understand that one. There follows the passage:

> Ah yes; your French is doubtless good,
> And French we know is understood
> By polished people everywhere;
> But then her land, though rich and fair,
> Lies far beyond the continents
> Of civilized accomplishments;
> And she could sooner learn to speak
> Persian or Sanskrit, Norse or Greek,
> Than this delightful brilliant witty
> Tongue of delightful Paris city,
> ("The devil's paradise, the hell
> Of angels,"—Heine loved it well!)[15]

The last two lines are taken directly from the *Babylonische Sorgen* in Heine's *Letzte Gedichte,* and the entire passage in Thomson is but an adaptation from the following lines in *Babylonische Sorgen:*

> Glaub mir, mein Kind, mein Weib, Mathilde,
> Nicht so gefährlich ist das wilde
> Erzürnte Meer und der trotzige Wald,
> Als unser jetziger Aufenthalt!
> Wie schrecklich auch der Wolf und der Geier,
> Haifische und sonstige Menschengeheuer:
> Viel grimmere, schlimmere Bestien enthält
> Das singende, springende, schöne Paris,
> *Die Hölle der Engel, der Teufel Paradies—*
> Dass ich dich hier verlassen soll,
> Das macht mich verrückt, das macht mich toll!

15. James Thomson, *Poetical Works,* I, 38.

The classic illustration of Heine's influence upon James Thomson occurs in the recital by the vision in *Vane's Story* of the well-known "Ich bin die Prinzessin Ilse." The instance occurs just after the initial appearance of the vision, and after the speaker has persuaded her to accompany him to the ball that night. While the speaker dresses, he entreats the vision to sing to him. Glancing about abstractedly in attempting to think of an appropriate song, his eye falls upon a copy of Heine:

> What book is this I held before,
> The gloaming glooming more and more,
> Eyes dreamed and hand drooped on the floor?
> The *Lieder*—Heine's—what we want!
> A lay of Heine's you shall chant,
> Our poor Saint Heinrich! for he was
> A saint here of the loftiest class,
> By martyrdom more dreadly solemn
> Than that of Simeon on the column.
> God put him to the torture; seven
> Long years beneath unpitying heaven,
> The body dead, the man at strife
> With all the common cares of life:
> A living Voice intense and brave
> Issuing from a mattress-grave.
> At length the cruel agony wrung
> *Confessions* from that haughty tongue;
> Confessions of the strangest, more
> Than ever God had bargained for;
> With prayers and penitential psalms
> That gave the angels grinning qualms,
> With jests when sharp pangs cut too deep
> They made the very devils weep.

The speaker then directs the vision to "sing that song of love and ruth the Princess Ilse sang his youth." There follows the German poem from *Die Harzreise* with the English translation sung to a tune of mild Bishop Heber. The blending of the pagan with the sacred is, in itself, highly reminiscent of Heine's manner, and Thomson quite appropriately exclaims:

> Oh what a quaintly coupled pair
> The poem and the music were!
> The Sunday School's old simple air,
> The heathen verses rich and rare!

The poem is quite obviously spoiled somewhat by Heinesque grossness, and Thomson admits as much, but excuses the fault, with Heine's example, in the Epilogue:

> Grossness here indeed is regnant.
> But it is the grossness pregnant;
> Heine growled it, ending thus
> His wild *Book of Lazarus*.

Shelley is undoubtedly Thomson's model in the first part of *Vane's Story*, but Heine dominates completely the second; and it must be admitted that *Die Prinzessin Ilse* fits in perfectly with its fabulous, heathen character.

Thomson's devotion to Heine has led him, too, to inject unexpected bits of humor and irony in the two idylls *Sunday at Hampstead* and *Sunday Up the River*. In these two idylls, says Arthur Lyttleton:

> ... Thomson has spoilt a very original and attractive subject by the most commonplace and almost coarse jocularity. He would retort, perhaps, that as a democratic poet he writes of the people for the people, and that if we do not like his Cockney merriment we need not read a Cockney poet. But it is because Thomson is a poet with a poet's delicacy and loftiness, that we protest against the intrusion of "Jameson's Irish Whiskey," with jocular laudations which are not comic but nauseous, into a poem which in many parts is a revelation of the pure and bright side of many a hard-worked life.[16]

There is no doubt but that Thomson is attempting again to conjure with the style and voice of Heine, and succeeds so well that he reaps the same harvest of criticism which fell to Heine's lot!

The two idylls, however, bear closer similarity to the poetry of Heine than that of gross humor and satire. The lightness, grace, brevity, whimsical humor, and melody of

---

16. *Op. cit.*, pp. 241-242.

many of the lyrics of the two poems possess the charm and delightfulness of Heine's measures. The ninth lyric of *Sunday Up the River*, for example, is a little jewel; the twelfth is greatly suggestive of Heine in a general fashion; and the fourteenth is a direct adaptation of "Mit deinen blauen Augen":

> Mit deinen blauen Augen
> Siehst du mich lieblich an;
> Da ward mir so träumend zu Sinne
> Dass ich nicht sprechen kann.
>
> An deine blauen Augen
> Gedenk' ich allerwärts;—
> Ein Meer von blauen Gedanken
> Ergiesst sich über mein Herz.
>
> Those azure, azure eyes
> Gaze on me with their love;
> And I am lost in a dream,
> And cannot speak or move.
>
> Those azure, azure eyes
> Stay with me when we part;
> A sea of azure thoughts
> Overfloods my heart.

Thomson, in his shorter lyrics, is not often given to employing the *moralische Ohrfeige*, but in "Once in a Saintly Passion" is a splendid example of Heine's revulsion of mood:

> Once in a saintly passion
> I cried with desperate grief,
> "O Lord, my heart is black with guile,
> Of sinners I am chief."
> Then stopped my guardian angel
> And whispered from behind,
> "Vanity, my little man,
> You're nothing of the kind."[17]

William Ernest Henley (1849-1903).—Among Victorian poets, William E. Henley shares with James Thomson the

17. *Poems*, p. 121.

honor of being closest to Heinrich Heine. The German poet's influence is seen clearly in both the form and mood of Henley's poetry. The stanzaic form and the use of broken rhythm in the poetry of Henley are adopted directly from the verse of Heine. Like Heine, too, Henley treats the higher and lower aspects of love, and the sea plays a rôle in his work similar to that which it plays in the magnificent sea-poetry of Heine. Few poets of any clime or period have been more successful in paralleling the superb ability of the German song writer in depicting mood in shorter lyric poems. With equal facility, Henley is able to imitate Heine in lyric verse, in simple ballad structure, and in the tempestuous enthusiasm of sentiment.

Henley undoubtedly had an important influence on the employment of free verse forms, and in his use of them indicated the path that later poetry was to traverse. Many of the poems in his collection *In Hospital* are written in the short, irregular stanzaic and verse forms for which we must go to Heine for the original models. The *Song of the Sword*, too, is written in an adaptation of the broken, irregular verse form of Heine. In *London Voluntaries*, Heine again appears to have been the model for Henley's verses. Henley's effects in the collection are paralleled by the effects gained by Heine in the *Nordsee* poems in the *Buch der Lieder*. Not only does Henley make wide use of Heine's *freier Rhythmus*, but the English author also employs continuously Heine's regular stanza pattern without rhyme, as in *"Casualty"*:

> As with varnish sea and glistening
> Dripped his hair: his feet looked rigid;
> Raised, he settled stiffly sideways:
> You could see his hurts were spinal.

"This is the verse," says B. Ifor Evans, "of the Spanish ballads and folk-songs, with the modification that they are governed by a liberal conception of assonance, in place of Henley's abandonment of rhyme." The Spanish form was imitated by Heine in his *Romanzero*, and Henley quite probably adopted it from that source. "Heine would thus give a model for a form which would have the appearance of freedom without necessitating a complete break with tradition. Henley adds the novelty of brutal, unlovely themes, which seem to fit with the bare rhymeless verse."[18]

In the intricacies of poetic design, Henley also is deeply indebted to Heine. The English poet, obviously following Heine, makes large use of polysyndeton as, for example, in the first stanza of "The Pretty Washermaiden":

> The pretty washermaiden
> She washes on always!
> And as she rubs, and as she wrings,
> Her shapely body sways and springs
> As if to burst her stays.

Equally large use is made of another of Heine's favorite devices, epizeuxis, as is seen, for example, in "gentle and good and fair and kind" (*Echoes*, No. XIII), or "languishing, glorying, glowing" (*Hawthorn and Lavender*, No. XXVII). The same is true in the use of asyndeton and the repetition of synonyms for *Gefühlssteigerung*, as in "She bruised, she wrung, she tortured" (*Echoes*, No. XXXVI). Scores of other examples might easily be given.

Henley likewise follows Heine closely in his use of parallelism, contrast, and symmetry. In the ninth song in *Echoes*, for example, is a typically Heinesque instance of clever parallelism and contrast in the pictures of life and death:

> Madam Life's a piece in bloom
> Death goes dogging everywhere:
> She's the tenant of the room,
> He's the ruffian on the stair.
>
> You shall see her as a friend,
> You shall bilk him once and twice;
> But he'll trap you in the end,
> And he'll stick you for her price.

---

18. Evans, *English Poetry in the Later Nineteenth Century*, p. 267.

Major Influence 213

> With his kneebones at your chest,
> And his knuckles in your throat,
> You would reason—plead—protest!
> Clutching at her petticoat.
>
> But she's heard it all before,
> Well she knows you've had your fun,
> Gingerly she gains the door,
> And your little job is done.[19]

One of the finest examples of the Heinesque type of contrast in the English language is found in the first two stanzas of the "Envoy" to *Hawthorn and Lavender*, which, incidentally, is, as a whole, a superb illustration of typical Heinesque form and mood:

> My songs were once of the sunrise:
> They shouted it over the bar;
> First-footing the dawns, they flourished,
> And flamed with the morning star.
>
> My songs are now of the sunset:
> Their brows are touched with light,
> But their feet are lost in the shadows
> And wet with the dews of night.
>
> Yet for the joy in their making
> Take them O fond and true,
> And for his sake who made them
> Let them be dear to you.[20]

Henley shows clear derivations from the *Buch der Lieder* in general, and the *Lyrisches Intermezzo* in particular, in his many delightful parallels of Heine's mood. Especially is this true in the graceful short lyrics of *Echoes* and *Hawthorn and Lavender*. The thirteenth and eighteenth lyrics from the former collection together with the twenty-seventh from the latter are given as splendid examples of the Heinesque mood expressed in Heinesque fashion:

---

19. *Poems*, p. 87. All selections and extracts of Henley's poetry are from William E. Henley, *Poems*, reprinted by permission of the Macmillan Company, publishers.
20. *Ibid.*, p. 153.

ECHOES

XIII

Bring her again, O western wind,
Over the western sea:
Gentle and good and fair and kind,
Bring her again to me!

Not that her fancy holds me dear,
Not that a hope may be:
Only that I may know her near,
Wind of the western sea.[21]

XVIII

The nightingale has a lyre of gold,
The lark's is a clarion call,
And the blackbird plays but a boxwood flute,
But I love him best of all.

For his song is all of the joy of life,
And we in the mad, spring weather,
We two have listened till he sang
Our hearts and lips together.[22]

HAWTHORN AND LAVENDER

XXVII

It was a bowl of roses:
There in the light they lay,
Languishing, glorying, glowing
Their life away.

And the soul of them rose like a presence,
Into me crept and grew,
And filled me with something—someone—
O, was it you?[23]

What poems could be more truly Heinesque in their monosyllabic simplicity, in naïve expressiveness, in the simple *Volkslied* measure, in crystalline clearness, in grace, aroma, imagery, spontaneity, and in wonderful singing quality? To

---

21. *Ibid.*, p. 89.
22. *Ibid.*, p. 92.
23. *Ibid.*, pp. 175-176.

Major Influence

these lyrics might be added the thirtieth song in *Echoes* and the exquisite "O, gather me the rose, the rose" in which, in addition to the elusive Heinesque quality, is the use of the familiar Heinesque *Wiederholung und Häufung,* as in the final stanza:

>The myrtle and the rose, the rose
>The sunshine and the swallow,
>The dream that comes, the wish that goes,
>The memories that follow![24]

In all appear Heine's favorite figures and devices—the rose, the nightingale, sunshine, spring, song, the coupling of a background of nature with an undercurrent of love.

Henley's treatment of love, too, is quite similar to that of Heine. Both treat *höhere Liebe* and *niedrige Minne* although Henley's emphasis upon the latter is far below that of his German model. In the seventh lyric of *Echoes* appears the familiar Heinesque coupling of love and death so often seen in the pieces of the *Buch der Lieder.* Number sixteen in *Echoes* is done in Heine's best manner, in the treatment of *höhere Liebe:*

>While the west is paling
>Starshine is begun.
>While the dusk is failing
>Glimmers up the sun.
>
>So, till darkness cover
>Life's retreating gleam,
>Lover follows lover,
>Dream succeeds to dream.
>
>Stoop to my endeavour,
>O my love, and be
>Only and forever
>Sun and stars to me.[25]

In the songs descriptive of *niedrige Minne,* Heine's adjectives portraying the physical side appear in far greater abun-

24. *Ibid.,* p. 83. 25. *Ibid.,* p. 91.

dance than elsewhere. The same is true in the case of Henley, as is readily seen in "The Pretty Washermaiden":

> The pretty washermaiden,
> She washes on always!
> And as she rubs, and as she wrings,
> Her shapely body sways and swings
> As if to burst her stays.
>
> Her cheek is rich and shining
> And brown as any egg.
> And, when she dives into her tub
> To duck the linen she's to scrub,
> She shows the neatest leg!
>
> Her round arms white with lather,
> Her elbows fresh and red,
> Her mouth the rosiest of buds,
> Who would not risk a shower of suds
> To kiss her dainty head?[26]

The poem, however, in which Henley most nearly approaches Heine's attitude toward love is the thirty-seventh section of *Echoes*, which, in its tinge of melancholy, its *Schmerz*, and its portrayal of unrequited love, bears close resemblance to the *Junge Leiden* of Heine's early years:

> I gave my heart to a woman—
> I gave it to her, branch and root,
> She bruised, she wrung, she tortured,
> She cast it under foot.
>
> Under her feet she cast it,
> She trampled it where it fell,
> She broke it all to pieces,
> And each was a clot of hell.
>
> There in the rain and the sunshine
> They lay and smouldered along;
> And each, when again she viewed them
> Had turned to a living song.[27]

26. *Ibid.*, pp. 269-270.   27. *Ibid.*, p. 106.

The closing thought is strangely reminiscent of the opening one in "Aus meinen grossen Schmerzen Mach' ich die kleinen Lieder" from the *Lyrisches Intermezzo*.

In one other respect Henley shows marked kinship with Heine—in his love and treatment of the sea. As does Heine, Henley regards the sea as symbolic of human emotions, and couples with the surging main the personal element, as in these lyrics:

ECHOES

X

The sea is full of surging foam,
The sky of driving cloud;
My restless thoughts among them roam. . . .
The night is dark and loud.

Where are the hours that came to me
So beautiful and bright?
A wild wind shakes the wilder sea. . . .
O, dark and loud's the night![28]

XX

The surges gushed and sounded,
The blue was the blue of June,
And low above the brightening east
Floated a shred of moon.

The woods were black and solemn,
The night winds large and free,
And in your thought a blessing seemed
To fall on land and sea.[29]

XXVII

She sauntered by the swinging seas,
A jewel glittered at her ear,
And, teasing her along, the breeze
Brought many a rounded grace more near.

So passing, one with waves and beam,
She left for memory to caress
A laughing thought, a golden gleam,
A hint of hidden loveliness.[30]

28. *Ibid.*, p. 88.   29. *Ibid.*, p. 93.   30. *Ibid.*, p. 98.

The same characteristic is evident in the seventeenth lyric from *Echoes*, with an additional Heinesque element added in the *Weltschmerz* of the concluding lines:

> While children romp in the surges,
> And sweethearts wander free,
> And the Firth as with laughter dimples. . . .
> I would it were deep over me![31]

Henry Baerlein (b. 1875).—Among our present-day English writers, the one that shows the most unmistakable and complete influence of Heinrich Heine is Henry Philip Bernard Baerlein, who has also written a very creditable biography of the German poet. In no other collection of English poems are there found so many traces and reminiscences of the great German poet as in Baerlein's slender volume, *Windrush and Evenlode.* Practically every poem is written in the simple, unaffected style so thoroughly cultivated by Heine, and the volume attests, in addition, the author's rare ability of simulating the style, mannerisms, subject matter, and moods of the German lyricist. It is the Heine of the *Lyrisches Intermezzo* that so thoroughly invades the work of Henry Baerlein—the mocking, ironical, playful Heine, the poet of melancholy and unrequited love, the victim of *Weltschmerz*, the creator of unforgettable crystalline gems.

For a few of the poems of Henry Baerlein, we can readily find the individual sources in Heine; for the majority, however, we are forced to consider the "total" Heine as the springs from which Baerlein's poems arise. Among those poems which may be traced to original sources is the piece called "You Are the White of April," the first stanza of which parallels that of the familiar "Du bist wie eine Blume":

> You are the white of April
> Which on the branch is laid.
> I gaze at you, my darling,
> And I am sore afraid.

---

31. *Ibid.,* p. 92.

Major Influence

> Du bist wie eine Blume,
> So hold und schön und rein;
> Ich schau' dich an, und Wehmut
> Schleicht mir ins Herz hinein.

Another piece based upon an equally famous poem, "Ein Fichtenbaum steht einsam," is the little poem called "The Lovers":

> A lonely peak is brooding
> In the wild, northern day,
> What time his jagged fingers
> Each passing cloud do slay.
>
> He knows that in the southland
> A slender palm tree sighs,
> So wearily she gazes
> Into the burnished skies.
>
> And lo! he stands entreating
> The clouds that on their flight
> They will with messages of love
> Upon the palm alight.

"A Solitary Pool" would seem also to have found its inspiration in the same German lyric:

> A solitary pool
> Sleeps on the mountain-side
> And many times the peering sun
> Says that she must have died.
>
> But as the purple hours
> Fold her in their embrace
> A ripple wrought of silver
> Trembles upon her face.
>
> For so in sleep she dreameth
> Of what she loves the best,
> How once a star came singing,
> Into her singing breast.

While Henry Baerlein's ballad "The Grand Armée" differs widely in content from Heine's immortal *Die Grenadiere,* the English ballad may very likely have been suggested by that of Heine with which Baerlein was undoubtedly familiar. There exists, however, no doubt as to the source of "An Old Story," for, with the exception of a few minor changes, the theme set forth here is unmistakably that of "Ein Jüngling liebt ein Mädchen":

> A young man loved a maiden
> With such a humble grace
> That he could never trust himself
> To look her in the face.
>
> Another boy came laughing
> At either land or sea,
> And when his eye fell on her eye
> 'Twas laughing—so was she.
>
> No doubt that is a story
> As old as are the hills,
> Whom lover March is making young
> With kiss of daffodils.

Equally apparent is the fact that Heine's "Wenn zwei von einander scheiden" is nearly perfectly reproduced in "When Two Friends Leave Each Other":

> When two friends leave each other
> They deepen all the pain
> By carefully arranging
> How they shall meet again.
>
> And when that hour of parting
> Arrives for me and you,
> Shall we not have, my dearest,
> Far better things to do?

In matters of structure, the poems of Henry Baerlein bear close affinity to those of his German predecessor. Like Heine, Baerlein is a master of such devices as parallelism, contrast, repetition, antithesis, symmetry, *Gefühlssteigerung* and *freier Rhythmus*. In such songs as "Since All Things Pass Away," "Those Who Live," "Farewell," and "A Night Piece," Baerlein adopts the short-lined irregular stanzaic form employed as aptly by Heine in the *Nordsee* cycles. For the condensation of thought found in "O Daughter of the Twilight" and "Shall I Regret the Day," we must seek in Heine the equal and prototype. Two very fine instances of the Heinesque devices of parallelism, contrast, repetition, and symmetry are to be found in the poems "The Brothers" and "My Lady," both of which, incidentally, close after the manner of Heine on a pathetic and personal note.

It would be a tedious and lengthy task to quote the many poems of Henry Baerlein which owe to Heine their stylistic traits. Three examples alone are cited as representative of Baerlein's debt to Heine in the matter of structure. The first, "A Night Piece," with its typically Heinesque close, employs the monosyllabic simplicity and irregular form characteristic of Heine's verse:

> We rode along the sand
> In the night—
> I felt a hand upon my hand
> Alight.
>
> Not any single word
> The silence broke,
> And what I heard
> The maiden's finger spoke.
>
> The light you fear, I said,
> Upon the gloomy, rolling sea—
> 'Tis love. . . . Ah yes, the tear, she said
> Which God has wept for you and me.

The remaining two examples illustrate the dexterity with which Baerlein handles the devices of parallelism and contrast. In "If," not only is parallelism used in Heine's manner, but the figures used in the structural device are among Heine's favorites; the concluding stanza with its light humor is typical of Heine:

> If I were a swallow
> That breaks along the sky,
> Fair lands, fair lakes and unheeding—
> I know where I should fly.
>
> Were I the star prevailing
> In beauty overall,
> Filled with a radiant passion—
> I know where I should fall.
>
> And if I were a lover
> And my heart were sore,
> I'd meet with star and swallow
> Outside a certain door.
>
> If I looked from the window,
> Maiden, if I were you,
> No verses would be written
> On what I ought to do.

In "Hyacinth Gazed in the Waters" is found one of the finest examples in English of Heine's use of parallelism and contrast. The poem, too, in its self-mockery, is in Heine's best tradition.

> Hyacinth gazed in the waters
> Which reflected back so clearly
> That his image gave him joy
> And he loved it very much.
>
> In that inkpot am I gazing
> And I see a thousand verses
> And a grim nose in the blackness
> And I love them very little.

One of the few poems of Henry Baerlein modeled on the Heine of the *Junge Leiden* is "Beyond the Borderland of Sleep," which, in its use of the reverie motif, its symbols, its simplicity, and its personal element, is highly reminiscent of the youthful song-writer:

> Beyond the borderland of sleep
> She flies to me, she flies to me
> And what the lips imprisoned keep
> Is murmured by her eyes to me.

> They fade—alas! the dream is done,
> The dream which had no guile for me,
> And now the moon and stars and sun
> Are shadows of her smile for me.

Few English poets have dared to ridicule the sacred, to satirize the Church in any of its forms in the mocking voice of the cynical Heine so disliked by the "respectable" Englishman of the past century. In one poem, "The Reward," Henry Baerlein very closely approaches the attitude of the archmocker in this regard:

> So you cannot tell the lady
> What's in your devoted heart,
> As in fear of such a passion
> She would hastily depart.
>
> I have heard of other people
> Who the naked truth abhorred,
> And apparently the draping
> Has not been its own reward.
>
> In Jerusalem a tourist
> May, with moderate research
> Find the cave of Ananias
> Now the new Franciscan Church.

In poems too numerous to mention, Henry Baerlein shows himself a master of Heine's use of revulsion of mood or *Stimmungsbrechung*. In the following quatrain is a splendid example of Heinesque terseness as well as the use of the surprising close:

> "There is no God," a sporting man averred.
> "By God there is," another one replied.
> It would have been delightful but a bird
> Rose and they shot and both of them were wide.

In no other wise is Henry Baerlein so completely akin to Heine as in the tone and mood of his verse. The English writer has managed to capture with an unusual degree of success the quiet, unaffected grace and simplictiy of Heine coupled with that author's lightness of touch and sheer singing quality, in such lyrics as "Maid of the Farm of Heather," "Eugenics," "Duet," "Finisterre," "A Sad Song," "The Bride of the World," and "Once Upon a Time." Three short poems which might have come from the pen of Heine himself, are given here as examples of Baerlein's mastery of the naïvety, crystal-line clearness, and flavor of his German model. Each of the pieces concludes on that note of *Schmerz* which rounded off the vast majority of Heine's songs.

Those Little Feet Have Passed

Those little feet have passed
Away for evermore,
Now they are loitering
Upon a pallid shore.

Ah, no, they tread, they tread
Upon this heart of me—
I did not know that little feet
Could fall so heavily.

The Golden Chambers of My Heart

The golden chambers of my heart
Took every pilgrim from the road,
Thus Hope would enter—and depart
With sorry thanks for his abode.

Sometimes I hear those artful hands
Come knocking softly at the door,
But now a solemn porter stands
Where locks were all-unknown before.

The Flower-Folk Which in the Garden Play

The flower-folk which in the garden play
Have never laughed as they laugh today—
O love, my love, but they cannot see
What of laughter there is in me.

In the delicacy of his humor, his whimsicality, his glorification of the commonplace, Baerlein, too, reveals himself as a close student of Heine, as is evidenced by such poems as "I

Love You Like the Morning Star," "Limitations," "Retribution," "Tragedy," "Starlight and Lamplight in Sofia," "Very French," and "La Bonne Cuisinière." The first-named, primarily because of its brevity, is cited here as an instance of Baerlein's lightness of touch in humor:

> I love you like the morning star
> Which trembles in the sky,
> And so the shepherd of the dawn
> Is joyful, so am I.
>
> But if you disregarded
> My knocking at the door
> A little while,—I fancy
> That I would love you more.

In the incongruous mixture, too, of humor and pathos, of the grave and the gay, there is a close resemblance between Baerlein and Heine. The two pieces, "There Was a Wild-Rose Blossom" and "Nothing," are done in the typically Heinesque manner:

> THERE WAS A WILD-ROSE BLOSSOM
>
> There was a wild-rose blossom,
> That hung her fragile head
> And through the day's long splendour
> Was wishing that she were dead.
>
> She thought of her proud cousin,
> The cultivated rose,
> Who laughs with every sunbeam
> Which through the garden goes.
>
> Who gives her heart to many,
> Her heart to three or four,
> And always has another heart
> Behind another door.
>
> NOTHING
>
> She was a pallid Fräulein
> Who kept the little shop
> Where you could buy goloshes
> Or Lessing or a chop.

>In every single sentence
>She said "Herr Doktor" twice
>And in return I thought I would
>Give medical advice.
>
>I leant across the counter
>My look was darkling, and
>Against the pallid Fräulein's heart
>I swiftly put a hand.
>
>Then spoke, "A certain weakness—"
>But she, "Not once in there!"
>Poor little one! I turned away
>My look of dark despair.

William Sharp (1858-1905).—Few Victorians were more familiar with the life and writings of Heinrich Heine than was William Sharp, and few English poets show greater influence from the German poet than does his great biographer. In form, mood, subject matter, and method of treatment, Sharp shows unmistakable derivations from Heine.

In the matter of form, Sharp is influenced by Heine more, perhaps, than in any other respect. The broken-lined form of the German poet is used to large extent in such poems as "Oona of the Dark Eyes and the Crying of Wind," "The Founts of Song," and "On a Redbreast Singing at the Grave of Plato." In *Transcripts from Nature* selected from *The Human Inheritance* and *Earth's Voices*, each poem consists of two parts—a sestet and couplet in iambic tetrameter with the rime scheme *a b b a c c d d*—a form not original with Heine but strangely reminiscent of him. For the monosyllabic simplicity of form in such poems as "The Star of Beauty," "Sheiling Song," and "The Mystic's Prayer," Sharp is undoubtedly indebted to Heine. Sharp's use of Heine's *freier Rhythmus* appears to greatest advantage and extent in the collection *Sospira di Roma* found in the volume *Flower o' the Vine*, published in the spring of 1891 during the English poet's stay in Rome. Concerning his use of unrhymed, irregular meters in the collection,

Sharp wrote to a friend that "What can be done in Greek and German can be done in English."[32] The German referred to is, in all likelihood, that of Heinrich Heine. The little poem "At the Last" may be given as a typical instance of Sharp's use of *freier Rhythmus:*

> She cometh no more:
> Time, too, is dead.
> The last tide is led
> From the last shore
> Eternity. . . .
> What is eternity?
> But the sea coming,
> The sea going,
> For evermore.[33]

Sharp, too, makes occasional use of Heine's device of parallelism and contrast as in the poem "Day and Night":

> From gray of dusk, the veils unfold
> To pearl and amethyst and gold—
> Thus is the new day woven and spun:
>
> From glory of blue to rainbow-spray,
> From sunset-gold to violet-grey—
> Thus is the restful night re-won.[34]

Sharp is unusually successful in imitating Heine's moods—a feat which, in itself, is deserving of none but the highest commendation. The little poem "Phantasy" (from *Poems of Phantasy*), for example, is a graceful, musical thing with its subtle mixture of sweet pain and delicate sensuousness, leaving the reader with a sense of utter incompleteness, and is done in the typical Heinesque manner of the gems of the *Lyrisches Intermezzo*. In the poem "Time," Sharp even manages the revulsion of mood for which Heine is famous:

> I saw a happy Spirit
> That wandered among flowers:
> Her crown was a rainbow,
> Her gown was wove of hours.

---

32. William Sharp, *Poems*, p. ix.
33. *Poems and Dramas*, p. 60.   34. *Ibid.*, p. 73.

> She turned with sudden laughter,
> *I was, but am no more!*
> And as I followed after
> Time smote me on the brow.[35]

Heine's treatment of love in its many and varied aspects finds a close parallel in the love songs of William Sharp. The pure, sweet sadness of the poem called simply "Song" finds its counterpart in the *Weltschmerz* and *Liebesschmerz* of the songs to Amalie and Therese. "The Summer Woman" with its picture of despair, doubt, and caprice, and its intermingling of bitter and sweet, joy and anguish, might have stepped from the pages of the *Lyrisches Intermezzo* or *Junge Leiden*. "It Happened in May" is typical of Heine's lighter moments in pondering the problem of love:

> A Maid forsaken
> A white prayer offered
> Under the snow of the apple-blossom:
> To whom was it proffered?
> By whom was it taken?
> Well, I suppose
> Nobody knows.
> But somehow, the snows
> Of the apple-blossom
> Were changed one day.
> A kiss was offered,
> A kiss was taken:
> And lo! when the maid looked shyly away,
> Of bloom of the apple the boughs were forsaken!
> But whiter and sweeter grew orange-blossom!
> Now this is quite true, I say,
> And it happened in May.[36]

"The Death Child" gives fundamentally the same picture as that of Heine's *Lorelei*. Instead of the golden-haired siren high upon the rock, Sharp shows us the Death Child sitting under an elder-tree on a desolate moor. Her hair is as dark as starless night and offers strange contrast to her flower-

---

35. *Ibid.*, p. 286.   36. *Poems* (1912), p. 295.

crowned face as she sings an eerie song by a dark pool. The two girls are direct contrasts; the setting is different; but the theme is related to that of Heine's poem, for:

> Few ever cross that dreary moor,
> Few see that flower-crown'd head;
> But whoso knows that wild song's lure
> Knoweth that he is dead.[37]

Few closer relationships with the nature poetry of Heine are found than in the volume *Earth's Voices* by William Sharp. The English poet is thoroughly impressed with the sacred freedom of nature and regards her not in a Wordsworthian sense but with the same sort of self-indulgence displayed by Heine. Sharp's yearning and passion for nature are particularly well expressed in "The Song of the Thrush." The English poet shares with Heine a definite and passionate love for the sea, as his longer poem *Oceanus* attests. Perhaps, the two poems in which Sharp most definitely reveals kinship with Heine in the celebration of nature are "The Norland Wind" and "White Rose." Both are given here—the first because of its kinship with the exultant poems of *Die Nordsee,* and the second because there is no poem in the entire range of English literature which captures so completely the Heinesque mood in the treatment of nature:

THE NORLAND WIND

> The south wind on the hill,
> And the west wind on the lea,
> But better than these I love
> The north wind on the sea!
>
> For the north wind on the sea
> Is fearless and elate;
> The ocean vast and free
> Is not more great.
>
> On the hill the south wind laughs
> Where the blue cloud-shadows flee:

---

37. *Flower of the Vine,* p. 78.

The west wind takes the mead
With a ripple of glee:

But the north wind on the deep
Is the wind of winds for me,
Spirit of dauntless life
And Lord of liberty.[38]

WHITE ROSE

Far in the inland valleys
The spring her secret tells;
And roses live on the bushes,
The lilies shake their bells.

To a lily of the valley
A white rose leans from above:
"Little white flower o' the valley,
Come up and be my love."

To the lily of the valley
A speedwell whispers, "No!
Where the roses live are thorns,
'Tis safe below."

The lily clomb to the rose-bush,
A thorn in her side:
The white rose has wedded a red rose,
And the lily died.[39]

Owen Meredith (1831-1891).—No English poet of the past century shows greater success in the use of Heine's *moralische Ohrfeige* than does Owen Meredith, who is also discussed elsewhere.[40] From Heine, Meredith has mastered completely the knack of twisting sharply the original trend of his verse in a pointed, epigrammatical close. In the section called *In Holland* from *The Wanderer*, the poems "Bluebeard," "Fatima," and "Going Back Home" all reveal a clever use of Heine's favorite device, the *moralische Ohrfeige*. The concluding two verses of each offer a sharp, surprising, yet

38. *Songs and Poems Old and New*, p. 188.
39. *Poems* (1912), p. 292.
40. See section on Informal Opinion.

Major Influence

conclusive twist to the remainder of the poems. A somewhat modified use of Heine's revulsion of mood is seen, too, in the concluding stanza of "The Mermaiden":

> I could not help but love him, love him,
> Till my love grew pain to me.
> And tomorrow he weds the Princess
> In that palace beside the sea.[41]

In "King Limos," also from *The Wanderer*, there is a similar use of Heine's revulsion of mood. The poem tells the story of an old king buried hundreds of years ago—an old king whose wicked old heart had grown so chill that he drank each night a goblet filled with a virgin's blood to warm it. The revulsion occurs in the application of the moral, the law of the world declares that the strong must devour the weak, and in the implication that the same law prevails in the world of souls:

> The law of the one is still to absorb:
> To be absorbed is the other's lot:—
> The lesser orb by the larger orb,
> The weak by the strong . . . why not?
>
> My want's at the worst: so why should I spare
> (Since just such a thing my want supplies)
> This little girl with the silky hair,
> And the love in her two large eyes?[42]

The poem "Medio De Fonte Leporum Surgit Amari Aliquid," from the English section of *The Wanderer*, offers in the final two verses the finest English example of Heine's use of *kalte Dusche*. The inspiration may have come from the *Herrn von Schnabelowopski* or the lyrico-satirical pieces of the German poet. The English poem is in Heine's best satirical manner:

> We walked about at Hampton Court,
> Alone in sunny weather,
> And talked—half earnest, and half sport,
> Linked arm in arm together.

41. *Poetical Works*, p. 442.   42. *Ibid.*, pp. 270-271.

I pressed her hand upon the steps.
Its warmest light the sky lent,
She sought the shade: I sought her lips:
We kissed: and then were silent.

Clare thought, no doubt, of many things,
Besides the kiss I stole there;—
The sun, in sunny founts in rings,
The bliss of soul with soul there,

The bonnet fresh from France, she wore,
My praise of how she wore it,
The arms above the carven door,
The orange-trees before it;—

But I could only think, as mute
I watched her happy smile there,
With rising pain, of this curst boot
That pinched me all the while there.[43]

From the section *In Holland* from *The Wanderer* are two poems, "Metempsychosis" and "Small People," which show clearly evidence of the sparkling wit of Heine. In the first, "Metempsychosis," appear a typical Heinesque self-mockery and a typical Heinesque theme. In Heine's ingenious, sparkling fashion, Meredith tells the tale of a lover done to death by the charms of a golden-haired, blue-eyed woman and seeking revenge in a humorously unique way. The story is but another variation of the popular theme so often used by the German poet in his youthful poems. The light, fantastical treatment is in Heine's favorite manner, and the easy yet striking wit—particularly that of the third stanza—coupled with a suggestion of self-mockery is reminiscent of the humorous pieces of the *Nachlese*:

> She fanned my life out with her soft little sighs:
> She hushed me to death with her face so fair:
> I was drunk with the light of her wild blue eyes,
> And strangled dumb in her long gold hair.

43. *Ibid.*, p. 240.

Major Influence

So now I'm a blessed and wandering ghost,
Though I cannot quite find my way up to heaven:
But I hover about o'er the long reedy coast,
In the wistful light of a low red even.

I have borrowed the coat of a little gray gnat:
There's a small sharp song I have learned how to sing:
I know a green place she is sure to be at:
I shall light on her neck there, and sting and sting.

Tra-la-la, tra-la-la, life never pleased me!
I fly where I list now, and sleep at my ease.
Buzz, buzz, buzz! the dead only are free.
Yonder's my way now. Give place, if you please.[44]

The same delicate, Heinesque wit is used by Meredith in "Small People," which is too long to quote in full. The sudden outburst of the final two verses, in which the poet wishes he could find, among all the "small people," "A man,—to insult and to shoot" is a typically Heinesque mental twist.

In still another respect Meredith shows the influence of Heinrich Heine, in the extensive use of that author's reverie motif. The grave and specter-lovers play a great part in the poetry of Meredith—particularly in *The Wanderer* and the *Minor Poems*—and we are often reminded of the use Heine made of the same in the *Traumbilder* and *Romanzen* of the *Junge Leiden*. Meredith often couples, as does Heine, love and death, and mingles pessimism, joy, pain, sentiment, sentimentality, and mockery. In treating the grave and specter-lovers, Meredith avoids the lasting impression of horror by following Heine's method of a deliberate and conscious mockery and the use of revulsion of mood to destroy purposefully the tone of the original illusion. One of the finest examples in Meredith of the influence of Heine's *Traumbilder* and *Romanzen* is "A Ghost Story," also from *The Wanderer*:

I lay awake past midnight:
The moon set o'er the snow;

---

44. *Ibid.*, pp. 267-268.

The very cocks for coldness,
Could neither sleep nor crow.

There came to me near morning
A woman pale and fair;
She seemed a monarch's daughter,
By the red gold round her hair.

The ring upon her finger
Was one that well I know;
I knew her fair face also,
For I had loved it so!

But I felt I saw a spirit,
And I was sore afraid;
For it is many and many a year
Ago, since she was dead.

I would have spoken to her,
But I could not speak for fear;
Because it was a homeless ghost
That walked beyond its sphere;

Till her head from her white shoulders
She lifted up: and said . . .
"Look in! you'll find I'm hollow
Pray do not be afraid!"[45]

Mary Elizabeth Coleridge (1861-1907).—In the work of Mary Elizabeth Coleridge there is frequent reminiscence of Heine's familiar lyric form and matter. Few poets have been able to manage the concentration of mood for which Heine is so famous as well as has Mary Coleridge. Writing without effort and in the monosyllabic simplicity of Heine's finest lyrics, she, too, is a master of condensation. The themes upon which the English writer wrote are likewise strongly reminiscent of Heine. Heine's pathos, *Weltschmerz*, longing, sentimentality, melancholy, love, despair, and simplicity all find a place in the lyrics of the English poetess, who employs the same verse form found in the German poet and manages

45. *Ibid.*, p. 267.

quite successfully to catch the true Heinesque quality in her lines.

In the little gem, "Two Songs," written with the same effortless ease and grace so characteristic of Heine's best pieces, Mary Coleridge celebrates love in a typically Heinesque fashion. Especially should be noted the symmetry and parallelism offered by the two stanzas—traits for which Heine is famous as a lyricist. The first and last lines offer a typical Heinesque contrast while the two short stanzas themselves illustrate the general parallelism:

> The blossoming of love I sang.
> The streams adown the mountain spring,
> And all the world with music rang.
>
> A cloud has darkened Heaven above,
> I only hear a moaning dove.
> I sing the withering of love.[46]

Written in the same parallel style as Heine's "Es liegt der heisse Sommer," and illustrative of the stanzaic parallelism and contrast peculiar to the songs of the *Lyrisches Intermezzo*, is the little poem "Sun and Wind":

> Deep in the heart of Winter lies a day
> Bright from the treasuries of perfect Spring,
> Life stirs and wakes in each created thing,
> December sleeps, and dreams, and dreams of May.
>
> Deep in the heart of Spring, when every flower
> Is radiant, comes a day of bitter wind.
> A blossom-laden bough, untimely thinned,
> Groans, for December holds no darker hour.[47]

Here, Heine's familiar contrast of the seasons of the year as well as the monosyllabic quality of his verse are equally evident in the English lyric.

Written in close imitation of Heine's favorite form, the little poem "Now" also illustrates the German poet's wide use

---

46. *Poems*, p. 19.   47. *Ibid.*, p. 90.

of contrasts in an intra-stanzaic manner. In the last stanza is the familiar seasonal parallelism:

> A crazy fool am I, and mad
> As the maddest dreams of sleep.
> I laughed when I was very sad,
> And now for joy I weep.
>
> The cold is here, the darkness drear,
> The yellow gloom, the rain
> And, lo, in the winter of the year
> 'Tis Spring with me again.[48]

One of the finest examples of Heinesque parallelism is found in the poem "Gifts"; there is in each stanza the odd twist or use of antithesis in which Heine so delighted:

> I tossed my friend a wreath of roses, wet
> With early dew, the garland of the morn,
> He lifted it—and on his brow he set
> A crackling crown of thorn.
>
> Against my foe I hurled a murderous dart,
> He caught it in his hand—I heard him laugh—
> I saw the thing that should have pierced his heart
> Turn to a golden staff.[49]

Heine's typical antithetical close in ironic vein—the *kalte Dusche*—which is one of the truly distinctive qualities of his verse, is used to great advantage by Mary E. Coleridge in the poems, "In London Town" and "Wind and Sea." In fact, the former is marked throughout by the subtle irony and undertone of mockery which characterize the verse of the strange genius of Heine. The form, too, of "In London Town" is quite reminiscent of that used by Heine in the *Buch der Lieder*. Because of the comparative length of the first-named poem, the shorter piece, "Wind and Sea," only is given here. Few English poems are more truly Heinesque in all respects. Attention should be called, especially, to the Heinesque parallelism

---

48. *Ibid.*, p. 207.   49. *Ibid.*, p. 17.

in the first stanza and to the abrupt change to mockery in the last stanza:

> The wind and the sea are sisters
> They moan forevermore,
> One in the pine tree branches
> And one against the shore.
> One for the land behind her
> And one for the land before.
>
> The wind is the sea's young brother
> The self-same voice have they,
> Sunlight and moonlight kiss them,
> And then they kiss and play,
> Sometimes they hate each other,
> And then they fight all day.
>
> "What silly stuff you scribble!"
> My fair love said to me.
> "As if such things as those are
> Could ever strive or agree:
> They are neither brothers nor sisters,
> But just the Wind and the Sea!"[50]

One of the chief traits of Heine's lyric verse is that which is called in German *Häufung und Wiederholung*, a means by which effect is gained by accumulative repetition. In such a poem as "Beware," this Heinesque repetition (seen in the repeated emphasis on the idea of "softness") is employed. In the concluding verse of each stanza, too, is the parallelism or contrast typical of Heine. The piece celebrates woman after the fashion of Heine's songs springing from his unrequited love for Amalie:

> Her yellow hair is soft, and her soft eyes
> Are as the doe's for meekness. Only feel
> The softness of the hand in mine that lies!
> The sheath is velvet, but the sword is steel.
>
> Soft are her footsteps, and her low replies
> The lover's woe like softest music heal.
> Ah, let him still remember and be wise,
> The sheath is velvet, but the sword is steel.[51]

50. *Ibid.*, p. 182.   51. *Ibid.*, p. 71.

In the highly concentrated little poem, "The Haven," appears a similar sort of repetition with the emphasis upon the idea of "grayness." One of the chief means by which Heine gains effect through *Häufung und Wiederholung* is through the inversion of terms. Mary Elizabeth Coleridge applies the same method in "Over the Hills and Far Away." The first two verses of each stanza are given below as illustrative of the method:

> All around was dumb and still
> Dumb and still as any stone.
>
> All around was gray and dun,
> Gray and dun by sea and shore.
>
> All around was barren ground,
> Barren ground lay far and near.
>
> When she asks me what befell,
> What befell on Lady Day.
>
> All around was dumb and still,
> Dumb and still as any stone.[52]

One of the finest specimens of true Heinesque verse in English literature is the poem "Slowly" in which are apparent at a glance the Heinesque traits of repetition, inversion, monosyllabic simplicity, and the like. Here, too, is the gemlike quality of the German poet's shorter lyrics:

> Heavy is my heart,
> Dark are thine eyes.
> Thou and I must part
> Ere the sun rise.
>
> Ere the sun rise
> Thou and I must part.
> Dark are thine eyes
> Heavy is my heart.[53]

In addition, it might be noted that while the lyric "Wasted" shows no direct influence of Heine, in its suggestion of grief it

---

52. *Ibid.*, p. 15.   53. *Ibid.*, p. 3.

is strangely reminiscent of the yearning of the German poet. Mary Elizabeth Coleridge may well have had Heine the apostle of love, Heine the brave soldier in the liberation war of humanity, Heine the poet of "Ich bin das Schwert, ich bin die Flamme," in mind when she wrote in the concluding stanza of "Say This":

> Say that I spent on love my latest breath,
> And spent it well.
> Say that I died a happy soldier's death
> And fighting fell.[54]

Robert Louis Stevenson (1850-1894).—It was in the period of his student days (1867-1873) that Robert Louis Stevenson first manifested a definite interest in German language and literature. In 1872, the English youth proposed to take a summer session at some German university with Sir Walter Simpson, who was also studying law; but, because of the nervousness of Stevenson's mother, the plan was abandoned, and the two friends contented themselves with a two or three weeks' stay in Frankfurt. From Frankfurt, Stevenson went to Baden-Baden where he was joined by his parents. A walking tour of the Black Forest completed his visit to Germany.[55] It was during this time that Stevenson turned his attention seriously to the study of German literature.

As early as 1869 or 1870 occur occasional references to Heinrich Heine in the correspondence of Robert Louis Stevenson. In a notebook of 1871-1872, in a list of Stevenson's favorite readings *(Catalogus Librorum Carissimorum)*, Heine is the only German author mentioned.[56] From no writer does Stevenson quote more freely than from Hazlitt, whom he couples with Sterne and Heine as the best of companions on a walking tour.[57] The first published book by the English writer, *An Inland Voyage,* shows the influence of both *A*

---

54. *Ibid.*, p. 178.
55. G. Balfour, *The Life of Robert Louis Stevenson*, I, 126-127.
56. *Ibid.*, I, 117.   57. *Ibid.*, I, 230.

Sentimental Journey by Sterne and the *Reisebilder* of Heine.[58] In Stevenson's early agnosticism and revolt against orthodoxy, too, there is undoubtedly the influence of the arch-mocker Heine.[59]

It is in the poems especially of Stevenson's youth, together with a few later pieces, that reminiscences of Heine are most apparent. Credit must go to B. Ifor Evans for pointing out the fact that the English poet found in Heine the model for some aspects of his open-air romanticism and for his exaggerated gestures in sentiment and the contrasting excess of buoyancy. The following poem is cited as an instance in which Stevenson parallels closely some of the moods of Heine's lyrics:[60]

> The infinite shining heavens
> Rose and I saw in the night
> Uncountable angel stars
> Showering sorrow and light.
>
> I saw them distant as heaven,
> Dumb and shining and dead,
> And the idle stars of the night,
> Were dearer to me than bread.
>
> Night after night in my sorrow
> The stars stood over the sea,
> Till lo! I looked in the dusk
> And a star had come down to me.

Attention, too, is called to the following brief lyric written in truly Heinesque manner:

> I have trod the upward and the downward slope;
> I have endured and done in days before;
> I have longed for all, and bid farewell to hope;
> And I have lived and loved, and closed the door.

Lightness of touch is probably Stevenson's chief trait as a poet. Even in treating nature and more serious subjects, grace

---

58. J. A. Stewart, *R. L. Stevenson: Man and Writer*, I, 187.
59. *Ibid.*, I, 105-106.
60. B. Ifor Evans, *op. cit.*, pp. 274-275.

and a certain daintiness are ever present. In the pleasant, playful love, the self-indulgence with which he treats of the open air and other themes, and in grace, condensation, and spontaneous melody, a great many of Stevenson's lyrics are strongly suggestive of Heine.

The delicacy and grace of "To Minnie," for example, are highly reminiscent of Heine's finer love songs, and the delicate humor and pathos of many of the children's pieces such as, for example, "Bed in Summer," suggest the German poet of "Mein Kind, wir waren Kinder" and similar songs. And, indeed, for that matter, the well-known "Requiem" bears in common with Heine's finest lyrics a gemlike quality of crystallized thought in graceful and melodious form.

Two of the shorter lyrics of Stevenson are given below as exemplary of the grace and lightness for which the lyrics of his great predecessor are famous. The poems sing themselves as do Heine's finest songs. The Heinesque whimsicality of "Looking Forward" is particularly striking. Both pieces possess Heine's naïvety:

Singing

Of speckled eggs the birdie sings
And nests among the trees;
The sailor sings of ropes and things
In ships upon the seas.

The children sing in far Japan,
The children sing in Spain;
The organ with the organ man
Is singing in the rain.

Looking Forward

When I am grown to man's estate
I shall be very proud and great,
And tell the other girls and boys
Not to meddle with my toys.

Richard Monckton Milnes, Lord Houghton (1809-1885).
—Few English writers enjoyed a more thorough acquaintance-

ship with German life and letters than did Richard Monckton Milnes. In 1830, Milnes visited Germany during the summer and studied for several months at the University of Bonn. The visit marked his first intimate introduction to German life. Thereafter, until his death, he lived off and on in Germany, and with each succeeding visit his interest in the country and its people increased. From 1848 to 1860, he wrote articles on German politics and an occasional study of German letters. Among his many German friends are found Freiligrath, Gräfin Hahn-Hahn, Fanny Lewald, Hartmann, and the Varnhagens to whom Heine was so indebted during his stay in Berlin. Among German writers he was most impressed with the Schlegels, Tieck, Schiller, Goethe, and Heine, whom he met through Lady Duff Gordon in 1840 and upon whom he wrote an extensive article discussed earlier in this study.[61] Milnes and Lady Duff Gordon must be regarded as Heine's closest English friends.[62]

Walther Fischer, in his admirable and thorough study on the relations of Milnes to Germany,[63] has pointed out already the English writer's indebtedness to Heine, and we can do little more here than to recount briefly his findings. The work in which the influence of Heine is greatest is Milnes' poetic cycle, *The Goddess Venus in the Middle Ages,* a lengthy work in which the sources are drawn primarily from Heine's *Elementargeister*. The poem opens with a treatment of Venus much after the fashion of Heine; thereupon follows a somewhat free version of the Tannhäuser theme as Heine himself treated it; and at the close is a long-winded story in verse called *The Northern Knight in Italy* which is, in reality, nothing more than an unsuccessful version of Heine's delightful prose story of the knight "der wegen seiner Unerfahrenheit, oder auch seiner schlanken Gestalt wegen, von den Unholden mit besonders lieblichen Listen umgarnt wird." One other

---

61. See section on Criticism.   62. See section on Informal Opinion.
63. *Die persönlichen Beziehungen Richard Monckton Milnes zu Deutschland.*

work of Milnes is a direct derivation from Heine, *The Brownie*, which is taken largely from the first book of *Zur Geschichte der Religion und Philosophie in Deutschland*. Aside from source material, Milnes derives little from Heine in either form, manner, or matter.

Ernest Dowson (1867-1900).—To Professor Warr, who was in search of an accomplished young fellow to read German and play the violin to an old invalid gentleman, Victor Plarr tells us that Ernest Dowson, who, it seems, was always in search of employment, was recommended. Dowson, whose ability as a violinist was practically nil, and whose German was quite problematical, failed to get the post upon application.[64] A little later, Plarr tells us, he wanted Dowson to translate Heine and other modern Teuton poets into English for the late Professor Buchheim, but it appears that the English poet's lack of German again proved troublesome, for he writes:

Caro Mio—I return your letter with abundant thanks for the offer. Alas! that it should be so, but my knowledge of German is so limited that I should be an encumbrance rather than an aid, if I accepted it. I could only translate Heine from French translations, and that is scarcely what your friend would desire. And where would appreciation of the Heinesque style come in? I am afraid you must pass on the attractive opportunity to some one more competent.[65]

Ernest Dowson, to be sure, owes little to German literature. As a poet, he stands probably midway between Keats and Swinburne; yet more than once we are reminded of the lyrics of Heine despite the fact that he appears to have been unable to read the German poet in the original. Particularly is this true in the love poems of Dowson, in which are evident the same evenness and intrinsic grace found in Heinrich Heine. Dowson's "April Love," "Amor Umbratilis," "Ad Domnulam Suam," and "Vitae summa brevis spem nos vetat incohare longam" celebrate love much after the manner of Heine. There is a subtle anguish, a graceful longing, in the English

---

64. Victor Plarr, *Ernest Dowson*, p. 71.
65. *Ibid.*, pp. 74-75.

verses such as Heine, too, expressed. And, as in the case of Heine's lyrics, Dowson's feeling is rendered all the more poignant by the light, delicate touch with which he softens the *Schmerz*.

One poem, particularly, strikes us as being unusually reminiscent of Heine in its simplicity of form, in its organic structure, and in the matter expressed. In "Soli Cantare Periti Arcades," Dowson uses a typical Heinesque short-verse form. The piece has the usual Heinesque smooth beginning, moves through parallels, and closes delightfully. The third stanza with its hatred of London, the fourth and fifth dealing with Parisian ladies, and the sixth with its hint of voluptuousness might well have been written by Heine himself:

> Oh, I would live in a dairy,
> And its Colin I would be,
> And many a rustic fairy
> Should churn the milk with me.
>
> Or the fields should be my pleasure,
> And my flocks should follow me,
> Piping a frolic measure
> For Joan or Marjorie.
>
> For the town is black and weary,
> And I hate the London Street;
> But the country ways are cheery,
> And country lanes are sweet.
>
> Good luck to you, Paris ladies!
> Ye are over fine and nice;
> I know where the country maid is,
> Who needs not asking twice.
>
> Ye are brave in your silks and satins,
> As ye mince about the Town;
> But her feet go free in pattens
> If she wear a russett gown.
>
> If she be not queen nor goddess
> She shall milk my brown-eyed herds,
> And the breasts beneath her bodice
> Are whiter than her curds.

So I will live in a dairy,
And its Colin I will be,
And its Joan that I will marry,
Or, haply, Marjorie.[66]

William Allingham (1824-1889).—On April 5, 1865, Moncure Conway in acknowledging the receipt of *Fifty Modern Poems* and *The Dial* sent to him by William Allingham, who is discussed at greater length earlier in this study,[67] wrote: "You are not Heinesque, yet touched me thrice like Heine: i.e. 'The Poor Little Maiden,' 'His Town,' 'Down on the Shore.'"[68] And, indeed, the three poems mentioned are reminiscent of Heine—"The Poor Little Maiden" and "His Town" in their delicate yet poignant pathos, and "Down on the Shore" in its celebration of the sea after the manner of *Die Nordsee*.

Allingham, however, shows a more definite suggestion of Heine in still other poems. The German poet's irregular, short-lined form is used somewhat by the English poet in "These Little Songs," "The Little Dell," and "On the Longest Day." The poem, "The Fairies," employs not only the short-lined form of Heine but is written with a similar grace, lightness, and delicacy. In the poem, too, are delicate shadings of humor and fancy cleverly intermingled after the fashion of Heine. In Allingham's *Day and Night Songs*—and especially in the pieces, "The Fields in May" and "A Holiday"—nature is celebrated in Heinesque fashion. Heine's favorite figures, roses, violets, bird-songs, rejoicing brooks, hedges, green fields, cuckoos, sunshine, fragrant breezes, flowers, linnets, elms, brooklets, pairs of lovers, tender lips, warm hearts, and love, are used to good advantage by the English writer. The poem, "Invitation to a Painter," beginning "Flee from London, good my Walter! boundless jail of bricks and gas," expresses a typically Heinesque distaste for British city life.

66. *Poems and Prose*, p. 57.   67. See section on Informal Opinion.
68. *Letters to William Allingham*, ed. by H. Allingham and E. B. Williams, p. 166.

Arthur Hugh Clough (1819-1861).—In Arthur Hugh Clough and Matthew Arnold, we have the first conscious introduction of Heine's influences in English poetry. These influences, which are fundamentally stylistic in nature, are seen primarily in an English imitation of Heine's cadences. Clough, himself, is not particularly a Heine enthusiast despite the fact that he had a fairly good acquaintanceship with German literature. It is known that he read Goethe and Schiller in the originals—and his occasional quotations in his letters from the German together with his translations from Goethe and his predilection for German titles for his own verse assure us that he was no stranger to German letters. Mention of Heine is noticeably wanting in the works of the Victorian poet; yet the free, irregular form of such poems as "Selene" and "The Shadow" gives the suggestion that Heine's *freier Rhythmus* was not unknown to him. Among the more conventional verse forms, such poems, too, as "In the Depths" and "O ship, ship, ship" from *Songs in Absence* are reminiscent of the German poet in their quiet, smooth beginnings, their melody, their simplicity, and their ease of movement.

Fundamentally, Clough is a serious poet, one who is conscious to the extreme, perhaps, of "the gravity of this world" and "the uncertainty of the other." A mind as complex and balanced as Clough's rarely lends itself to irony; yet when it does, there results an irony both peculiar and unique. In the infrequent yet nonetheless striking moments of irony Clough permitted himself, he is oddly akin to the arch-mocker and master of ironical expression, Heinrich Heine. In the later stanzas of "Men of Galilee"—the stanzas beginning "Ye poor deluded youths go home," etc.—Clough captures Heine's remarkable gift of a subtle irony fading gradually into a mere shade and yet seeming in the fading all the more pervading.

In the poem "Duty" (from *Poems on Life and Duty*), which is unfortunately too long to quote here, Clough, especially in the first half, mocks with the voice of Heine the conventional and Philistine attitude toward the virtue, duty. In "The Latest Decalogue," perhaps Clough's most excellent piece in the ironical style, is found the same type of mocking irony for which Heine was so severely scored. It is not too bold an assumption, I think, to believe that Clough found his model in the bitterness, the mockery, and irony of the great German poet. "The Latest Decalogue," which is comparatively brief, is given here:

> Thou shalt have one God only; who
> Would be at the expense of two?
> No graven images may be
> Worshipped, except the currency:
> Swear not at all; for, for thy curse
> Thine enemy is none the worse:
> At church on Sunday to attend
> Will serve to keep the world thy friend:
> Honour thy parents; that is, all
> From whom advancement may befall;
> Thou shalt not kill; but needs't not strive
> Officiously to keep alive;
> Do not adultery commit;
> Advantage rarely comes of it:
> Thou shalt not steal; an empty feat,
> When it's so lucrative to cheat:
> Bear not false witness; let the lie
> Have time on its own wings to fly:
> Thou shalt not covet, but tradition
> Approves all forms of competition.[69]

Matthew Arnold (1822-1888).—The question of Heine's influence upon the poet Matthew Arnold is one that must be approached with extreme care, for in the entire range of literature, it would be, indeed, difficult to find two poets more diametrically opposed. Arnold, whose knowledge of and relationship to German life and literature are discussed at length in the section on Criticism, stands, as poet, for the opposite of that for which Heine stood. The materials, methods, and

---

69. A. H. Clough, *Poems*, p. 184.

experiences of the two writers are as different as day and night. And yet, both poets possess some things in common. Both, for example, are embodiments of the mixture of Hellenism and Hebraism although the two are revealed in different ways in the respective poets. Of Heine's Hellenism and Hebraism already much has been said. In Arnold, Hellenism stands mainly for intellectual power, Hebraism for moral power. Even in the elements they hold in common, there is an abyss that cannot be bridged between the vacillating, irresolute, and uncontrolled Heine and the English poet whose creed was Goethe's formula for ideal life, "Im Ganzen, Guten, Wahren resolut zu leben."

In one respect only does Arnold show clearly the influence of Heine—in his assimilations of that poet's use of *freier Rhythmus*. Arnold undoubtedly followed Heine in his use of the broken-line and short-verse form, although there is by no means even a suggestion of slavish imitation. In such pieces as *Rugby Chapel* and *Heine's Grave* the influence is fairly unmistakable. In other poems the adaptation is not so well marked, and it is merely a fair guess to say that Arnold approaches Heine's *freier Rhythmus* and short-verse form in such poems as "Consolation," "A Question," "The Voice," "The Strayed Reveler," "Philomela," and "Dover Beach."

In a few of Arnold's lighter lyrics, the English poet impresses us at times with a vague sort of Heinesque quality. This is seen particularly in the lilt and grace and the surprising close of "Meeting" from the *Switzerland* group, in the reverie motif of "Longing" from *Faded Leaves*, in the crystalline lyricism of "Despondency" and "Requiescat," and in the abrupt close of "Pis-Aller."

Humor is a quality foreign to the poems of Matthew Arnold; yet in "A Wish" there is a suggestion of it. To say that the suggestion of humor here is akin to that of Heine would indeed be stretching matters a bit, but it can be said quite truthfully that the sentiment—especially of stanzas four

Major Influence

to eight—expresses exactly that of Heine as he lay on his mattress-grave:

> Spare me the whispering, crowded room,
> The friends who come, and gape, and go;
> The ceremonious air of gloom—
> All, which makes death a hideous show!
>
> Nor bring, to see me cease to live
> Some doctor full of phrase and fame,
> To shake his sapient head, and give
> The ill he cannot cure a name.
>
> Nor fetch, to take the accustom'd toll
> Of the poor sinner bound for death,
> His brother doctor of the soul,
> To canvass with official breath,
>
> The future and its viewless things—
> That undiscover'd mystery
> Which one who feels death's winnowing wings
> Must needs read clearer, sure, than he!
>
> Bring none of these; but let me be,
> While all around in silence lies,
> Moved to the window near, and see
> Once more, before my dying eyes,
>
> Bathed in the sacred dews of morn
> The wide aerial landscape spread—
> The world which was ere I was born,
> The world which lasts when I am dead.

Arthur Symons (b. 1865).—Because the lyrics of Arthur Symons often resemble those of Heine in their delicate grace and crystal-like condensation, a word might be said of Symons here. Of his knowledge of German literature practically nothing is known. We do know, however, that he was to some extent acquainted with the work of Heinrich Heine, for in *Days and Nights,* first published in 1889, appears a translation of *Die Wallfahrt nach Kevlaar.* In more than a few lyrics, Symons closely parallels the mood of the German song-writer.

In the little poem "The Fisher's Widow," there is close resemblance to Heine's treatment of the sea in *Die Nordsee*—a resemblance seen particularly in the absence of color and in the use of the sea fundamentally as a background for the interpretation of human emotion. The monosyllabic simplicity and the effortless ease of movement, too, are both suggestive of *Die Nordsee*:

> The boats go out and the boats come in
> Under the wintry sky;
> And the rain and foam are white in the wind,
> And the white gulls cry.
>
> She sees the sea when the wind is wild
> Swept by the windy rain;
> And her heart's a-weary of sea and land
> As the long days wane.
>
> She sees the torn sails fly in the foam,
> Broad in the sky-line grey;
> And the boats go out and the boats come in,
> But there's one away.[70]

The poem "Night" parallels closely the mood of Heine in the lyrics of *Lyrisches Intermezzo* and the *Letzte Gedichte*. The English lyric, too, follows closely the form of Heine's shorter lyric of mood, in its simplicity of wording and in its condensation of verse and stanzaic form:

> The night's held breath,
> And the star's steady eyes:
> Is it sleep, is it death,
> In the earth, in the skies?
>
> In my heart of hope,
> In my restless will,
> There is that should not stop
> Though the earth stood still,
>
> Though the heavens shook aghast,
> As the frost shakes a tree,

---

70. *Days and Nights*, p. 120.

Major Influence

And a strong wind cast
The stars in the sea.[71]

In the poems called *Regrets*, Symons matches the ability of Heine to condense and crystallize a mood and a story in eight short lines. The second of the poems, "Rispetto," is given below as an example of typical Heinesque simplicity and condensation and of the ability of Symons to portray in the succinct fashion of Heine, in two short stanzas, contrasting situations under the same circumstances:

> We went into the woods the first of May,
> And all the birds were singing in the trees;
> Together did we go the livelong day,
> We two and Love, and plighted promises.
>
> Ah wellaway! here's Spring, and here we are,
> And in the woods two walking joylessly;
> Ah wellaway! the birds still sing above,
> And we're together still: but where is Love?[72]

In two pieces, Arthur Symons avails himself of Heine's peculiar use of ironic antithesis in order to destroy deliberately the impression given by the opening lines of his poems. In the first of the *Scènes de la Vie de Bohème*, Symons makes a typical Heine beginning in regard to both quietness and smoothness and paints a delicately tinted picture of an exquisite night in May. Next, a young couple is introduced, it would seem, for the purpose of enjoying the beauties of the delightful evening. There is every indication of a charming, romantic scene, but with a typically Heinesque twist the illusion is destroyed as we find:

> She jarred his nerves; he bored her—and so soon.
> Both were polite, and neither cared to say
> The word that mars a perfect night of May.
> They watched the waning moon.[73]

The same type of Heinesque ironical antithesis—the odd twist at the end—is used by Symons in the third of his *Songs of the*

71. *The Fool of the World and Others Poems*, p. 23.
72. *Days and Nights*, p. 140.   73. *Ibid.*, p. 87.

Poltescal Valley, where, after painting in the first three stanzas a joyous picture of nature in which the laughing woodpecker, the friendly rain, the thunder, the voice of the sea, the leaves of the valley, and the birds all unite to give us a picture of unbounded joy and enthusiasm, he closes with the stanza:

> Only you at the window, with rueful lips
> Half pouting,
> Stand dumb and doubting,
> And drum with your finger-tips.[74]

In form, too, Symons often bears close resemblance to Heine. Especially is this true in the condensation, the evenness and grace, the crystal clearness, the monosyllabic simplicity, the short-verse form, and the brevity of the impressionistic lyrics of *The Fool of the World and Other Poems*.

74. *The Fool of the World*, p. 30.

VII. *Minor Influence*

ASIDE FROM THE POETS who in one way or another show the influence of Heinrich Heine upon their creative verse, there is a small group of English poets who have adapted directly from the work of the German singer. They have done little else than interpret after their own fashion, parody, or reapply the materials of Heine in the English tongue. Their own verse may show, occasionally, traces of the influence of Heine, but it is for the most part of too little value to cause extended comment. Those instances, however, in which the writers themselves have tapped directly the springs of Heine's genius in the matter of adaptation are far more interesting and valuable bits of evidence in showing the tremendous spread of the German poet's popularity among his English contemporaries and followers. Insofar as adaptation is concerned, it is interesting to note that nearly every English adaptation of Heine is one of the famous song, *Die Lorelei*. No less than seven poets have attempted English versions of the original concept, some few of which are quite closely related to the German original in mood and idea while others, possessing only the nucleus of Heine's idea, vary to great extent from Heine's legend of the Rhine maiden.

William Sawyer.—William Sawyer, in a volume of verse which he calls *The Legend of Phyllis* (1872), has an English poem which he calls "The Lorelei." The poem represents no attempt whatsoever at translation on the part of Sawyer, but it is undoubtedly based on Heine's famous original. The story of the English poem is essentially that of the German; but, unfortunately, the author lacked both the skill and art of

Heine, and the English piece is, consequently, uninspiring and uninteresting.

Walter Scott Carmichael.—In *Miscellanea Poetica* (1883), Walter Scott Carmichael has included a short sentimental song entitled "The Fisherman"[1] which, while it bears absolutely no resemblance to *Die Lorelei*, treats of a fisherman and his two sons out at sea on a stormy night in the exact meter of the great German song. The poem was written to the air of *Die Lorelei*.

Amelia B. Edwards.—In "The Rhine Maiden," Amelia B. Edwards paints swiftly the picture of a maiden standing on the banks of the Rhine singing a beautiful song amid the distant pealing of an organ and chapel bells.[2] The singing is interrupted suddenly as the maiden takes an arrow from her hair and shoots the speaker in the poem through the heart. While the poem deviates widely from the original German concept, the general idea of the English version is, in the main, that of Heine's piece.

John Stuart Blackie (1809-1895).—John Stuart Blackie had by far a greater knowledge of German letters than the average English writer of his age. As a youth, Blackie studied both in Göttingen and Berlin and later in life paid numerous visits to Germany. He is said to have been able to speak the German language quite as well as he could speak English. Among his literary works is a translation of Goethe's *Faust* and a volume called *War Songs from the German*. Although his knowledge of Heine appears to have been limited, he has left one English poem, "The Jungfrau of the Lurlei," which, while it does not bear much resemblance to Heine's *Lorelei*, was probably inspired by that work. The poem is found in the volume *Musa Burschicosa*.

G. S. Cautley (d. 1880).—In a short poem, the "Lorelei,"[3] undoubtedly derived from Heine's poem of the same name,

---

1. Pp. 38-39.
2. *Ballads*, pp. 39-41.
3. *The Three Fountains*, p. 131.

Minor Influence

George Spencer Cautley paints in English the German siren with her beautiful eyes and "tresses of light" as she sat harping on high and enthralling the crowd below with the glamour of song. Cautley, too, has another poem, "The Siren," which in concept owes much to Heine's *Lorelei:*

> A Siren on a rocky isle,
> A youth upon the cliff is seen;
> She tries his fancy to beguile,
> The deep dark water moans between.
>
> "Gentle thou art," he saith, "and fair,
> Yet naught thine azure eyes avail,
> Amid the golden coils of hair,
> Gleams weirdly forth the fish's tail."
>
> Yet still he gazed, she smiled the more:
> She sang a wondrous witching strain.
> He groaned and sighed, he laughed and swore,
> Then plunged into the deadly main.[4]

William Stigand (1825-1915).—William Stigand, who has been discussed at length as a translator of Heinrich Heine, has written the following interesting sequel to the German *Lorelei.* It is called merely "The Fate of the Lorelei" and needs no special comment:

> Turn to me, child, thy guileless eye,
> And lay thy hand in mine,
> I'll tell thee the fate of Lorelei,
> The Siren of the Rhine.
>
> Year after year, age after age,
> Her voice came down the deep,
> And maidens pale had many a page
> And many a knight to weep.
>
> Oh, little reck'd she of the bleaching bones,
> Or the last reproachful look,
> But still to the joy of her dulcet tones
> The waves in the sunbeam shook.

4. *A Century of Emblems.*

In starlike beauty on the rocks,
Just o'er the whirlpool's foam,
One morn she dress'd her sweeping locks
With a golden, gleaming comb.

The sun hung low upon the hill,
The dew still gemm'd the plain,
And she sang still a song to kill
The soul within the brain.

A song so sweet, it seem'd to make
The small waves mad with glee;
Heaven him I pray in its guard to take
Who hears that minstrelsy.

A bark with sail all silken white
Comes dancing down the stream,
There sits at the helm as fair a knight
As ever was maiden's dream.

Oh, spare him, spare him, Lorelei!
Alas! he draws full near;
And the magic might of the melody
Rings out more strange and clear.

The yearning waters hiss with joy,
The boat hangs on the verge;
One swerve of the helm might whelm the boy,
Beneath the hungry surge.

The helm with firm right hand he grips,
In his left a scarf does lie,
He presses it upon his lips,
And he looks on Lorelei.

"By thy love's strength, O Bertha dear,
I will this fiend o'ercome."
He looked on her and knew no fear,
Pale Lorelei was dumb.

He looked a glance so pure and strong,
With Bertha's love serene,
She shrieked and leaped the waves among,
And never more was seen.[5]

5. *Anthea: Poems and Translations*, pp. 121-122.

Minor Influence

Sir Francis Hastings Doyle (1810-1888).—Sir Francis Hastings Doyle, discussed earlier in this study as a translator of Heine, has written in connection with his admirable translation of Heine's "Ein Fichtenbaum steht einsam" the following stanzas suggested by the German original:

"EIN FICHTENBAUM STEHT EINSAM"

A Pine-Tree standeth lonely
On a bleak northern hill.
And sleeps with ice surrounded
With snow that falleth still.

There is one palm he dreams of,
Far in the morning land,
Who mourns alone, and silent,
Mid rocks and burning sand.

STANZAS SUGGESTED BY THE ABOVE

They dream, but dreams are of the night;
Will not the sun rise by-and-by?
Or is the hope that thirsts for light
Only a mocking lie?

O wondrous dawn may wake, and turn
To floods of life the phantom snows,
Whilst desert sands that drift and burn
Shall blossom as the rose.

The pine and palm may feel that then
Both cold and heat, and Time and Space,
One polar crag, in tropic glen,
To other laws give place.

Through them, whilst the young heavens grow rife
With joy, and airs divinely sweet,
Distance dies off from spirit-life,
That severed hearts may meet.

Oh leave that thought to float above,
Each parching leaf, each blighted bough;
It breathes of hope, it breathes of love,
It worketh on—even now,

In that dark pine's despairing breast,
To melt the bitter frost of pain;
And on his drooping palm-tree's crest
Falls like the early rain.[6]

H. W. Garrod (b. 1878).—Heathcote William Garrod, well known as a literary critic and historian, editor and classical scholar, has included in his *Oxford Poems*[7] a parody of Heine's "Mein Kind, wir waren Kinder":

> Dear child, when we were children
> Content with children's toys,
> We had more than children's wisdom
> In the ways of girls and boys;
>
> We married and gave in marriage
> Our men and our women-dolls,
> Rehearsing then with puppets
> What now is a drama of souls;
>
> We wore them thin with pleasure
> And white with secret pain,
> And married them and broke them
> And mended them again:
>
> And vainly tried to fancy
> Some patched and plastered doll
> As pretty and bewitching
> As when it once was whole;
>
> Just as today we marry
> And play our different parts
> And love and hate and end by
> Breaking our silly hearts:
>
> And then we patch and plaster
> With bottle and brush and glue
> Hearts that once old and broken
> Nothing can make look new.
>
> Would God we still were children,
> Still pleased with children's toys,
> Without the bitter wisdom
> Of grown-up girls and boys.

6. *Lectures on Poetry, Second Series*, pp. 282-283.
7. Pp. 70-71.

Eva Gore-Booth (1870-1926).—Among the posthumous poems of Eva Gore-Booth is found a fragment in German, based probably on Heine's *Lorelei:*

> DIE RHEINBAHN
>
> Als sie beendet war,
> Ein junger Fischer sah,
> Im hellen Mondenschein,
> Von ihrem Fels, mit wild Geschrei,
> Das schönste Mädchen Lorelei
> Sich toll hinunter stürzen in den Rhein.[8]

Other Poets Influenced by Heine.—Dante Gabriel Rossetti (1828-1882) can scarcely be said to have been influenced by any German author. Hall Caine assures us that while in Rossetti's library most poets were adequately represented, the German poets were conspicuously absent. Indeed, we are told that Goethe's *Faust* and Carlyle's translation of *Wilhelm Meister* were about the only notable German works included.[9] And Rossetti himself, writing to Hall Caine concerning the possibility of a German origin for Coleridge's name "Christobel," admitted in no uncertain terms that he did not know the German language at all.[10] And yet, we find Rossetti writing as early as January 23, 1855, to William Allingham about the original of a ballad by Heine which, it would seem, he was quite anxious to find.[11] The only influence, it would appear, that Heine exerted upon the English poet was by way of art rather than letters, in inspiring him to paint *The Queen's Page* from the German author.[12]

Robert Browning (1812-1889) mentions Heinrich Heine in three of his poems: "Christmas Eve," "Dis Aliter," and "Development." No trace of Heine's influence upon the English poet is apparent although Browning in "Pisgah Sights" employs the short-lined verse form so typically Heine's.

8. *Poems,* p. 119.
9. Hall Caine, *Recollections of Dante Gabriel Rossetti,* p. 234.
10. *Ibid.,* p. 153. 11. Hill, *Letters of Dante Gabriel Rossetti,* p. 96.
12. Esther Wood, *D. G. Rossetti and the Pre-Raphaelite Movement,* p. 117.

Mathilde Blind points out that George Eliot (1819-1880) in her *Spanish Gypsy* deals with the eternal dualism between the Hellenic and the Christian ideals of which Heine was the original and incomparable expounder.[13] In the verse of George Eliot otherwise, however, there are no discernible traces of the German poet's influence.

"A people with so fine a literature,"[14] is the only remark George Meredith (1828-1909) permitted himself upon German literature as a whole; yet, as far as individual German authors are concerned, Meredith speaks frequently and at length upon the merits and faults of practically every German writer of consequence. His letters and works reveal many allusions to men like Harnack, Mommsen, Niebuhr, Mörike, Hoffmann, Richter, Zschokke, etc., in addition to extensive comments and references to the foremost literary names. Carlyle is mentioned as having encouraged him in his study of German, and, with the years, his interest in German letters, scholarship, politics, education, music, customs, and the like increased steadily. His literary works include translations from Heine and Mörike. *Farina*, a youthful work, is, as Lees points out, broadly speaking a German fairy-tale, and such works as *The Empty Purse, Harry Richmond, One of Our Conquerors*, the *Tragic Comedians*, and *The Ordeal of Richard Feverel* reveal clearly German characteristics.

Meredith had passed probably the two most impressionable years of his life (from 1842-1844) at the Moravian school at Neuwied on the Rhine, near Cologne, and had later traveled extensively throughout Germany—all of which makes more easily understandable his enthusiasm for things and persons German. In regard to Heine, Meredith knew quite well Miss Fiona MacLeod and the Duff Gordons from whom he must have received firsthand information regarding the great German writer. In his *Essay on the Idea of Comedy*, Meredith alludes definitely to Heine when referring to the lack of the

---

13. Mathilde Blind, *George Eliot*, p. 225.
14. John Lees, *George Meredith's Literary Relations with Germany*, p. 432.

comic spirit which he considered one of the weak spots in German letters. German attempts at comedy remind him of the dancing of Atta Troll, and he feels that Heinrich Heine alone has not been enough to discipline the Germans in the much-needed comic spirit.[15]

Among the great German names, we are told, none was so dear to Meredith as that of Heine.[16] The one work of Meredith's (which unfortunately falls outside the scope of this study) that shows the greatest influence of Heine is *The Tragic Comedians*. In the fourth chapter of the work, Alvan's talk with Clothilde is about statesmen, European politics, and literature. We are told they capped verses of the "incomparable Heinrich" which Meredith describes as "lucid metheglin, with here and there no dubious flavour of acid, and a lively sting in the tail of the honey. Sentiment, cynicism, and satin impropriety and scabrous," continues Meredith, "are among those verses, where pure poetry has a recognized voice; but the lower elements constitute the popularity in a cultivated society inclining to wantonness out of bravado as well as by taste." Somewhat earlier, in 1868, he had said:

Heinrich Heine added a new element to his songs and ballads: an irritant exile breathed irony into them, and shaped them into a general form and significance. He is the unique example of a man who made himself his constant theme, and he pursued it up to the time when he was rescued from his "mattress-grave." By virtue of a cunning art he caused it to be interesting while he lived. I feel the monotony of it begin to grow on me often now when I take up the Buch der Lieder, the Neuer Frühling, and the Romanzero.[17]

Sir Henry Head (b. 1861) is undoubtedly far better known in his connection with the practice of medicine than as a purely literary figure. In one of his few literary efforts, a volume called *Destroyers*, is included a number of poems called *Songs of La Mouche*[18]—supposedly the poems of Camille

15. *Ibid.*, pp. 432-433.
16. R. E. Sencourt, *The Life of George Meredith*, p. 16.
17. *Miscellaneous Prose*, pp. 144-145.
18. *Destroyers and Other Verses*, pp. 19-54.

Selden. The poems are divided into two sections, the first containing five poems based on Camille Selden's relationship to Alfred Meissner and the second containing twenty-one poems based on her relationship to Heinrich Heine.

Although Richard LeGallienne (b. 1866) is without doubt English by birth, the question of including him in this study is a doubtful one because of the claim America has upon him. Certainly, however, it will do no harm to mention that in his *Old Love Stories Retold* is found an account of Heine and Matilda[19] among a collection that includes the stories of Dante and Beatrice, Shelley and Mary Godwin, Keats and Fanny Brawne, etc.

Maurice Baring (b. 1874), discussed also as a translator of Heine, has written a delightful, imaginary account of a very pleasant and agreeable evening at Madame Jaubert's in Paris on the occasion of which a distinguished group including Prince and Princess Belgiojoso, Madame de Vergennes, M. de Musset, and Herr Heinrich Heine gathered to meet the celebrated Bellini.[20]

A. E. Housman (1859-1936) and George Bernard Shaw (b. 1856) both show unmistakable influences of Heine. The form of Housman, who is a sort of blend of Baudelaire and Heine, often resembles closely that of his German predecessor. As an iconoclastic critic, as the mocker of Philistinism, as a wit, humorist and satirist, George Bernard Shaw is in more than one respect the natural and logical successor of the brilliant and original Heine. Maurice Bourgeois tells us that if a literary parallel be sought for the sardonic humor, the tragicomic expression, the utter disillusionment, the total renouncement, and the note of passionate, exuberant revolt in the works of John Millington Synge (1871-1909), we should turn to Heinrich Heine.[21]

19. Pp. 69-83.
20. Maurice Baring, *Dead Letters*, pp. 183-189.
21. *John Millington Synge and the Irish Theater*, p. 218.

CONCLUSION

IT IS EVIDENT that but a mere handful of translators possessed the requisite lyric gift to render the superb lyric gems of Heine. Of all of the translations attempted, those of Heine's exquisite lyrics of purely subjective mood prove the least satisfactory and gratifying. Perhaps the reason lies in the fact that English poetry can boast such a wealth of exquisite lyrics of her own, that the mere imitation of Heine's gems finds no ecstatic welcome. The reason, however, probably lies in the fact that the English lyric, in its robust and crystal-clear nature, is so utterly foreign to the dreamy, speculative, and passive quality of Heine's delightful songs, that the yawning gulf between is not to be bridged—even by translation. In most instances, greater success is noted in the versions of Heine's longer pieces— notably his ballads—which is probably accounted for by their kinship to the English ballad form.

Even if an excellent stylist, the translator is seldom able to reproduce accurately the rhythm and rhyme of his original upon which so often depend the nuances which make the original so rich and effective. And so it is in the case of the English translators of Heine. Much of the delicate humor, elusive pathos, shy satire, and sudden wit are hopelessly lost in the English versions. The gauzelike delicacy and the butterfly grace of the originals is almost invariably lost, and far too many of the English versions are marred by cumbersome, unwieldy Germanisms and inelegant English phraseology.

A great majority of the translators have taken Heine's simplicity merely as a matter of course and have failed absolutely to realize that the naïve quality of his work was arrived at only after the most conscientious effort. "Spare not the critical amputating knife. Be severe with yourself," Heine wrote to Steinmann and Rousseau as early as 1820. "That is the artist's first commandment."[1] The Spartan-like rigor in the matter of style was an important question to Heine who, like Flaubert and Thomas Mann, believed that the manner in which a thing is said is of far greater importance than the thing itself. "In art the form is everything, the substance nothing," states an aphorism in his *Gedanken und Einfälle*.[2] The German lyric in the hands of Brentano, Novalis, Uhland, and even Eichendorf had passed the flowering stage and was on the road to decay when Heine discovered simplicity and made of it a studied and conscious art. It is in reproducing this simplicity—the simplicity of "Ein Fichtenbaum steht einsam" and "Du bist wie eine Blume"—that the great majority of the translators fail so miserably.

Little success, too, is noted in the extremely difficult reproduction of the ironic antithesis which so thoroughly characterizes the work of Heine. The sting of the bee lurking in the rose—often merely the "shrill laughter of utter despair," often the brave, mocking humor of a being who spurns self-pity, often, too, the result of the established psychological fact that any given emotion if carried to an extreme has the natural tendency to veer sharply toward an opposite feeling—is impossible to reproduce even by the most skilful translator. "Je wichtiger ein Gegenstand ist," says Heine, "desto lustiger muss man ihn behandeln; das blutige Gemetzel der Schlachten, das schaurige Sichelwetzen des Todes wäre nicht zu ertragen, erklänge nicht dabei die betäubende türkische Musik mit ihren freudigen Pauken und Trompeten."[3]

The translators of Heine are, as Henley would say, too often mere "graveyard masons that would play the sculptor."[4]

1. *Heinrich Heines Briefwechsel*, ed. by F. Hirth, I, 157.
2. *Heinrich Heines sämtliche Werke*, ed. by Ernst Elster, VII, 413.
3. Erich Eckertz, *Heine und sein Witz*, pp. 10-11.
4. W. E. Henley, *Works*, V, 96.

Conclusion

In many instances the versions are clever, but they are not Heine. To translate the German lyricist demands genius akin to that of Heine himself, and but few of the English translators can boast that quality. Heine's "anguish dipped in honey" defies the ordinary craftsman.

Of Heine one may say, as Schiller said of Wallenstein, "Von der Parteien Gunst und Hass verwirrt, Schwankt sein Charakterbild in der Geschichte," for, as yet, a purely objective verdict of the poet and man has still to be given The critics of England, though, have gone a long way toward blazing the path of true appreciation for the works and for the life of Heinrich Heine. A number of the criticisms are purely biographical in nature, others are historical, others attempt to analyze the work of the poet, and still others seek to delineate the character of the man Heine. There is scarcely a phase of the work and character of the poet that remains untouched. Practically each critic has something interesting and something original to say of the many factors which shaped the character and work of the great German genius—his Bonapartism, his Saint-Simonism, his Hellenism, his Romanticism, his Orientalism, etc.—and the judgments passed are in most cases exceedingly sound and appropriate.

The major emphases are upon the biography, the art, and the religious and political views of the poet. The biographical details are unusually accurate, considering the fact that many of the intimate facts concerning Heine were not available at the time most of the reviews were written. In the later criticisms, the works of Stigand and Strodtmann are depended upon to a large extent. Extremely courageous and, for the most part, successful efforts are made to trace Heine's religious and political views through the difficult and confusing maze of the poet's vacillating convictions. Equal success is met with in the attempt of the critics to render verdicts upon the art of Heine.

Occasionally, errors are made in attempting to read into

Heine things that are simply not there. "Il n'y a," said Heine, "qu'une chose qui puisse me blesser, et de la manière la plus douloureuse, c'est qu'on veuille expliquer l'esprit de mes poésies par l'histoire (vous savez ce que ce mot signifie) de l'auteur . . . et surtout de son vivant."[5] To proclaim Heine, as most of the critics have done, the rightful successor of Goethe, and to see in his work the reactions of the age in which he lived are both intelligent and well-warranted criticisms. To declare Heine the interpreter of his age, as a few critics would have us to believe, is an honor the German poet does not deserve. It is true that Heine exercised a more vital influence than Goethe; it is true that Heine is a more genuine representative of the age with its aspirations, its despair, and its revolts against traditions and dogma. It is for this reason that Matthew Arnold calls him the paladin of the modern spirit.

But Heine is not the interpreter of the age; he is its mirror. And those who attempt to read into him an active participation in the affairs of his time strike wide of the mark, for Heine is fundamentally only an artist whose chief concern is art. "I am for the autonomy of art," he writes in *Salon IV*. "It is not to be regarded as the hand-maiden of religion or politics; it is its own definitive justification, just as the world is."[6] And again, in a letter to Karl Gutzkow, he states, "My motto remains: Art is the purpose of art, as love is the purpose of love, and even as life itself is the purpose of life."[7] In a remarkable passage in *Lutezia*, he defines the "supreme consideration of art as the self-conscious freedom of the spirit, just as it is the highest in all other manifestations of life."[8] No, Heine with his impish gaiety, his maudlin sentiment, his bitter pessimism is "no Hebrew prophet singing in the wilderness but a sophisticated child of his time."[9]

While the opinions found in the bits taken from the English letters, diaries, notebooks, lectures, and conversations are

---

5. Gauthiez, *op. cit.*, p. 81.
6. Elster, *op. cit.*, IV, 524 ff.
7. Hirth, *op. cit.*, II, 241 ff.
8. Elster, *op. cit.*, VI, 348.
9. Wood, *op. cit.*, p. 6.

mostly those representing a favorable attitude toward the German writer, there are, too, frequent references of a disparaging nature. Heine, because of his vacillating and unstable outlook upon the serious problems of his time, has found alike both friends and enemies among his English readers. No other German writer has been both so highly praised and so deeply censured as Heinrich Heine.

The vast majority of Englishmen, who, following the lead of Matthew Arnold, George Eliot, and other enthusiasts, have spoken in terms of wild and unmitigated enthusiasm of the German poet attest the high esteem in which the writer has been held in England. Aside from the innumerable critics and translators of Heine's works, it is fundamentally to those individuals who have mentioned him in passing that Heine owes his immense popularity in Britain. No less is this fame due to the handful of poets who, in commemorative verses, have sung the name of Heinrich Heine in glowing and passionate tones throughout the length and breadth of the English realm.

Heine also found his enemies in England. What man would not have so done who left himself exposed in so many vulnerable spots as did Heine? Ludwig Börne once said that "Nature has luckily given the rest of us wretched mortals only one back apiece, so that we have only to fear the blows of fate from one direction; but poor Heine has two backs; he is afraid of being struck by aristocrats on the one side and by democrats on the other, and in order to evade both he has to move forward and backwards at the same time."[10] Upon these "two backs" have fallen the brunt of many attacks, some of which have no doubt been merited. On purely religious, political, and social grounds, Heine has had much to fear from English writers. In a few instances, the disfavor and disrepute in which Heine has been held have their roots primarily in racial antipathy. Like the truculent Bartels, a few English writers have never quite put beyond them the fact that Heine was funda-

10. Ludwig Marcuse, *Heine: A Life Between Love and Hate*, pp. 246-247.

mentally a Jew and, as such, deserving of little but scorn and contempt. They have denied him a deep and sympathetic understanding and knowledge of German character, and have alluded to the Oriental and Hebraic coloring of many of his poems, and have thereby satisfied themselves, if not the world, that Heine was not a German poet but merely a "dirty blaspheming Jew." In a letter to J. Lehmann (June 25, 1823), Heine once wrote: "Es liegt in meinem Charakter, oder besser gesagt in meiner Krankheit, dass ich in Momenten des Missmuts meine besten Freunde nicht schone und sie sogar auf die verletzendste Weise persifliere und malträtiere."[11] It is this absolute disregard on Heine's part of the sacred bonds of friendship, decency, religion, and the finer impulses that has brought upon him the wrath of so many "respectable" Englishmen who have entirely overlooked the fact that Heine can scarcely be blamed for using the weapons nature so readily placed at his disposal, his wit and his scorching satire, to ward off the attacks to which he was exposed all of his life. "What sustains me," he says, "is the pride of my mental superiority which I received at birth, and the consciousness that no man in the world can with fewer strokes of the pen avenge himself more effectively."[12]

While Heinrich Heine has by no means exerted an influence upon English literature comparable to that of his great predecessor and contemporary, Johann Wolfgang Goethe, there are nevertheless unmistakable evidences of the great *Liederdichter's* style in English poetry. A larger number of poets than at first might be thought have often approached the Heinesque mood in short English lyrics. A great many, too, have obviously followed Heine in his treatment of love, the sea, and nature. As far as mechanical devices are concerned, there are numerous instances of influence in such matters as cadence, parallelism, contrast, *Häufung und Wiederholung*, and *freier Rhythmus*. Occasionally, the more subtle qualities

---

11. Elster, *Works*, I, 30.   12. H. Walter, *Heinrich Heine*, p. 30.

of Heine's poetry have been successfully reproduced—revulsion of mood, subtle anguish, poignancy, monosyllabic simplicity, and the like. In addition to those poets who show direct influence, there are, too, a few who, in one way or another, have adapted from the German singer or made reference to him.

Victoria's most distinguished critic once said, "Heine is in the European literature of that quarter of a century which follows the death of Goethe, incomparably the most important spirit." Despite Matthew Arnold's broad statement, the eminent critic could scarcely have realized the full significance of Heinrich Heine to Victorian England alone, and could certainly not have suspected the enthusiasm with which the present century would greet him. In the isolated field of translation, it is seen that over a hundred poets have thought the German bard worthy of English dress. The number of critics who have treated Heine as man and writer is nearly equally large. Practically every English writer of any prominence whatsoever appears to have been acquainted with the life and works of the great German singer, and the letters, diaries, notes, and conversations recorded attest the widespread popularity of the German writer. Although Heine's influence upon the poetry of England is, perhaps, not so great as that of a few other poets, it is nonetheless unmistakable and in full evidence and significance.

To England, Heine is undoubtedly the singer of the *Buch der Lieder* with its wild passion and naïve simplicity—the singer from whose lips emanates in a strange, unattempted minor key the melancholy tale of love sung in a thousand variations. In the *Romantische Schule*, Heine once described Sterne in words strangely applicable to himself, and it is this Heine who has so endeared himself to England:

He was the foster child of the pale tragic Muse. Once in a transport of gruesome tenderness, she kissed his young heart so mightily, so passionately, with such fiery absorption, that it began to bleed, and all at once to understand the sufferings of the world, and to be filled with infinite pity. Poor young poet's heart! But then the younger daughter of Mnemosyne, the rosy goddess of laughter, came quickly running, took the aching child in her arms, and strove to cheer him with mirth and singing; and she gave him for a toy to play with the comic mask, and the bells of the fool's cap, and soothingly kissed his lips, and printed on them all her lightness, all her defiant pleasure, all her witty mocking. And ever since his heart and his lips are in strange contradiction; and many a time when he was tragically moved, and he is fain to pour out the deepest feelings of that bleeding heart, then, to his own astonishment, from his lips come forth the most amusing, the most laughable sayings.

This is the Heine that England has taken to its heart in so amazing a fashion. Heinrich Heine will long continue to interest not Germany alone but Europe in general, for he is fundamentally a European poet, and to him more than to Wallenstein applies Schiller's famous line, "His life was a battle and a march."

APPENDIX
BIBLIOGRAPHY

Appendix

HEINE'S GRAVE

by

MATTHEW ARNOLD

"*Henri Heine*"—'tis here!
The black tombstone, the name
Carved there—no more! and the smooth,
Swarded alleys, the limes
Touch'd with yellow by hot
Summer, but under them still
In September's bright afternoon
Shadow, and verdure, and cool!
Trim Montmartre! the faint
Murmur of Paris outside;
Crisp everlasting-flowers,
Yellow and black, on the graves.

Half blind, palsied, in pain,
Hither to come, from the streets'
Uproar, surely not loath
Wast thou, Heine!—to lie
Quiet! to ask for closed
Shutters, and darken'd room,
And cool drinks, and an eased

Posture, and opium, no more!
Hither to come, and to sleep
Under the wings of Renown.

Ah! not little, when pain
Is most quelling, and man
Easily quell'd, and the fine
Temper of genius alive
Quickest to ill, is the praise
Not to have yielded to pain!

No small boast, for a weak
Son of mankind, to the earth
Pinn'd by the thunder, to rear
His bolt-scathed front to the stars;
And, undaunted, retort
'Gainst thick-crashing, insane,
Tyrannous tempests of bale,
Arrowy lightnings of soul!
Hark! through the alley resounds
Mocking laughter! A film
Creeps o'er the sunshine; a breeze
Ruffles the warm afternoon,
Saddens my soul with its chill.
Gibing of spirits in scorn
Shakes every leaf of the grove,
Mars the benignant repose
Of this amiable home of the dead.

Bitter spirits! ye claim
Heine?—Alas, he is yours!
Only a moment I long'd
Here in the quiet to snatch
From such mates the outworn
Poet, and steep him in calm.
Only a moment! I knew
Whose he was who is here
Buried, I knew he was yours!
Ah, I knew that I saw
Here no sepulchre built
In the laurell'd rock, o'er the blue
Naples bay, for a sweet

Tender Virgil! no tomb
On Ravenna sands, in the shade
Of Ravenna pines, for a high
Austere Dante! no grave
By the Avon side, in the bright
Stratford meadows, for thee,
Shakespeare! loveliest of souls,
Peerless in radiance, in joy.

What so harsh and malign,
Heine! distils from thy life,
Poisons the peace of thy grave?

I chide with thee not, that thy sharp
Upbraidings often assail'd
England, my country; for we,
Fearful and sad, for her sons,
Long since, deep in our hearts,
Echo the blame of her foes.
We, too, sigh that she flags;
We, too, say that she now,
Scarce comprehending the voice
Of her greatest, golden-mouth'd sons
Of a former age any more,
Stupidly travels her round
Of mechanic business, and lets
Slow die out of her life
Glory, and genius, and joy.
So thou arraign'st her, her foe;
So we arraign her, her sons.

Yes, we arraign her! but she,
The weary Titan! with deaf
Ears, and labor-dimm'd eyes,
Regarding neither to right
Nor left, goes passively by,
Staggering on to her goal;
Bearing on shoulders immense,
Atlantean, the load,
Wellnigh not to be borne,
Of the too vast orb of her fate.

But was it thou—I think
Surely it was—that bard
Unnamed, who, Goethe said,
Had every other gift, but wanted love;
Love, without which the tongue
Even of angels sounds amiss?

Charm is the glory which makes
Song of the poet divine;
Love is the fountain of charm.
How without charm wilt thou draw,
Poet! the world to thy way?
Not by the lightnings of wit!
Not by the thunder of scorn!
These to the world, too, are given;
Wit it possesses, and scorn—
Charm is the poet's alone.
*Hollow and dull are the great,
And artists envious, and the mob profane.*
We know all this, we know!
Cam'st thou from heaven, O child
Of light! but this to declare?
Alas! to help us forget
Such barren knowledge awhile,
God gave the poet his song.

Therefore a secret unrest
Tortured thee, brilliant and bold!
Therefore triumph itself
Tasted amiss to thy soul.
Therefore, with blood of thy foes,
Trickled in silence thine own.
Therefore the victor's heart
Broke on the field of his fame.

Ah! as of old, from the pomp
Of Italian Milan, the fair
Flower of marble of white
Southern palaces—steps
Bordered by statues, and walks
Terraced, and orange bowers

Heavy with fragrance—the blond
German Kaiser full oft
Long'd himself back to the fields,
Rivers, and high-roof'd towns
Of his native Germany; so
So, how often! from hot
Paris drawing-rooms, and lamps
Blazing, and brilliant crowds,
Starr'd and jewell'd, of men
Famous, of women the queens
Of dazzling converse, and fumes
Of praise—hot, heady fumes, to the poor brain
That mount, that madden!—how oft
Heine's spirit outworn
Long'd itself out of the din
Back to the tranquil, the cool
Far German home of his youth!

See! in the May afternoon,
O'er the fresh short turf of the Hartz,
A youth, with the foot of youth,
Heine! thou climbest again.
Up, through the tall dark firs
Warming their heads in the sun,
Chequering the grass with their shade—
Up, by the stream with its huge
Moss-hung boulders and thin
Musical water half-hid—
Up, o'er the rock-strewn slope,
With the sinking sun, and the air
Chill, and the shadows now
Long on the grey hillside—
To the stone-roof'd hut at the top.

Or, yet later, in watch
On the roof of the Brocken tower
Thou standest, gazing! to see
The broad red sun, over field,
Forest and city and spire
And mist-track'd stream of the wide
Wide German land, going down

In a bank of vapors—again
Standest! at nightfall, alone.

Or, next morning, with limbs
Rested by slumber, and heart
Freshen'd and light with the May
O'er the gracious spurs coming down
Of the Lower Hartz, among oaks,
And beechen coverts, and copse
Of hazels green in whose depth
Ilse, the fairy transform'd,
In a thousand water-breaks light
Pours her petulant youth—
Climbing the rock which juts
O'er the valley, the dizzily perch'd
Rock! to its Iron Cross
Once more thou cling'st; to the Cross
Clingest! with smiles, with a sigh.

Goethe, too, had been there.
In the long past winter he came
To the frozen Hartz, with his soul
Passionate, eager, his youth
All in ferment;—but he
Destined to work and to live
Left it, and thou, alas!
Only to laugh and to die.

But something prompts me: Not thus
Take leave of Heine, not thus
Speak the last word at his grave!
Not in pity and not
With half censure—with awe
Hail, as it passes from earth
Scattering lightnings, that soul.

The spirit of the world
Beholding the absurdity of men—
Their vaunts, their feats—let a sardonic smile
For one short moment wander o'er his lips.
That smile was Heine! for its earthly hour
The strange guest sparkled; now 'tis pass'd away.

That was Heine! and we,
Myriads who live, who have lived,
What are we all, but a mood,
A single mood, of the life
Of the Being in whom we exist,
Who alone is all things in one.

Spirit, who fillest us all!
Spirit, who utterest in each
New-coming son of mankind
Such of thy thoughts as thou wilt!
O thou, one of whose moods,
Bitter and strange, was the life
Of Heine—his strange, alas!
His bitter life—may a life
Other and milder be mine!
May'st thou a mood more serene,
Happier, have utter'd in mine!
May'st thou the rapture of peace
Deep have embreathed at its core!
Made it a ray of thy thought!
Made it a beat of thy joy!

Bibliography

I. MATERIAL ON HEINE

1. Books

Allen, S. A. "Heine and the Schnaderhüpfel." *Studies in Popular Poetry*. Chicago: University of Chicago Press, 1902.

Atkins, H. G. *Heine*. London: George Rutledge & Sons, 1929.

Bacon, Grace M. The Personal and Literary Relations of Heinrich Heine to Karl Immermann. Ph.D. Thesis: University of Michigan, 1910.

Baerlein, Henry. *Heine the Strange Guest*. London: Geoffrey Bles, 1928.

Bartels, Adolph. *Heinrich Heine Auch ein Denkmal*. Dresden: C. A. Kochs, 1906.

Bellaigue, Camille. *Un Siècle de musique française*. Paris: Ch. Delograve, 1887.

Berendsohn, W. A. *Der Lebendige Heine im Germanischen Norden*. Kopenhagen: Det Schonbergske, 1935.

Betz, Louis P. *Heine in Frankreich*. Zürich: J. Schabelitz, 1894.

Beyer, Paul. *Der junge Heine*. Berlin: G. Grote, 1911.

Bossert, Ä. *Essais de littérature française et allemande*, 1913.

Bottacchiari, Rodolfo. *Heine*. Torino: Fratelli Bocca, 1927.

Brandes, Georg. *Hauptströmungen der Literatur des 19ten Jahrhunderts*. Berlin: Erich Reiss, 1924.

Braun, Wilhelm A. *Types of Weltschmerz in German Poetry*. New York: Columbia University Press, 1905.

Brod, Max. *Heinrich Heine*. Amsterdam: Allert de Lange, 1935.

Browne, Lewis. *That Man Heine*. New York: Literary Guild of America, 1927.

Butler, Eliza M. *The Saint-Simonian Religion in Germany*. Cambridge: University Press, 1926.

Chiles, James A. *Ueber den Gebrauch des Beiwortes in Heines Gedichten*. Ph.D. Thesis: University of Illinois, 1908.

Ducros, Louis. *Henri Heine et son temps.* Paris: Didot et Cie., 1886.
Eckertz, Erich. *Heine und sein Witz.* Berlin: Emil Felber, 1908.
Eggert, Carl E. *Heine's Poems.* New York: Ginn & Co., 1906.
Elster, Ernst, ed. *Heinrich Heines sämtliche Werke.* 7 vols. Leipzig: Bibliographisches Institut, 1890.
Embden, Ludwig von. *The Family Life of Heinrich Heine.* Tr. by Chas. DeKay. New York: Cassell Publ. Co., 1892.
Ense, Varnhagen von. *Aus dem Nachlass Varnhagens von Ense.* Leipzig: F. A. Brockhaus, 1865.
Evans, Thomas W. *The Memoirs of Heinrich Heine.* London: George Bell & Sons, 1884.
Faust, Albert B., ed. *Heine's Prose.* New York: The Macmillan Co., 1899.
Fischer, August W. *Ueber die volkstümlichen Elemente in den Gedichten Heines.* Berlin: E. Ebering, 1905.
Franzos, Karl E. *Heines Geburtstag.* Berlin: Concordia, 1900.
Gautier, Théophile. *Portraits et souvenirs littéraires.* Paris: Michel Levy Frères, 1875.
Gauthiez, Pierre. *Henri Heine.* Paris: Bloud & Cie., 1913.
Goedeke, Karl. *Grundriss zur Geschichte der deutschen Dichtung.* 12 vols. Dresden: L. Ehlermann, 1905. VIII, 526-64.
Grenier, Edouard. *Souvenirs littéraires.* Paris: Alphonse Lemerre, 1894.
Grisebach, Eduard. *Das Goethesche Zeitalter der deutschen Dichtung.* Leipzig: W. Engelmann, 1891.
Heine, Heinrich. *Briefe.* Hamburg: Hoffmann & Campe, 1863.
Heine, Henri. *Correspondance inédite.* Paris: Calmann Lévy, 1877.
Heine, Maximilian. *Errinnerungen an Heinrich Heine.* Berlin: Ferd. Dümmler, 1868.
Hess, John A. *Heine's Views on German Traits of Character.* New York: G. E. Stechert & Co., 1929.
Hirth, Friedrich, ed. *Heinrich Heines Briefwechsel.* 3 vols. München: Georg Müller, 1914-1920.
Houben, H. H. *Gespräche mit Heine.* Frankfurt am Main: Rütten & Loening, 1926.
Karpeles, Gustav. *Heinrich Heine. Aus seinem Leben und aus seiner Zeit.* Leipzig: Adolf Titze, 1899.
——. *Heinrich Heines Autobiographie nach seinen Werken, Briefen und Gesprächen.* Berlin: Robert Oppenheim, 1888.
——, ed. *Heinrich Heines gesammelte Werke.* 9 vols. Berlin: G. Grote, 1893.

———. *Heinrich Heine's Memoirs.* Tr. by Gilbert Cannan 2 vols. New York: John Lane Co., 1910.

Kauffmann, Max. *Heines Charakter und die moderne Seele.* Zürich: Albert Müller, 1902.

Launay, Robert. *Les Pères de la démocratie.* Paris: Perrin & Cie., 1903.

Lees, John, ed. *'Buch der Lieder' von H. Heine.* London: Longmans, Green & Co., 1920.

Marcuse, Ludwig. *Heine: A Life Between Love and Hate.* New York: Farrar & Rinehart, 1933.

———. *Heinrich Heine, ein Leben zwischen Gestern und Morgen.* Berlin: E. Rowohlt, 1932.

Mauclair, Camille. *La Vie humilié de Henri Heine.* Paris: Libraire Plon, 1930.

Meissner, Alfred. *Heinrich Heine Erinnerungen.* Hamburg: Hoffmann & Campe, 1856.

Meyer, Friedrich. *Verzeichnis einer Heine-Bibliothek.* Leipzig: Dyksche Buchhandlung, 1905.

Meyer, Richard M. *Grundriss der neueren deutschen Literaturgeschichte.* Berlin: Georg Bondi, 1902.

Monahan, Michael. *Heinrich Heine: Romance and Tragedy of the Poet's Life.* New York: Nicholas L. Brown, 1924.

Moos, Eugen. *Heine und Düsseldorf.* Ph.D. Thesis: University of Marburg, 1908. n.p.

Mücke, Georg. *Heinrich Heines Beziehungen zum deutschen Mittelalter.* Berlin: Alex. Duncker, 1908.

Nassen, J. *Heinrich Heines Familienleben.* Fulda: Fulda Actiendruckerei, 1895.

Puetzfeld, Carl. *Heinrich Heines Verhältnis zur Religion.* Berlin: G. Grote, 1912.

Ras, Gerard. *Börne und Heine als politische Schriftsteller.* Groningen: J. B. Wolters, 1926.

Sachs, Henry B. *Heine in America.* Publications of the University of Pennsylvania, 1916.

Salluste. *Les Origines secrètes du Bolchevisme: Henri Heine et Karl Marx.* Paris: Jules Tallandier, 1930.

Selden, Camille. *Les Derniers jours de Henri Heine.* Paris: Calmann Lévy, 1884.

Sharp, William. *Life of Heinrich Heine.* London: Walter Scott, 1888.

Steinmann, Friedrich. *H. Heine: Denkwürdigkeiten und Erlebnisse aus meinem Zusammenleben mit ihm.* Prag: J. L. Kober, 1857.
Stigand, William. *The Life, Work, and Opinions of Heinrich Heine.* 2 vols. London: Longmans, Green & Co., 1875.
Strodtmann, Adolf. *Heinrich Heines Leben und Werke.* Berlin: F. Duncker, 1873-1874.
Topin, A. *Heine 1797-1856: La Vie de Heine—L'homme, l'œuvre —Heine et son temps.* Paris: Larousse, 1911.
Tournoux, Georges. *Les Mots étrangers dans l'œuvre poétique de Henri Heine.* Lille: Faculté Catholique, 1920.
Untermeyer, Louis. *Heinrich Heine: Paradox and Poet.* 2 vols. New York: Harcourt, Brace & Co., 1937.
Vallentin, Antonina. *Henri Heine.* Paris: Gallimard, 1934.
Victor, Walther. *Mathilda: Ein Leben um Heinrich Heine.* Leipzig: E. P. Tal & Co., 1931.
Walter, H. *Heinrich Heine: A Critical Examination of the Poet and His Works.* New York: E. P. Dutton & Co., 1930.
Weckmüller, Arthur. *Heines Stil.* Breslau: Priebatsch, 1934.
Weidekampf, Ilse. *Traum und Wirklichkeit in der Romantik und bei Heine.* Leipzig: Mayer & Müller, 1932.
Weill, Alexandre. *Souvenirs intimes de Henri Heine.* Paris: E. Dentu, 1883.
Wood, Frank H. *Heine as a Critic of His Own Works.* New York: New York University Press, 1934.
Zianitska, K. *Heinrich Heine der Liederdichter.* Leipzig: C. E. Kollmann, 1864.

2. *Periodicals*

Anonymous (listed chronologically):
"Recent German Lyrical Poetry," *Edinburgh Review*, LVI (October, 1832), 37-51.
Athenaeum, No. 278 (1833), pp. 115-116.
"Reminiscences of Men and Things," *Fraser's Magazine for Town and Country*, XXVI (December, 1842), 733-736.
"Heine, His Works and Times," *Tait's Edinburgh Magazine*, XVIII (1851), N. S., 679-683.
"The Life and Writings of Heinrich Heine," *Sharpe's London Magazine*, XVI (1852), 291-298, 362-369.
"Heinrich Heine," *Edinburgh Review*, CIV (1856), 192-209.
"The Last Days of a Poet," *New Monthly Magazine*, CXVII (1859), 363-370.

Dublin University Magazine, LIV (1859), 590-598.
"The Sharpshooters of the Press," *Cornhill Magazine*, VII (1862), 246-251.
Dark Blue Magazine, I (1871), 486.
Blackwood's Edinburgh Magazine, CXXII (1877), 75-89.
"Life and Works of Heinrich Heine," *London Quarterly Review*, LVIII (1882), 411-438.
"Heine's Reisebilder," *Athenaeum*, 1883, pp. 115-116.
"Heine's Reisebilder," *Spectator*, LX (1887), 77-78.
"Heinrich Heine," *Westminster Review*, CXXIX (1888), 426-441.
"Heinrich Heine," *Quarterly Review*, CLXIX (1889), 399-430.
"Heine's Works in English," *Spectator*, LXVIII (1892), 92-93.
"Choice Poems of Heinrich Heine," *Athenaeum*, No. 3649 (1897), p. 453.
"Heine's Mouche," *Academy*, LV (1898), 110-111.
"The Ideals of Heinrich Heine," *Quarterly Review*, CLXXXIX (1899), 424-452.
"Heine's Frau Mathilde," *Temple Bar*, CXX (1900), 395-405.
Athenaeum, No. 4019 (1904), p. 617.
"Heinrich Heine: Emotion and Irony," *Edinburgh Review*, CCVII (1908), 151-177.
"Heine," *Spectator*, CLVI (1936), 299.
Beard, Charles. "Heinrich Heine," *Theological Review*, XIII (1876), 174-201.
Black, G. A. "James Thomson: His Translations of Heine," *Modern Language Review*, XXXI (1936), 48-54.
Buchheim, Dr. "Heine's Centenary," *Athenaeum*, No. 3660 (1897), p. 855.
Butler, E. M. "Heine and the Saint Simonians," *Modern Language Review*, XVIII (1923), 68-85.
Davy, E. M. "Some Passages in the Life of Heine," *Belgravia London Magazine*, LXXXIII (1894), 291-299.
Eliot, George. "German Wit: Heinrich Heine," *Westminster and Foreign Quarterly*, LXV (1856), 1-33.
Embden, Ludwig von. "Some Unpublished Letters of Heine," *New Review*, VIII (1893), 139-150.
Fane, Julian. "Heinrich Heine: Poet and Humorist," *Saturday Review*, I, 13-14.
Garry, Jaye. "Heine in London," *Gentleman's Magazine*, CCXCV (1903), 231-243.

Bibliography

Gordon, Lucie Duff. "Some Translations of Heine," *Murray's Magazine*, IX (1891), 769-776.
Gordon, Samuel. "Heine, the German and the Jew," *Contemporary Review*, CXXVII (1925), 230-236.
Gosse, Edmund. "The Centenary of Heine," *Saturday Review*, LXXXIV (1898), 705-706.
Grant, Charles. "Heinrich Heine," *Contemporary Review*, XXXVIII (1880), 372-395.
Hayens, Kenneth. "Heine, Hazlitt and Mrs. Jameson," *Modern Language Review*, XVII (1922), 42-49.
Henderson, James. "Heine and Sir Walter Scott," *Temple Bar*, CXXIX (1904), 284-290.
Hewlett, Henry G. "Heinrich Heine's Life and Work," *Fraser's Magazine*, XCIV (1876), 600-623.
Hillard, Kate. "Heinrich Heine," *Victoria Magazine*, XXII (1874), 501-515.
Japp, A. H. "Heine," *British Quarterly Review*, LXXIII (1881), 137-154.
———. "Recurrent Ideas in Heine," *Gentleman's Magazine*, CCLII (1882), 71-78.
Kennard, Nina H. "Henri Heine: A Family Portrait," *Contemporary Review*, XLI (1882), 981-993.
Kernahan, Coulson. "Some Aspects of Heine," *Gentleman's Magazine*, CCLXI (1886), 233-253.
Lester, J. D. "Heinrich Heine," *Fortnightly Review*, XII (1869), 287-303.
Lytton, Robert. "Heinrich Heine's Last Poems and Thoughts," *Fortnightly Review*, XIII (1870), 257-277.
McLintock, R. "The Works of Heinrich Heine," *Academy*, XL (1891), 256-257.
———. "Heinrich Heines Familienleben," *Academy*, XLIII (1893), 364-365.
Magnus, Laurie. "Songs from Heine," *Fortnightly Review*, LXXX (1903), 525-528.
Montefiore, L. A. "Heinrich Heine in Relation to Religion and Politics," *Fortnightly Review*, XXVIII (1877), 325-339.
Peterson, Franklin. "Heine on Music and Musicians," *Fortnightly Review*, C (1913), 296-313.
Pryde, Thomas. "Heine's Visit to London," *National Review*, X (1887), 542-548.

Ransom, Arthur. "About Heine," *Westminster Review*, CLXXV (1911), 62-68, 149-155.
Royston, Alice G. "The Book of Ideas," *Universal Review*, VII (1890), 437-452.
Samuel, H. B. "Heinrich Heine," *Fortnightly Review*, LXXXV (1906), 854-870.
Shuldham, E. B. "Heinrich Heine," *Temple Bar*, XXIX (1870), 210-225.
———. "Heine as an Impressionist," *Temple Bar*, CXXI (1900), 420-430.
Sichel, Walter. "The Letters of Heinrich Heine," *Nineteenth Century*, XVI (1884), 118-133.
Smith, Garnet. "Heine as an Art-Critic," *Magazine of Art*, X (1887), 402-404.
Soissons, Count de. "The Jews as a Revolutionary Leaven," *Quarterly Review*, CCXXXIII (1920), 172-187.
W., O. "The Centenary of the Birth of Heine," *Academy*, LII (1897), 553-554, 576-577.
Williams, Orlo. "The Heine of the Harzreise," *Cornhill Magazine*, LIX (1925), 407-422.
Wolfe, Humbert. "Three Poems from Heine," *Spectator*, CXXXIX (1927), 661.

II. GENERAL

Abbott, Claude C., ed. *The Letters of Gerald Manley Hopkins to Robert Bridges*. 2 vols. London: Oxford University Press, 1935.
Allingham, H. and Williams, E. B., eds. *Letters to William Allingham*. London: Longmans, Green & Co., 1911.
Allingham, William. *A Diary*. Ed. by H. Allingham & D. Radford. London: Macmillan & Co., 1907.
———. *Fifty Modern Poems*. London: Bell & Daldy, 1865.
———. *The Music Master*. London: G. Routledge & Co., 1855.
———. *Poems*. Boston: Ticknor & Fields, 1891.
———. *Robin Redbreast and Other Verses*. New York: The Macmillan Co., 1930.
———. *Songs, Ballads and Stories*. London: George Bell & Sons, 1877.
———. *Varieties in Prose*. 3 vols. London: Longmans, Green & Co., 1893.

Bibliography

Anderson, David. *Edith Cavell and Other Poems.* London: Longmans, Green & Co., 1918.
Archer, Charles. *William Archer: Life, Work and Friendships.* London: George Allen and Unwin, 1931.
Armour, Margaret, tr. *The Works of Heinrich Heine.* Vols. X, XI, XII. London: W. Heinemann, 1905.
Arnold, Matthew. *Essays in Criticism.* Boston: Ticknor & Fields, 1865.
———. *Poetical Works.* London: Macmillan & Co., 1913.
Ashe, Thomas. *Poems.* London: Geo. Bell & Sons, 1886.
Axon, William E. A. *The Ancoats Skylark and Other Verses Original and Translated.* London: John Heywood, 1894.
Baerlein, Henry. *Windrush and Evenlode.* London: Methuen & Co., 1915.
Baker, James. *Literary and Biographical Studies.* London: Chapman & Hall, 1908.
Balfour, Lady Betty, ed. *Personal and Literary Letters of Robert, First Earl of Lytton.* 2 vols. London: Longmans, Green & Co., 1906.
Balfour, Graham. *The Life of Robert Louis Stevenson.* New York: Charles Scribner's Sons, 1901.
Baring, Maurice. *Dead Letters.* New York: Doubleday, Page & Co., 1925.
Barry, William. *Heralds of Revolt.* London: Hodden & Stoughton, 1904.
Battersea, Constance, ed. *Lady de Rothschild: Extracts from Her Notebooks.* London: A. L. Humphreys, 1912.
Bennett, Arnold. *Journal of Arnold Bennett.* New York: Garden City Publishing Co., 1935.
Binyon, Lawrence, ed. *The Letters of Maurice Hewlett.* London: Methuen & Co., 1926.
Blackie, John S. *Notes of a Life.* Ed. by A. Stodart Walker. London: William Blackwood & Sons, 1910.
Blathwayt, William. *Collected Poems.* London: Sir Isaac Pitman & Sons, 1932.
Blind, Mathilde. *George Eliot.* Boston: Roberts Bros., 1885.
Booth, Eva Gore. *Poems.* London: Longmans, Green & Co., 1929.
Bourdillon, Francis W. *Verses.* London: Simpkins, Marshall & Co., 1910.
Bourgeois, Maurice. *John Millington Synge and the Irish Theater.* London: Constable & Co., 1913.

Bowring, E. A., tr. *The Poems of Heine.* London: H. G. Bohn, 1861.
Bowring, Sir John. *A Memorial Volume of Sacred Poetry.* London: Longmans, Green, Reader & Dyer, 1873.
Bowring, Lewin B. *Autobiographical Recollections of Sir John Bowring.* London: H. S. King & Co., 1877.
Boyd, Percy, tr. *A Book of Ballads from the German.* Dublin: James McGlashan, 1848.
Braybrooke, Patrick. *Oscar Wilde: A Study.* London: Braithwaite & Miller. n.d.
Brereton, John Le Gay. *The Travels of Prince Legion and Other Poems.* London: Brown, Green, Longmans & Roberts, 1857.
Brooks, A. B. and Harlan, J. L., eds. *Letters from Owen Meredith to Robert and Elizabeth Browning.* Baylor: University Press, 1937.
Brooks, Van Wyck. *John Addington Symonds: A Biographical Study.* New York: Mitchell Kennerley, 1914.
Brooksbank, Thomas, tr. *The Works of Heinrich Heine.* Vol. IX. London: William Heinemann, 1904.
Broughton, Lewlie N., and Stelter, B. F. *A Concordance to the Poems of Robert Browning.* New York: G. E. Stechert & Co., 1924.
Brown, Horatio F. *John Addington Symonds: A Biography.* 2 vols. New York: Charles Scribner's Sons, 1895.
———, ed. *Letters and Papers of John Addington Symonds.* London: John Murray, 1923.
Browning, Elizabeth B. *Poetical Works.* London: Humphrey Milford, 1932.
Browning, George. *Footprints: Poems Translated and Original.* London: J. C. Hotten, 1871.
Browning, Oscar. *Life of George Eliot.* London: Walter Scott, 1890.
Browning, Robert. *Complete Poetic and Dramatic Works.* New York: Houghton Mifflin Co., 1896.
Buchanan, Robert. *A Look Round Literature.* London: Ward & Downey, 1887.
———. *A Poet's Sketch Book.* London: Chatto & Windus, 1883.
———. *David Gray and Other Essays, Chiefly on Poetry.* London: Sampson Low, Son & Marston, 1868.
———. *Master Spirits.* London: H. S. King & Co., 1873.

Burdett, Osbert. *The Idea of Coventry Patmore.* London: Humphrey Milford, 1921.
Burt, Mary Anne, tr. *Specimens of the Choicest Lyrical Productions of the Most Celebrated German Poets from Klopstock to the Present Time.* London: Arthur Hall, Virtue & Co., 1856.
Butler, E. M. *The Saint Simonian Religion in Germany.* Cambridge: University Press, 1926.
Cain, Henry E. James Clarence Mangan and the Poe-Mangan Question. Ph.D. Thesis: Catholic University, 1929.
Caine, T. Hall. *Recollections of Dante Gabriel Rossetti.* Boston: Roberts Brown, 1883.
Call, Wathen M. W. *Golden Histories.* London: Smith, Elder & Co., 1871.
Carlyle, Thomas. *The Last Words of Thomas Carlyle.* New York: D. Appleton & Co., 1892.
Carmichael, W. S. *Miscellanea Poetica.* Edinburgh: Colston & Son, 1883.
Cautley, G. S. *A Century of Emblems.* London: Macmillan & Co., 1878.
———. *The Three Fountains with Other Verses.* London: Longmans, Green & Co., 1869.
Champneys, Basil. *Memoirs and Correspondence of Coventry Patmore.* 2 vols. London: Geo. Bell & Sons, 1900.
Charlton, William H. *Poems and Plays Original and Translated.* London: Longmans Green & Co., 1868.
Chawner, Edward. *Gleanings from the German and French Poets.* London: Ward, Lock & Co., 1879.
Chislett, William. *George Meredith: A Study and an Appraisal.* Boston: The Gorham Press, 1925.
Clough, Arthur Hugh. *Letters and Remains of Arthur Hugh Clough.* London: Spottiswoode & Co., 1865.
———. *Poems.* London: Macmillan & Co., 1920.
Clough, Mrs. A. H., ed. *Prose Remains of Arthur Hugh Clough.* New York: Macmillan & Co., 1888.
Cohen, Lucy. *Lady de Rothschild and Her Daughters.* London: John Murray, 1935.
Coke, Henry J. *Tracks of a Rolling Stone.* London: Smith, Elder & Co., 1905.
Coleridge, Mary E. *Poems.* London: Elkin Mathews, 1918.
Conrad, Hermann. *George Eliot: Ihr Leben und Schaffen.* Berlin: Georg Reimer, 1887.

Cotterill, H. B. *Poems.* London: William Blackwood & Sons, 1873.
Craigmyle, Elizabeth. *German Ballads.* London: Walter Scott, 1892.
———. *Poems and Translations.* Aberdeen: Edmond & Spark, 1886.
Cross, J. W., ed. *George Eliot's Life as Related in Her Letters and Journals.* 3 vols. New York: Houghton Mifflin Co., 1909.
Crump, Lucy, ed. *Letters of George Birkbeck Hill.* London: Edward Arnold, 1906.
D., G. E. *A Song of Caedmon and Other Poems.* Oxford: Wheeler & Day, 1871.
D'Anvers, Nancy, ed. *English Echoes of German Song.* London: Marcus Ward & Co., 1877.
Darlow, T. H. *Francis Ridley Havergal: A Memoir.* London: Nisket & Co., 1927.
Deakin, Mary H. *The Early Life of George Eliot.* Manchester: The University Press, 1913.
Dennis, John. *Verses.* London: Privately Printed, 1898.
Dexter, Charles. *Versions and Verses.* Cambridge: Sever & Francis, 1865.
Dilke, Charles W. *The Papers of a Critic.* 2 vols. London: John Murray, 1875.
Douglas, James. *Theodore Watts-Dunton: Poet, Novelist, Critic.* London: Hodder & Stoughten, 1904.
Dowden, Edward. *Essays Modern and Elizabethan.* London: J. M. Dent & Sons, 1910.
Dowden, E. D., ed. *Fragments from Old Letters.* 2 vols. New York: E. P. Dutton & Co., 1914.
———. *Letters of Edward Dowden and His Correspondents.* New York: E. P. Dutton & Co., 1914.
Dowson, Ernest. *The Poems and Prose of Ernest Dowson.* Memoir by Arthur Symons. New York: Boni & Liveright, 1919.
Doyle, Sir Frances. *Lectures on Poetry.* 2nd Series. London: Smith, Elder & Co., 1877.
———. *Reminiscences and Opinions.* London: D. Appleton & Co., 1887.
Dulcken, H. W. *The Book of German Songs from the Sixteenth to the Nineteenth Century.* London: Ward & Lock, 1856.
Eckert, R. P. *Edward Thomas.* London: J. M. Dent & Sons, 1937.
Eckley, Sophia Mae. *Minor Chords.* London: Bell & Daldy, 1869.
Egan, T. S., tr. *Atta Troll and Other Poems by Heine.* London: Chapman & Hall., 1876.

Eliot, George. *Complete Poems.* Boston: Estes & Lauriat.
———. *Works.* 24 vols. London: William Blackwood & Sons, 1895.
Ellis, Havelock. "Heine," *The New Spirit.* London: Walter Scott, 1892. Pp. 68-88.
———, ed. *The Prose Writings of Heinrich Heine.* London: Walter Scott, 1887.
———. *Sonnets with Folk-Songs from the Spanish.* Cambridge: Riverside Press, 1925.
Elton, Oliver. *A Survey of English Literature 1830-1880.* 2 vols. London: Edward Arnold, 1920.
Esher, Reginald Viscount. *Ionicus.* London: John Murray, 1923.
Evans, B. Ifor. *English Poetry in the Later Nineteenth Century.* London: Methuen & Co., 1933.
F., C. K., tr. *Selections of Ballads Translated Chiefly from German Authors.* Privately Printed, 1873.
Fane, Julian. *Poems.* London: William Pickering, 1852.
———, tr. *Poems by Heinrich Heine.* (Not Published), 1854.
Finlayson, T. C. *Essays, Addresses, and Lyrical Translations.* London: Macmillan & Co., 1893.
Fischer, Walther. *Die Briefe von Richard Monckton Milnes, ersten Barons Houghton, an Varnhagen von Ense.* Heidelberg: Carl Winter, 1922.
———. *Die persönlichen Beziehungen Richard Monckton Milnes, ersten Barons Houghton, zu Deutschland.* Würzburg, 1918.
Fleckenstein, Edgar. *Die literarischen Anschauungen und Kritiken Elizabeth Barrett Brownings.* Heidelberg: Carl Winter, 1913.
Flower, Desmond, ed. *The Poetical Works of Ernest Christopher Dowson.* London: Cassell & Co., 1934.
Frisa, Heinrich. *Deutsche Kulturverhältnisse in der Auffassung W. M. Thackerays.* Wien: Wilhelm Braumüller, 1908.
Garnett, Richard. *Poems from the German.* London: Bell & Daldy, 1862.
Garrod, H. W. *Oxford Poems.* London: John Lane, 1912.
Gill, Wilfred A. *Edward Cracroft LeFroy: His Life and Poems.* London: John Lane, 1897.
Gillies, Robert P. *Memoirs of a Literary Veteran.* 3 vols. London: Richard Bentley, 1851.
Gissing, A. & E., eds. *Letters of George Gissing to Members of His Family.* London: Constable & Co., 1927.

Goedeke, Karl. *Grundriss zur Geschichte der deutschen Dichtung.* Vol. VIII, pp. 526-564. Dresden: Edmund Goetze, 1905.

Goldberg, Isaac. *Havelock Ellis: A Biographical and Critical Survey.* New York: Simon & Schuster, 1926.

Goldschmidt, H. E., ed. *German Poetry with English Versions of the Best Translators.* London: Williams & Norgate, 1869.

Gordon, Lucie Duff. *Letters from the Cape.* London: Humphrey Milford, 1927.

———. *Letters from Egypt.* London: Macmillan & Co., 1875.

———. *Last Letters from Egypt.* London: Macmillan & Co., 1875.

Gosse, Edmund. *More Books on the Table.* London: William Heinemann, 1923.

Gostwick, Joseph. *The Spirit of German Poetry.* London: William Smith, 1845.

———. *Outline of German Literature.* London: Williams & Norgate, 1873.

———. *German Poets.* New York: Stroefer & Kirchner, 1874.

Gray, Alexander. *Arrows.* Edinburgh: Grant & Murray, 1932.

Gretton, Mary S. *The Writings of George Meredith.* London: Humphrey Milford, 1926.

Haldane, Elizabeth. *George Eliot and Her Times.* New York: D. Appleton & Co., 1927.

Hardy, Thomas. *Collected Poems.* London: Macmillan & Co., 1919.

Harlan, A. B. and Harlan, J. L., eds. *Letters from Owen Meredith to Robert and Elizabeth Barrett Browning.* Baylor University, 1936.

Harris, Frank. *Contemporary Portraits.* New York: Published by the author, 1919.

———. *Jahre der Reife.* Berlin: S. Fischer, 1930.

———. *Mein Leben.* Berlin: S. Fischer, 1926.

Harrison, Frederick. *John Addington Symonds.* New York: Macmillan & Co., 1896.

Havergal, Frances R. *Golden Thoughts.* New York: E. P. Dutton & Co., 1892.

———. *Poetical Works.* London: James Nisket & Co., 1894.

———. *Swiss Letters and Alpine Poems.* London: James Nisket & Co., 1881.

Head, Henry. *Destroyers and Other Verses.* London: Humphrey Milford, 1919.

Hellman, Geo. S. *The True Stevenson: A Study in Appreciation.* Boston: Little, Brown & Co., 1925.

Henderson, M. Sturge. *George Meredith: Novelist, Poet, Reformer*. New York: Charles Scribner's Sons, 1907.
Henley, William E. *Poems*. London: Macmillan & Co., 1921.
———. *Views and Reviews: Essays in Appreciation*. New York: Charles Scribner's Sons, 1906.
Hill, George B., ed. *Letters of Dante Gabriel Rossetti to William Allingham*. New York: F. A. Stokes & Co.
Howitt, Margaret, ed. *Mary Howitt: An Autobiography*. 2 vols. London: William Isbister, 1889.
Howitt, Mary. *Ballads and Other Poems*. New York: George P. Putnam, 1848.
Huxley, Leonard, ed. *Elizabeth Barrett Browning: Letters to Her Sister*. London: J. Murray, 1929.
Ingleby, C. M. *Poems and Epigrams*. London: Trübner & Co., 1887.
Ince, Richard B. *Calverley and Some Cambridge Wits of the Nineteenth Century*. London: Richards & Toulman, 1929.
Irwin, H. C. *Rhymes and Renderings*. London: David Stott, 1886.
Ishill, Joseph, ed. *Havelock Ellis in Appreciation*. Berkeley Heights: Oriole Press, 1929.
Jacks, L. P. *Life and Letters of Stopford Brooke*. 2 vols. New York: Charles Scribner's Sons, 1917.
Japp, A. H. *German Life and Literature*. London: Marshall Japp & Co.
———. *Occasional Verses*. Printed for the author, 1893.
Johnson, R. B., ed. *The Letters of George Eliot*. London: John Lane, 1926.
Joyce, James A. *James Clarence Mangan*. London: Privately printed, 1902.
Keene, H. G. *Verses Translated and Original*. London: W. H. Allen & Co., 1886.
Kelley, Bernard. *The Mind and Poetry of Gerald Manley Hopkins*. London: Pepler & Sewell, 1935.
Kelso, Alex P. *Matthew Arnold on Continental Life and Literature*. Oxford: B. H. Blackwell, 1914.
Kenyon, F. G., ed. *The Letters of Elizabeth Barrett Browning*. 2 vols. New York: The Macmillan Co., 1897.
Kettle, R. M., ed. *Memoirs and Letters of Charles Boner*. 2 vols., London: Richard Bentley & Son, 1871.
Kingsmill, Hugh. *Frank Harris*. New York: Farrar & Rinehart, 1932.

―――. *The Life of D. H. Lawrence*. New York: Dodge Publishing Co., 1938.
―――. *Matthew Arnold*. New York: The Dial Press, 1928.
Kraeger, H. "Carlyles Stellung zur deutschen Sprache und Literatur," *Anglia*, XXII (1899), 145-342.
Kroeker, Kate F., ed. *Poems Selected from Heinrich Heine*. London: Walter Scott, 1887.
Lambert, Charles R. *Poems and Translations from the German*. London: Whittaker & Co., 1850.
Langford, John A. *The Lily of the West and Other Poems*. London: Marshall, Hamilton, Kent & Co.
Lawrence, Sir Alexander. *Aliunde*. London: Humphrey Milford, 1938.
Lees, John. "George Meredith's Literary Relations with Germany," *Modern Language Review*, XII (1917), 428-439.
LeGallienne, Richard. *Old Love Stories Retold*. New York: Dodd, Mead & Co., 1925.
Levy, Amy. *A Minor Poet and Other Verse*. London: T. Fisher Unwin, 1891.
Lindsay, Lord A. W. C. *Ballads, Songs and Poems Translated from the German*. Wigan: C. S. Simms, 1841.
Lindsay, James. *Autobiography*. London: William Blackwood & Sons, 1924.
―――. *Essays Literary and Philosophical*. London: William Blackwood & Sons, 1896.
Locker-Lampson, Frederick. *The Poems of Frederick Locker*. New York: F. A. Stokes & Brother, 1889.
―――. *My Confidences*. London: Smith, Elder & Co., 1896.
Lowry, H. F., ed. *The Letters of Matthew Arnold to Arthur Hugh Clough*. New York: Oxford University Press, 1932.
Lucas, E. V. *Reading, Writing and Remembering*. London: Harper & Brothers, 1932.
Lucas, Frank L. *Marionettes*. Cambridge: University Press, 1930.
Lyttleton, A. T. *Modern Poets of Faith, Doubt and Paganism and Other Essays*. London: John Murray, 1904.
Lytton, Robert. *Julian Fane: A Memoir*. London: John Murray, 1871.
Maanen, Willem van. *Maarten Maartens, Poet and Novelist*. Groningen: P. Noordhoff, 1927.
MacDonald, George. *Exotics*. London: Strahan & Co., 1876.

Bibliography 293

MacMechan, Archibald. *Late Harvest.* Toronto: The Ryerson Press, 1934.

Magnus, Lady Katie. "Heinrich Heine: A Plea." *Jewish Portraits.* London: T. Fisher Unwin, 1888.

Magnus, Laurie. *A Dictionary of European Literature.* London: George Routledge & Sons, 1927.

Maitland, F. W. *The Life and Letters of Leslie Stephen.* New York: G. P. Putnam's Sons, 1906.

Martin, Theodore. *Memoir of William Edmonstoune Aytoun.* London: William Blackwood & Sons, 1867.

Martin, Theodore, tr. *Poems and Ballads of Heinrich Heine.* London: William Blackwood & Sons, 1894.

Martin, Theodore, and Bowring, E. A., trs. *Heine's Book of Songs.* New York: F. A. Stokes Co., 1892.

Martin, W. Wilsey. *By Solent and Danube.* London: Trübner & Co., 1885.

Matheson, Annie. *The Religion of Humanity and Other Poems.* London: Percival & Co., 1890.

Meeker, J. Edward. *The Life and Poetry of James Thomson.* New Haven: Yale University Press, 1917.

Meredith, George. *Letters.* Ed. by his son. 2 vols. New York: Charles Scribner's Sons, 1912.

———. *Letters to Alice Meynell.* London: The Nonesuch Press, 1923.

———. *Poems.* New York: Charles Scribner's Sons, 1923.

Meredith, Owen. *Poetical Works.* New York: Thomas Crowell & Co.

Maynell, Wilfred. *Benjamin Disraeli: An Unconventional Biography.* 2 vols. London: Hutchinson & Co., 1903.

Miall, A. Bernard. *Nocturnes and Pastorals.* London: Leonard Smithers, 1896.

Mills, J. Saxon. *Fasiculus Versiculorum.* London: Swan Sonnenschein & Co., 1895.

Milnes, R. Monckton. *Monographs, Personal and Social.* New York: Holt & Williams, 1873.

Morgan, B. Q. *A Bibliography of German Literature in English Translation.* Madison: University of Wisconsin Studies, 1922. No. 16.

Morton, J. B. ("Beachcomber"). *By the Way.* London: Sheed & Ward, 1931.

Nevinson, H. W. "Heinrich Heine." *Books and Personalities*. London: John Lane, 1905.
———. *Essays in Freedom*. London: Duckworth & Co., 1909.
Nicoll, W. R. *A Bookman's Letters*. London: Hodder & Stoughton, 1913.
———. *Memories of Mark Rutherford*. London: T. Fisher Unwin, 1924.
Noyes, Alfred. *Poems*. London: Macmillan & Co., 1906.
Noyes, Thomas H. *An Idyll of the Weald with Other Legends and Lays*. London: J. C. Hotten, 1868.
O'Donoghue, D. J. *The Life and Writings of James Clarence Mangan*. Dublin: T. G. O'Donoghue, 1897.
———, ed. *Poems of James Clarence Mangan*. London: A. H. Bullen, 1903.
———, ed. *The Prose Writings of James Clarence Mangan*. London: A. H. Bullen, 1904.
Page, Frederick. *Patmore: A Study in Poetry*. London: Humphrey Milford, 1933.
Palgrave, Francis T. *Idylls and Songs*. London: J. W. Parker & Son, 1854.
Palmer, Herbert. *Post-Victorian Poetry*. London: J. M. Dent & Sons, 1938.
Paston, George. *Little Memories of the Nineteenth Century*. London: Grant Richards, 1902.
Paterson, Arthur. *George Eliot's Family Life and Letters*. London: Selwyn & Blount, 1928.
Patmore, Coventry. *Courage in Politics and Other Essays*. London: Humphrey Milford, 1921.
Paul, C. Kegan. *On the Wayside*. London: Kegan, Paul, Trench, Trübner & Co., 1899.
Paul, Herbert W. *Matthew Arnold*. New York: The Macmillan Co., 1902.
Payne, John. *Autobiography*. Olney, 1926.
Peterson, Houston. *Havelock Ellis: Philosopher of Love*. New York: Houghton Mifflin Co., 1928.
Pfeiffer, Emily. *Flowers of the Night*. London: Trübner & Co., 1889.
———. *Quarterman's Grace and Other Poems*. London: C. Kegan Paul & Co., 1879.
Pfeiffer, Sibilla. *George Eliots Beziehungen zu Deutschland*. Heidelberg: Carl Winter, 1925.

Bibliography

Photiades, Constantin. *George Meredith: His Life, Genius, and Teaching.* Tr. by Arthur Price. New York: Charles Scribner's Sons, 1913.
Plarr, Victor. *Ernest Dowson.* London: Elkin Mathews, 1914.
Pollock, W. H. *Old and New.* London: Eden, Remington & Co., 1890.
Radford, Ernest. *Chambers Twain.* London: Elkin Mathews, 1890.
———. *Old and New.* London: T. Fisher Unwin, 1895.
———. *Poems.* London: Gibbings & Co., 1906.
———. *Translations from Heine and Other Poems.* Cambridge: E. Johnson, 1882.
Raleigh, Lady, ed. *The Letters of Sir Walter Raleigh (1879-1922).* London: Methuen & Co., 1926.
———. *A Selection from the Letters of Sir Walter Raleigh (1888-1922).* London: Methuen & Co., 1928.
Reid, T. Wemyss. *The Life, Letters and Friendships of Richard Monckton Milnes.* 2 vols. London: Cassell & Co., 1890.
Renwanz, Johannes. *Matthew Arnold und Deutschland.* Greifswald: Julius Abel, 1927.
Rhys, Ernest. *A London Rose and Other Rhymes.* London: Elkin Mayhews & John Lane, 1894.
Robertson, J. M. *Essays Towards a Critical Method.* London: T. Fisher Unwin, 1889.
Robinson, Tracy and Lucy, eds. *Selections from the Poetry of John Payne.* New York: John Lane, 1906.
Rodd, Rennell. *Rose Leaf and Apple Leaf.* Portland, Maine: T. B. Mosher, 1906.
———. *Songs in the South.* London: David Bogue, 1881.
———. *The Unknown Madonna and Other Poems.* London: David Stott, 1888.
Ross, Janet. *Three Generations of English Women.* London: T. Fisher Unwin, 1893.
Russell, Charles. *Sonnets, Poems and Translations.* London: W. Thacker & Co., 1920.
Russell, Rollo. *Break of Day and Other Poems.* London: T. Fisher Unwin, 1893.
Salt, Henry S. *The Life of James Thomson.* London: Watts & Co., 1914.
Savage, Henry. *Richard Middleton.* London: Cecil Palmer, 1922.
Sawyer, William. *The Legend of Phyllis.* London: Longman's, Green, Reader & Dyer, 1872.

Schreiner, S. C. Cromwright, ed. *The Letters of Olive Schreiner (1876-1920)*. Boston: Little, Brown & Co., 1924.
Schwartz, J. M. W. *The Morning of a Love and Other Poems*. London: Remington & Co., 1885.
———. *The Letters of Maarten Maartens*. Ed. by his daughter. New York: R. R. Smith, 1930.
Scully, William Charles. *Poems*. London: T. Fisher Unwin, 1892.
Sencourt, R. E. *The Life of George Meredith*. London: Chapman & Hall, 1929.
Sendall, W. J. *The Literary Remains of Charles Stuart Calverley*. London: George Bell & Sons, 1885.
———, ed. *Complete Works of C. S. Calverley*. London: G. Bell & Sons, 1913.
Shapcott, R., ed. *The Autobiography of Mark Rutherford*. London: Humphrey Milford, 1936.
Sharp, Elizabeth A. *William Sharp: A Memoir*. New York: Duffield & Co., 1912.
Sharp, William. *Flower o' the Vine*. New York: C. L. Webster & Co., 1892.
———. *Poems*. New York: Duffield & Co., 1912.
———. *Poems and Dramas*. New York: Duffield & Co., 1914.
———. *Songs and Poems, Old and New*. London: Elliot Stock, 1909.
Sheehan, Patrick A. *Parerga*. London: Longmans, Green & Co., 1908.
Sherman, Stuart P. *Matthew Arnold: How to Know Him*. Indianapolis: Bobbs-Merrill Co., 1917.
Sichel, Walter. *The Sands of Time*. London: Hutchinson & Co., 1923.
———. *Types and Characters*. London: Hutchinson & Co., 1925.
Smith, Garnet, ed. *The Melancholy of Stephen Allard*. New York: Macmillan & Co., 1895.
Snodgrass, John, tr. *Heine's "Religion and Philosophy in Germany."* London: Trübner & Co., 1882.
———. *Wit, Wisdom and Pathos from the Prose of H. Heine with a Few Pieces from the Book of Songs*. London: Trübner & Co., 1879.
Sorley, W. R., ed. *The Letters of Charles Sorley*. Cambridge: University Press, 1919.
Stephen, Leslie. "The Importation of German." *Studies of a Biographer*. London: Duckworth & Co., 1898.

Stevenson, R. L. *Poems.* New York: Thomas Crowell & Co., 1900.
Stewart, J. A. *Robert Louis Stevenson: Man and Writer.* London: Sampson Low, Marston & Co., 1924.
Stigand, William. *A Vision of Barbarossa and Other Poems.* London: Chapman & Hall, 1860.
———. *Anthea.* London: Kegan, Paul, Trench, Trübner & Co., 1907.
Stoddart, Anna M. *John Stuart Blackie: A Biography.* 2 vols. London: William Blackwood & Sons, 1895.
Stoddart, R. H., ed. *Personal Reminiscences by Constable and Gillies.* New York: Scribner, Armstrong & Co., 1876.
Stork, Charles W. *Heine and Tennyson: An Essay in Comparative Criticism.* Haverford, Pa.: Privately printed, 1909.
Storr, Francis, tr. *"Travel Pictures" together with "The Romantic School."* London: G. Bell & Sons, 1912.
Swinnerton, Frank. *George Gissing: A Critical Study.* London: Martin Secker, 1912.
Symonds, J. A. *New and Old.* London: Smith, Elder & Co., 1880.
Symons, Arthur. *Days and Nights.* London: Martin Secker, 1923.
———. *The Fool of the World and Other Poems.* London: William Heinemann, 1906.
———. *Poems.* 2 vols. London: William Heineman, 1914.
Thomson, James. *The City of Dreadful Night.* Portland, Maine: T. B. Mosher, 1892.
———. *Poetical Works.* 2 vols. Ed. by Bertram Dobell. London: Reeves & Turner, 1895.
———. *Poems.* Ed. by Gordon H. Gerould. New York: Henry Holt & Co., 1927.
———. *Vane's Story, Weddah and Om-El-Bonain and Other Poems.* London: Reeves & Turner, 1881.
Todhunter, John, tr. *Heine's Book of Songs.* Oxford: Clarendon Press, 1907.
Tomlin, Edward L. *Gleanings.* London: Longmans, Green & Co., 1891.
Topin, A. I., and Gertz, Elmer. *Frank Harris: A Study in Black and White.* Chicago: Madelaine Mendelsohn, 1931.
Trench, R. C. *Poems.* 2 vols. London: Macmillan & Co., 1885.
Trotter, B. F. *A Canadian Twilight and Other Poems of War and Peace.* Toronto: McClelland, Goodchild & Stewart, 1917.
Tuckwell, G. M., ed. *The Life of the Rt. Hon. Sir Charles W. Dilke.* 2 vols. London: John Murray, 1917.

Untermeyer, Louis, tr. *Poems of Heinrich Heine*. New York: Henry Holt & Co., 1917.

Walker, A. S., ed. *The Letters of John Stuart Blackie to His Wife*. London: William Blackwood & Sons, 1909.

Walz, Heinz. *George Merediths Jugendwerke und ihre Bedeutung für die persönliche Entwicklung des Dichters*. Quackenbrück: C. Trute, 1932.

Watts-Dunton, Clara. *The Home Life of Swinburne*. London: A. M. Philpot, 1922.

Webb, Philip G. L., tr. *More Translations from Heine*. London: G. Allen & Unwin, 1920.

Weber, Anton. *George Gissing und die soziale Frage*. Leipzig: B. Tauchnitz, 1932.

Weissel, Josefine. *James Thomson der Jüngere: Sein Leben und seine Werke*. Wien: W. Braumüller, 1906.

Wilberforce, Edward, tr. *Dante's Inferno and Other Translations*. London: Macmillan & Co., 1903.

Williams, B. C. *George Eliot: A Biography*. New York: The Macmillan Co., 1936.

Williamson, Kennedy. *W. E. Henley: A Memoir*. London: Harold Shaylor, 1930.

Wilson, D. A. *Carlyle to Threescore and Ten*. London: Kegan, Paul, Trench, Trübner & Co., 1929.

Wilson, D. A., and MacArthur, D. W. *Carlyle in Old Age*. London: Kegan, Paul, Trench, Trübner & Co., 1934.

Wilson, James G. (Mrs.) *A Book of Verses*. London: Elliot Stock, 1901.

Wilson, James H. *Zalmoxis and Other Poems*. London: Elliot Stock, 1892.

Wise, T. J., ed. *Letters to Robert Browning by E. B. Browning*. London, 1916.

Wodehouse, Mrs., ed. *Matthew Arnold's Notebooks*. New York: The Macmillan Co., 1902.

Wolfe, Humbert. *Early Poems*. Oxford: Basil Blackwell, 1930.

———. *Shylock Reasons with Mr. Chesterton and Other Poems*. Oxford: Basil Blackwell, 1920.

———. *Snow*. London: Victor Gollancz, 1931.

———. *This Blind Rose*. London: Victor Gollancz, 1928.

Woolff, L. *George Meredith: poète et romancier*. Paris: Payot, 1924.

Wood, John D. *Poems in Rhyme and Blank Verse.* London: Melville & Mullen, 1903.
Wright, J. E. T. *W. Hale White.* Ph.D. Thesis: University of Pittsburgh, 1933.
Wright, Thomas. *The Autobiography of John Payne.* Olney: Thomas Wright, 1926.
———. *The Life of Walter Pater.* 2 vols. London: Everett & Co., 1907.
———. *The Life of John Payne.* London: T. Fisher Unwin, 1919.
———. *Thomas Wright of Olney: An Autobiography.* London: Herbert Jenkins, 1936.

Index

Abbreviations, key to, 40n
Academy, The, anonymous criticism of Heine in, 152-153, 155
"Ackerlos, John," as minor translator of Heine, 39-40; mentioned, 103n
Alfieri, Vittori, translated, 99n
Allingham, William, knowledge of German literature, 177; mentioned, 177, 259; views on Heine, 178; influence of Heine on, 245
Althaus, Friedrich, conversation with Carlyle on German literature, 176-177
Anacreon, translated, 52
Anderson, David, as minor translator of Heine, 40-41; other translations of, 40
Archer, William, as minor translator of Heine, 41-42; other translations of, 41
Aristophanes, 128
Armour, Margaret, as major translator of Heine, 6, 14-18; other translations of, 15; translations reviewed in *Athenaeum*, 159
Arndt, Earl Beck, translated, 90
Arnold, Matthew, as major critic of Heine, 113-116; condemned by Carlyle for his praise of Heine, 176; *Heine's Grave*, 187, 192-193; influence of Heine on, 246, 247-249; on Heine, 269; mentioned, 110, 120, 121, 137, 188, 204, 266, 267
Arnold, Mrs., 113
Ashe, Thomas, as minor translator of Heine, 42-43; other translations of, 42
Athenaeum, The, anonymous criticism of Heine in, 144-145, 153, 159
Auersperg, Graf von, translated, 84n
Austin, Lucie. *See* Duff Gordon, Lady
Axon, William E. A., as minor translator of Heine, 43-44; other translations of, 43

Baerlein, Henry, influence of Heine on, 218-226
Baker, James, as minor critic of Heine, 160
Baring, Maurice, imaginary account of Heine, 262
Barrett, Henrietta, 48
Barry, William Francis, as minor critic of Heine, 157-158
Bartels, Adolph, 175, 267
Baudelaire, Charles, translated, 96; mentioned, 178, 262
"Beachcomber," interest in Heine, 171
Beard, Charles, as minor critic of Heine, 137-138
Beck, translated, 50
Beethoven, Ludwig van, 164
Begas, Reinhold, 23
Belgiojoso, Princess, 262
Bellini, Vincenzo, 262
Bennett, Arnold, interest in Heine, 171
Béranger, Pierre Jean de, translated, 21; mentioned, 128
Berlioz, Hector, 164
Bion, translated, 42
Bismarck, 45
Black, G. A., as minor critic of Heine, 168
Black, William, conversation with Carlyle about Heine, 177
Blackie, John Stuart, as adaptor from Heine, 254; as translator from the German, 254
Blackwood's Magazine, anonymous criticism of Heine in, 139-140
Blathwayt, William, as minor translator of Heine, 44-45
Blind, Mathilde, 260
Bodenstedt, Friedrich, translated, 43, 99n
Boner, Charles, mentions Heine, 171; conversation with Carlyle about Heine, 175-176

[301]

Börne, Ludwig, mentioned, 124, 202; on Heine, 267
Bourdillon, Francis William, as minor translator of Heine, 45; other translations of, 45
Bourgeois, Maurice, 262
Bowring, Edgar A., as major translator of Heine, 6, 11-14; other translations of, 12; translations compared with Sir Theodore Martin's, 14; as minor critic of Heine, 129; mentioned, 129
Boyd, Percy, as minor translator of Heine, 45
Brawne, Fanny, 262
Bremer, Frederica, translated, 71
Brentano, Clemens, translated, 28, 66, 72; mentioned, 264
Brereton, John LeGay, as minor translator of Heine, 45-46
Brezzi, Signor, as teacher of George Eliot, 109
Bridges, Robert, mentions Heine, 170
Briggs, H. B., as translator of Heine, 103n
Brooke, Stopford A., as minor translator of Heine, 103
Brooksbank, Thomas, as major translator of Heine, 6, 14-18; translations reviewed in *Athenaeum*, 159
Browning, Elizabeth Barrett, as minor translator of Heine, 46-49; reading of German authors, 46; mentioned, 173
Browning, George, as minor translator of Heine, 49-51; other translations of, 50
Browning, Robert, mentioned, 183; mentions Heine, 259
Buchanan, Robert, on Sir Theodore Martin as a Heine translator, 7-8, 131; as minor critic of Heine, 130-131; mentioned, 156; poem to Heine, 191
Buchheim, Dr., as minor critic of Heine, 153; mentioned, 243
Bürger, Gottfried August, translated, 54, 55
Burne-Jones, Sir Edward, dedication of John Payne's translations to, 86
Burne-Jones, Mrs., 110
Burns, Robert, 128, 140
Burt, Mary Anne, as minor translator of Heine, 51-52

Butler, Eliza M., as minor critic of Heine, 166
Byron, George Gordon, Lord, *Weltschmerz* of contrasted with Heine's, 4; compared with Heine, 138, 142, 145; mentioned, 107, 108, 113, 114, 128, 149, 182

Caine, Hall, mentioned, 191-192; on D. G. Rossetti's knowledge of German, 259
Calderon, translated, 85
Call, Wathen Mark Wilks, as minor translator of Heine, 52-53; other translations of, 52
Calverley, Charles Stuart, as minor translator of Heine, 53-54; other adaptations of, 53
Campe, Julius, 126
Carlyle, Thomas, edited, 79; similarity with Heine, 174; antipathy to Heine, 174-177; mentioned, 116, 163, 171, 177, 181, 259
Carmichael, Walter Scott, as adaptor of Heine, 254
Cash, Mary, instructed by George Eliot in German, 109
Catullus, translated, 42, 52; mentioned, 140
Cautley, George Spencer, as adaptor of Heine, 254-255
Cellini, Benvenuto, translated, 94
Cervantes, Miguel de, 128
Chamisso, Adelbert von, translated, 63, 84n
Charlton, William Henry, as minor translator of Heine, 54; other translations of, 54
Chawner, Edward, as minor translator of Heine, 54
Chaworth, Mary, 4
Chiles, James Alburn, on Heine's stylistic traits, 203
Chopin, Frederic François, 164
Chorley, Henry, 71
Clough, Arthur Hugh, mentioned, 114; influence of Heine on, 246-247; readings and translations of German literature, 246
Coke, Henry J., mentions Heine, 170
Colburn's New Monthly Magazine, anonymous criticism of Heine in, 128
Coleridge, Mary Elizabeth, influence of Heine on, 234-239

Coleridge, Samuel Taylor, 259
Conway, Moncure, on William Allingham's indebtedness to Heine, 245
Cornhill Magazine, The, anonymous criticism of Heine in, 129-130
Corot, Jean Baptiste, 134
Cotterill, Henry Bernard, as minor translator of Heine, 54-55
Courthope, W. J., letter of J. A. Symonds to, 95
Craigmyle, Elizabeth, as minor translator of Heine, 55-56; other translations of, 55-56
Crashaw, Richard, translated, 42
Crawford, Alexander William, as minor translator of Heine, 56
Criticism, difficulties encountered by Heine critics, 105-107; of Heine, 265-266
Critics of Heine, division into major and minor groups, 107

"D., G. E.," as minor translator of Heine, 56-57
Dalkyrs, H. G., letter of J. A. Symonds to, 95
Dalziel, Edward, 57
Dalziel, George, 57
Dante, Alighieri, translated, 42, 85, 99; mentioned, 95, 204, 262
D'Anvers, Francis, as minor translator of Heine, 57; mentioned, 98
Davy, Mrs. E. M., as minor critic of Heine, 152
Delaroche, Hippolyte, 147
Delitzsch, F. J., translated, 98
Dennis, John, as minor translator of Heine, 57-58
De Quincey, Thomas, 204
Descamps, Jean Baptiste, 147
Deutsch, translated, 66
Dexter, Charles, as minor translator of Heine, 58-59
Dickens, Charles, 183
Dilke, Charles Wentworth, as personal friend of Heine, 183
Disraeli, Benjamin, 156, 167, 183
Dobell, Bertram, 168
Donizetti, Gaetano, 163
Dowden, Edward, similarity of Richard Monckton Milnes' essay to that of, 117; as major critic of Heine, 121-123; mentioned, 193

Dowson, Ernest, influence of Heine on, 243-245
Doyle, Sir Francis Hastings, as minor translator of Heine, 59; stanzas of suggested by a poem of Heine's, 257-258
Dryden, John, 118
Du Bellay, Joachim, translated, 96
Dublin University Magazine, The, anonymous criticism of Heine in, 128-129
Duff Gordon, Lady Lucie, as minor translator of Heine, 102-103, 150; as minor critic of Heine, 150; as personal friend of Heine, 183-187; acquaintanceship of George Meredith with, 260; mentioned, 117, 176, 242
Dulcken, Henry W., as minor translator of Heine, 59-60
Dürer, Albert, 45

Ebert, K. E., translated, 63
Eckermann, Johann Peter, 174
Eckley, Sophia May, as minor translator of Heine, 60
Edinburgh Review, The, anonymous criticism of Heine in, 124-125, 127-128, 161-162; translations of Julian Fane and John E. Wallis reviewed in, 127-128
Edwards, Amelia B., as adaptor of Heine, 254
Egan, Thomas Selby, as major translator of Heine, 34-36
Eichendorf, Joseph von, translated, 101; mentioned, 264
Eliot, George, as major critic of Heine, 108-113; interest in languages, 109; translations of, 109; interest in German literature, 110; ideas similar to Heine's, 260; mentioned, 124, 125, 267
Ellis, A. J., 52
Ellis, Havelock, as minor translator of Heine, 60-62; as minor critic of Heine, 140-141; mentioned, 180
Elton, Oliver, 174-175
Embden, Ludwig von, editing of correspondence of Heine reviewed in *The New Review*, 151-152
Enfantin, Barthélemy Prosper, 200
Ense, Varnhagen von, 175, 242
Esher, Reginald, Viscount, dissatisfaction with Heine, 174

Evans, B. Ifor, on the influence of Heine on the poems of W. E. Henley, 211-212; mentioned, 240
Evans, Mary Ann. *See* Eliot, George
Evans, Thomas, mentioned, 129; as minor critic of Heine, 146

"F., C. K.," as minor translator of Heine, 62-63; other translations of, 62
Fane, Julian, as major translator of Heine, 23-25; as major critic of Heine, 108; translations of reviewed in *The Edinburgh Review*, 127-128
Ferrand, translated, 63
Feuchtersleben, translated, 45
Fichte, Johann Gottlieb, 172
Finlayson, James, 63, 64
Finlayson, Thomas Campbell, as minor translator of Heine, 63-66; other translations of, 63
Fischer, Walter, on R. M. Milnes' indebtedness to Heine, 242
Fitzgerald, Edward, 183
Flaubert, Gustave, 264
Förster, Paul, translated, 43
Fraser's Magazine, anonymous criticism of Heine in, 125-126
Frederick the Great, 181
Freiligrath, Hermann Ferdinand, translated, 28, 55, 63, 66, 70, 72, 75; mentioned, 137, 242
Freiligrath-Kroeker, Kate, as major translator of Heine, 28-30; other translations of, 28; as minor critic of Heine, 146; mentioned, 40, 86, 87, 91, 93, 129
Freytag, Gustav, 46

Garnett, Richard, as minor translator of Heine, 66-67; other translations of, 66; on John Payne as translator, 85
Garrod, Heathcote William, parody on Heine, 258
Garry, Jaye, as minor critic of Heine, 157
Gautier, Théophile, translated, 96
Geibel, Emanuel, translated, 63, 84n
Geike, J., as translator of Heine, 103n
German literature, influence of on English literature, Foreword

Gillies, Robert Pearce, interest in German literature, 178; views on Heine, 178
Gissing, Ellen, 179
Gissing, George, interest in German literature, 179; views on Heine, 179
Gissing, William, 179
Giusti, Giuseppe, translated, 99n
Gleim, Johann Wilhelm Ludwig, translated, 63
Godwin, Mary, 262
Goethe, Frau von, entertains the Howitts, 71
Goethe, Johann Wolfgang von, translated, 12, 21, 32, 40, 42, 50, 55, 63, 66, 73, 74, 81, 82, 85, 86, 87, 94, 97, 99n, 246, 254; attitude toward the sea contrasted with Heine's, 29; compared with Heine, 112, 120; mentioned, 8, 46, 59, 60, 95, 106, 107, 110, 114, 115, 116, 118, 130, 136, 140, 144, 146, 148, 156, 173, 174, 175, 176, 178, 193, 201, 242, 248, 259, 266, 268, 269
Goldberg, Isaac, 61
Goldschmidt, Madame, 94
Gordon, Samuel, as minor critic of Heine, 167-168
Gore-Booth, Eva, fragment of based on Heine, 259
Gosse, Edmund, as minor critic of Heine, 153-155
Gosse, Mrs., letter of J. M. W. Schwartz to, 89
Gostwick, Joseph, as minor translator of Heine, 67-68; as minor critic of Heine, 135
Gottschall, Rudolf von, translated, 73
Gottsched, R., translated, 63
Götz, J. M., translated, 63
Grant, Charles, as major critic of Heine, 118-119
Gray, Agnes, letter of James Thomson to, 20-21
Gray, Alexander, as minor translator of Heine, 68-69
Grenier, Edouard, on Heine, 107
Grillparzer, Franz, 178
Groth, Klaus, translated, 32
Grün, Anastasius, translated, 54, 63
Gutzkow, Karl, 266

Hahn-Hahn, Ida, Gräfin, 242
Haldane, F. S., 111

Index

Halm, Friedrich, translated, 54, 63, 82
Hamlin, translated, 73
Hammer, Julius, translated, 73
Hardy, Thomas, as minor translator of Heine, 69
Harnack, 260
Harris, Frank, interest in Heine, 181-182
Hartmann, Moritz, 242
Hauptmann, Gerhart, translated, 41
Havergal, Frances, as minor translator of Heine, 69-70
Hayens, Kenneth C., as minor critic of Heine, 165
Hazlitt, William, 165, 239
Head, Sir Henry, on the poems of Camille Selden, 261-262
Hebbel, Christian Friedrich, translated, 66
Hegel, G. W. F., mentioned, 95, 130, 149, 164, 172; influence on Heine, 200
Heine, Amalie, 4, 140, 167, 228, 237
Heine, Henriette, letter of Mary Howitt about, 71
Heine, Maria Embden, 143
Heine, Mathilde, article about in *Temple Bar*, 156; mentioned, 138, 144, 262
Heine, Therese, 228
Heinemann, William, as publisher, 14; on Margaret Armour as translator, 16
Hellborn, H. von, translated, 99n
Hemans, Mrs., 71
Henderson, James, as minor critic of Heine, 158-159
Henley, William E., as minor critic of Heine, 156-157; influence of Heine on, 210-218; mentioned, 264
Hennell, Sarah, 110
Hensel, Wilhelm, 23
Herder, Johann Friedrich, translated, 43, 56, 84n
Herz, Heinrich, as minor translator of Heine, 70
Herzen, Alexander, compared with Heine, 164-165
Hewlett, Henry G., as minor critic of Heine, 138
Hewlett, Maurice, regard for Heine, 179-180
Hill, George Birkbeck, dislike of Heine, 172

Hillard, Kate, as minor critic of Heine, 135-137
Hindermann, Frau, 203
Hoffmann, E. T. A., 260
Hoffmann, Heinrich, translated, 84n
Hölderlin, Friedrich, *Weltschmerz* of contrasted to Heine's, 4; translated, 66
Hood, Thomas, compared with Heine, 160; mentioned, 183
Hopkins, Gerald Manley, mentions Heine, 170
Horace, translated, 42
Horschelt, Madame, mentions Heine, 171
Houghton, Lord. See Milnes, Richard Monckton
Housman, A. E., influence of Heine on, 262
Howitt, Anna, 71
Howitt, Mary, as minor translator of Heine, 70-72; other translations of, 70, 71
Howitt, William, literary work in Germany, 71
Hueffer, Francis Franz, as minor translator of Heine, 72-73
Hugo, Victor, translated, 45; mentioned, 149
Humboldt, Alexander, 23, 46
Huysmans, J. K., translated, 85

Ibsen, Henrik, translated, 41
Immermann, Karl Lebrecht, 106
Influence of Heine on English literature, 268-270
Informal opinion on Heine, grouping of, 169-170
Ingleby, Clement Mansfield, dedicates poem to Heine, 188
Irwin, Henry Crossley, as minor translator of Heine, 73-74; other translations of, 73; dedicates poem to Heine, 187-188

Jacobi, Georg, translated, 82
Jameson, Mrs., 47, 71, 165
Japp, Alexander H., as minor translator of Heine, 74-75; other translations of, 74; as minor critic of Heine, 141-143
Jarrett, H. S., as minor translator of Heine, 92-93, 103n

Jaubert, Madame, 262
Johnson, Lionel, on J. C. Mangan as translator, 81-82
Jordi, translated, 45
Jowett, Benjamin, 95

Kant, Immanuel, 172
Kaulbach, Wilhelm von, 71
Keats, John, Heine compared with, 128; mentioned, 134, 154, 183, 243, 262
Keene, Henry George, as minor translator of Heine, 75; other translations of, 75
Kennard, Nina H., mentioned, 120, 121; as minor critic of Heine, 143-144
Kernahan, Coulson, as major critic of Heine, 119-121
Kerner, Justinus, translated, 50, 101; mentioned, 80
Kingsley, Charles, on Heine, 177
Kingsmill, Hugh, 115, 181
Klopstock, Friedrich Gottlieb, 80
Körner, J., translated, 76
Körner, Karl Theodor, translated, 63; mentioned, 137
Kummer, Friedrich, on Heine's inconsistencies, 202-203

Lamb, Charles, 118
Lambert, Charles R., as minor translator of Heine, 75-76
Lange, J. Peter, translated, 98
Langford, John Alfred, as minor translator of Heine, 76; other translations of, 76
Lassalle, Ferdinand, 144, 165
Lawrence, Sir Alexander W., as minor translator of Heine, 76; other translations of, 76
Lawrence, D. H., interest in Heine, 171
Leaf, Lotta, letter of Maurice Hewlett to, 179-180
Lees, John, 260
Lefroy, Edward Cracroft, dedicates poem to Heine, 188-189
Le Gallienne, Richard, on Heine and Mathilde, 262
Lehmann, J., 268
Leland, Charles Godfrey, as translator of Heine, 14; translations of reviewed, 150-151; mentioned, 147, 159

Lemoine, translated, 45
Lenau, Nikolaus, *Weltschmerz* of contrasted to Heine's, 4; translated, 66, 101
Leopardi, Giacomo, Count, translated, 21; compared with Heine 158; mentioned, 140, 204
Lessing, Gotthold Ephraim, translated, 85
Lester, J. D., as minor translator of Heine, 76-77; as minor critic of Heine, 131-132
Levy, Amy, as minor translator of Heine, 77
Levy, Robert, 103n
Lewald, Fanny, statement of Heine to, 29; mentioned, 242
Lewes, George Henry, 95, 110, 163
Lewis, Veronica, correspondence of George Eliot with, 109
Lichtenberger, 201-202
Lindsay, James, mentions Heine, 170
Lingg, Hermann, translated, 66, 99n
Locker-Lampson, Frederick, poem of on Heine, 193-194
London Quarterly Review, The, anonymous criticism of Heine in, 144
Lucan, translated, 45
Lucas, Edward V., interest in Heine, 171
Lucas, Frank Lawrence, as minor translator of Heine, 77-78
Luther, Martin, 46, 139, 179
Lyttleton, Arthur, on Heine's influence upon James Thomson, 206, 209
Lytton, Robert, Earl of. *See* Meredith, Owen

"Maartens, Maarten," as minor translator of Heine, 89-90; other translations of, 89
Maccall, William, on the influence of Leopardi and Heine upon James Thomson, 206
MacDonald, George, as minor translator of Heine, 78-79
Macdougall, Mrs. W. B. *See* Armour, Margaret
MacLeod, Fiona, acquaintanceship of George Meredith with, 260
McLintock, R., as minor critic of Heine, 150-151; on the translations of C. G. Leland, 150-151

Index   307

MacMechan, Archibald, as minor translator of Heine, 79
MacMillan, Alexander, as minor translator of Heine, 79-80
Magnus, Edward, 23
Magnus, Lady, as minor critic of Heine, 148
Magnus, Laurie, as minor translator of Heine, 80
Mangan, James Clarence, as minor translator of Heine, 80-82; other translations of, 81
Mann, Thomas, 106, 264
Martin, Mrs., 47
Martin, Sir Theodore, as major translator of Heine, 6-11; translations of compared with Bowring's, 14; criticized as translator by Robert Buchanan, 131; mentioned, 11, 12, 144
Martin, W. Wilsey, as minor translator of Heine, 82; version of "Du bist wie eine Blume" compared with that of Charles Russell, 82
Marx, Karl, on James Thomson's translations of Heine, 23; mentioned, 165
Matheson, Annie, as minor translator of Heine, 82-83; other translations of, 82
Matthison, Friedrich, translated, 84n
Maurice, F. D., 118
Meissner, Alfred, mentioned, 25; Camille Selden's poems on, 262
Mendelssohn, Felix, 23
Meredith, George, as minor translator of Heine, 102-103; on German literary men, 260; influence of Heine on, 260-261
Meredith, Owen, on Julian Fane's translations of Heine, 24; as minor critic of Heine, 132; dislike of Heine, 172-174; influence of Heine on, 230-234
Meyer, H. A. W., translated, 98
Meyerbeer, Giacomo, 23, 164
Miall, A. Bernard, as minor translator of Heine, 83; other translations of, 83
Middleton, Richard, interest in Heine, 171
Mill, John Stuart, 181
Mills, J. Saxon, as minor translator of Heine, 83-84; other translations of, 83

Milnes, Richard Monckton, on Julian Fane's translations of Heine, 24; as major translator of Heine, 25-27; as major critic of Heine, 116-117; as personal friend of Heine, 183, 187; influence of Heine on, 241-243
Mitford, Miss, 47
Molimer, Auguste, translated, 85
Mommsen, Theodor, 260
Monaco, Alice, Princess of, 182
Monahan, Michael, on *Heine's Grave*, 193
Montaigne, Michel de, 60
Montefiore, L. A., as minor critic of Heine, 138-139
Morgan, Lady, 183
Mörike, Eduard, translated, 260
Morton, John B., interest in Heine, 171
Moschus, translated, 42, 52
Moser, Julius, translated, 90
Müller, Wilhelm, attitude toward the sea contrasted to Heine's, 29; Heine's similarity to in folk-song, 204
Müllner, Adolf, 178
Mulvaney, Charles Pelham, 18
Musset, Alfred de, translated, 60, 99n; mentioned, 107, 130, 140, 262

Napoleon, 67, 139, 145, 154, 156, 159
Neumann, Hermann, translated, 32, 63
Nevinson, Henry W., as minor critic of Heine, 159
New Review, The, anonymous criticism of Heine in, 151-152
Niebuhr, Barthold Georg, 260
Nietzsche, Friedrich, 106
Novalis, 204, 264
Noyes, Alfred, poem on Heine, 195-196
Noyes, Thomas Herbert, as minor translator of Heine, 84; other translations of, 84n

Oddie, J. W., as translator of Heine, 103n; translations of reviewed in *Athenaeum,* 153
Oehlenschläger, Adam, translated, 76
Opinion, informal, on Heine, 266-268
Ovid, translated, 42

Palgrave, Francis Turner, as minor translator of Heine, 84-85
Patmore, Coventry, on Heine, 177

Paul, Charles Kegan, as minor translator of Heine, 85; other translations of, 85
Payne, John, as minor translator of Heine, 85-86; other translations of, 85; on Heine, 178; poem on Heine, 194-195
Peterson, Franklin, mentioned, 147; as minor critic of Heine, 163-164
Petrarch, translated, 74
Pfeiffer, Emily, as major translator of Heine, 30-31; dedicates poem to Heine, 190-191
Plarr, Victor, 243
Platen, August, Graf von, translated, 55, 66, 73, 84n, 97; mentioned, 96, 116, 193
Poe, Edgar Allan, 82
Pollock, Walter Herries, dedicates poem to Heine, 189
Pope, Alexander, 118, 120
Powell, York, 18
Pryde, Thomas, as minor critic of Heine, 147-148
Puttlingen, Vesque, 24

Quarterly Review, The, anonymous criticism of Heine in, 148-149, 153-156

Rabelais, François, 128
Radford, Ernest, as major translator of Heine, 32-34; other translations of, 32
Raleigh, Sir Walter, interest in Heine, 171
Ransom, Arthur, as minor critic of Heine, 162-163
Renan, Ernest, 61
Rhys, Ernest, as minor translator of Heine, 88-89
Richter, Jean Paul, 128, 260
Rittershaus, Emil, translated, 63
Robert, 147
Roberts, Friederike, 5
Robertson, John M., mentions Heine, 170-171
Rodd, Rennell, as major translator of Heine, 31-32; dedicates poem to Heine, 190
Rodenberg, Julius, translated, 82
Rogers, A., mentioned, 75; as minor translator of Heine, 86; other translations of, 86

Ross, Janet, as minor critic of Heine, 150
Rossetti, Dante Gabriel, mentioned, 131, 191, 192; painting of from Heine, 259
Rossini, Gioachino, 163
Rothschild, Lady de, dislike of Heine, 172-173
Rousseau, Jean Jacques, 150, 264
Royston, Alice G., as minor critic of Heine, 149-150
Rückert, Friedrich, translated, 45, 50, 55, 63, 66, 82, 84n, 97; mentioned, 137
Ruge, Arnold, 201
Ruge, Franciska, as minor translator of Heine, 87
Russell, Charles, version of "Du bist wie eine Blume" compared with that of W. Wilsey Martin, 82; as minor translator of Heine, 87-88; other translations of, 87
Russell, Rollo, as minor translator of Heine, 88
Rutherford, Mark, interest in Heine, 171

Sachs, Hans, 79
St. Hilaire, Barthélemy, 185
St. Simon, Comte de, mentioned, 144, 164, 166; influence of upon Heine, 200
Salis, Johann von, translated, 75
Sallet, Friedrich von, translated, 73
Samuel, Horace Barnett, as minor critic of Heine, 160-161; dedicates poem to Heine, 189-190
Sappho, 140
Sartorius, Prof., on Heine, 105
Sawyer, William, as adaptor of Heine, 253-254
Schalles, Ernst August, 165
Schefer, Leopold, translated, 66
Scheffer, 147
Schelling, F. W. J. von, 172
Schiller, Johann Friedrich, translated, 12, 43, 50, 55, 62, 63, 73, 75, 81, 84n, 85, 87, 99n; mentioned, 46, 106, 173, 177, 242, 246, 265, 270
Schlegel, August Wilhelm, 172, 242
Schlegel, Friedrich, 242
Schopenhauer, Arthur, 174
Schreiner, Olive, as admirer of Heine, 180-181

Index

Schwab, Gustav, 71
Schwarzkopf, August, translated, 43
Schwartz, J. M. W., as minor translator of Heine, 89-90; other translations of, 89
Scott, Sir Walter, mentioned, 5; Heine's interest in, 158-159
Scully, William Charles, as minor translator of Heine, 90-91; other translations of, 90
Selden, Camille, poems of on Heine, 261-262; mentioned, 155
Shakespeare, William, 106, 110, 181, 182
Sharp, William, mentioned, 188; influence of Heine on, 226-230
Sharpe's London Magazine, anonymous criticism of Heine in, 127
Shaw, George Bernard, as successor to Heine, 262
Sheehan, Patrick A., interest in Heine, 171
Shelley, Percy Bysshe, 60, 118, 140, 180, 181, 204, 209, 262
Sherman, Stuart P., on *Heine's Grave*, 192-193
Shuldham, E. B., as minor translator of Heine, 91; as minor critic of Heine, 132-135
Sibree, Mary, 109
Sichel, Walter S., as minor critic of Heine, 145-146
Simpson, Sir Walter, 239
Simrock, Karl, letter of Heine to, 29
Skipsey, Joseph, interest in Heine, 171
Smith, Mrs. Francis, letter of Olive Schreiner on Heine to, 180-181
Smith, Garnet, as minor critic of Heine, 147
Smith, John Stores. See "Ackerlos, John"
Snodgrass, John, as minor translator of Heine, 91-92; on Charles Grant as Heine critic, 119; mentioned, 143, 144
Soissons, Count de, as minor critic of Heine, 164-165
Sorley, Charles, mentions Heine, 171
Spectator, The, anonymous review of Francis Storr's translations of Heine in, 147; anonymous review of C. G. Leland's translations of Heine in, 151; anonymous criticism of Heine in, 168

Spinoza, Baruch, 139, 164
Spontini, Gasparo Luigi Pacifico, 164
Stanley, Dean, 192
Steinmann, 264
Sterne, Laurence, compared with Heine, 158; mentioned, 128, 239, 240; Heine on, 269-270
Stern, Rabbi, translated, 43
Stevenson, Robert Louis, influence of Heine on, 239-241
Stigand, William, as major translator of Heine, 34; as minor critic of Heine, 138; sequel to Heine's *Lorelei*, 255-256; mentioned, 122, 137, 144, 188, 265
Stobbe, translated, 50
Stolberg, Graf zu, translated, 87
Storm, Theodor, translated, 50
Storr, Francis, translations of Heine reviewed in *Spectator*, 147
"Stratheir," as minor translator of Heine, 92-93; 103n
Strauss, David, mentioned, 46; translated, 109
Strettell, Alma, as minor translator of Heine, 93-94
Strodtmann, Adolf, 131, 134, 137, 140, 144, 158, 265
Sturm, Julius, translated, 50
Swift, Jonathan, 118, 128
Swinburne, Algernon Charles, 61, 243
Symonds, John Addington, as minor translator of Heine, 94-96; other translations of, 94-95; on the translations of Lady Duff Gordon, 150
Symons, Arthur, as minor translator of Heine, 96-97; other translations of, 96; influence of Heine on, 249-252
Synge, John Millington, 262

Tait's Edinburgh Magazine, anonymous criticism of Heine in, 126-127
Tanner, translated, 50
Temple Bar, The, anonymous criticism of Heine in, 156
Tennyson, Alfred, Lord, 79, 95, 114, 130, 136, 183
Theocritus, translated, 42; adapted, 53
Thiers, Adolphe, 8
Thomas, Edward, interest in Heine, 171
Thomson, James, 204
Thomson, James ("B. V."), as major translator of Heine, 20-23; aptitude

for languages, 20; other translations of, 21; translations reviewed by G. A. Black, 168; influence of Heine on, 204-210; mentioned, 11, 210
Tieck, Johann Ludwig, translated, 84n; Heine's similarity to in folksong, 204; mentioned, 71, 80, 242
Todhunter, John, as major translator of Heine, 6, 18-20; mentioned, 36
Tomlin, Edward Locke, as minor translator of Heine, 97
Translation, difficulties of evaluating, 3-6; requirements for, 5-6; difficulties in translating Heine, 263-265
Translators, division into groups, 6
Trench, Richard Chenevix, as minor translator of Heine, 97; other translations of, 97
Trotter, Bernard Freeman, as minor translator of Heine, 98
Turnbull, M. P., 103n
Tyrell, G., 103n

Uhland, Johann Ludwig, translated, 43, 55, 63, 66, 73, 76, 82, 83, 84n, 101; mentioned, 71, 137, 264

Vansittart, A. A., 35
Vergennes, Madame de, 262
Vergil, translated, 42; adapted 53
Vernet, 147
Villon, François, 140
Voltaire, Jean François, 128, 148

Wagner, Richard, 178
Wailly, Leon de, 187
Wallis, J. E., as major translator of Heine, 27-28, 103n; translations of reviewed in *Edinburgh Review*, 127-128
Wallis, R. E., as minor translator of Heine, 98; other translations of, 98
Warr, Prof., 243

Watts-Dunton, Theodore, mentioned, 6; sonnet to Heine, 191-192
Weatherley, Frederick E., as minor translator of Heine, 98-99
Webb, Philip G. L., as major translator of Heine, 36-38, 103n
Weckmüller, Artur, on Heine's stylistic traits, 203
Wellington, Arthur Wellesley, Duke of, 139
West, Miss, 122
Westminster Review, The, anonymous criticism of Heine in, 148
White, William Hale, interest in Heine, 171
Wilberforce, Edward, as minor translator of Heine, 99; other translations of, 99n
Wilde, Oscar, 182
Wilkie, 108
Williams, Orlo, as minor critic of Heine, 166-167
Wilson, Mrs. James Glenny, as minor translator of Heine, 100-101
Wilson, James H., as minor translator of Heine, 101; other translations of, 101
Wood, John Dennistoun, as minor translator of Heine, 102; other translations of, 102
Wolfe, Humbert, as minor translator of Heine, 101-102; poems of on Heine, 196-198
Wordsworth, William, 108, 134, 154, 181, 192
Wright, Thomas, on the translations of John Payne, 85-86; mentions Heine, 171; on John Payne's poem on Heine, 194-195

Zeller, Eduard, translated, 95
Zschokke, Heinrich, 260
Zuccalmaglio, 69

www.ingramcontent.com/pod-product-compliance
Lightning Source LLC
Chambersburg PA
CBHW021118300426
44113CB00006B/192